Trauma-Informed Practices With Children and Adolescents

Trauma-Informed Practices With Children and Adolescents

William Steele and Cathy A. Malchiodi

Routledge
Taylor & Francis Group
New York   London

Routledge
Taylor & Francis Group
711 Third Avenue
New York, NY 10017

Routledge
Taylor & Francis Group
27 Church Road
Hove, East Sussex BN3 2FA

Version Date: 20110805

International Standard Book Number: 978-0-415-89052-6 (Paperback)

Library of Congress Cataloging-in-Publication Data

Steele, William.
  Trauma-informed practices with children and adolescents / William Steele, Cathy A. Malchiodi.
      p. ; cm.
  Includes bibliographical references and index.
  Summary: "Trauma-Informed Practices with Children and Adolescents is a sourcebook of practical approaches to working with children and adolescents that synthesizes research from leading trauma specialists and translates it into easy-to-implement techniques. The approaches laid out address the sensory and somatic experiences of trauma within structured formats that meet the "best practices" criteria for trauma informed care: safety, self-regulation, trauma integration, healthy relationships, and healthy environments. Each chapter contains short excerpts, case examples, and commentary relevant to the chapter topic from recognized leaders in the field of trauma intervention with children and adolescents. In addition to this, readers will find chapters filled with easily applied activities, methods, and approaches to assessment, self-regulation, trauma integration, and resilience-building. The book's structured yet comprehensive approach provides professionals with the resources they need to help trauma victims not just survive but thrive and move from victim thinking to survivor thinking using the current best practices in the field"--Provided by publisher.
    ISBN 978-0-415-89052-6 (pbk. : alk. paper)
    1. Post-traumatic stress disorder in adolescence--Treatment. 2. Post-traumatic stress disorder in children--Treatment. 3. Child psychotherapy. I. Malchiodi, Cathy A. II. Title.
    [DNLM: 1. Stress Disorders, Traumatic--therapy. 2. Adolescent. 3. Child. 4. Crisis Intervention. 5. Psychotherapy--methods. 6. Resilience, Psychological. 7. Survivors--psychology. WM 172.5]
    RJ506.P55S74 2011
    616.85'2100835--dc23   2011018665

Visit the Taylor & Francis Web site at
http://www.taylorandfrancis.com

and the Routledge Web site at
http://www.routledgementalhealth.com

Printed and bound in Great Britain by
TJ International Ltd, Padstow, Cornwall

To those who keep me resilient and thriving

Joyce, Monika, Darren, Tina, Gunnar, Ema, Denny, Diane

William Steele

In memory of my mom and dad who always helped me feel safe.

Cathy Malchiodi

Contents

Foreword

I was fortunate to read *Trauma-Informed Practices With Children and Adolescents* as I was flying to Beirut, Lebanon, where I would be co-leading a seven-day intensive training program for adult survivors of land mine explosions. The 29 participants were coming from such land mine–infested areas as Kurdistan, Jordan, Yemen, Iraq, and Lebanon. The purpose of our program was to train these survivors to promote resilience in peer-to-peer projects back in their home communities.

Although the participants were adults, reading this manuscript was perfect preparation. It reinforced and enriched my perspective on the value of being a trauma-informed practitioner whose interventions are attachment grounded, resilience focused and strength based. Bill Steele and Cathy Malchiodi have assembled a great team of authors who bring conceptual acumen, a firm grasp of current research, and rich clinical experience in treating children who are trauma survivors.

The material is an exciting confluence of perspectives, including the concepts of resilience, attachment, the mind/body connection, and ecology. Each of these perspectives offers a unique and valuable point of view to those who work with survivors of trauma. The resilience lens reminded me to continue looking for strengths, rather than focusing on deficits, throughout the training. I came across one of the countless nuggets of resilience at the very start of the program, the day after I read the book. One land-mine explosion survivor introduced himself to our Beirut group by asserting, "I am not a victim of a land mine. The land mine is a victim of me. I survived—the land mine didn't."

Attachment is another valuable perspective that permeates the book. Attachment theory does much more than sensitize us to the profound and pervasive harm that childhood traumas leave in their wake. It also guides our healing practices by promoting a sense of safety, highlighting the centrality of the therapeutic relationship, emphasizing the power of attunement, and underscoring the importance of human connectedness for a thriving life. An event in the Beirut program beautifully demonstrated how attachment leads to dramatic change. One participant had lost his left arm about halfway to the elbow, leaving a gnarled stub, while he was working to clear land mines in his home country. On the fourth day of the workshop, he deeply thanked the group for unconditionally accepting him. He then shared that he was wearing a short-sleeve shirt in public for the first time since his accident.

The book's third perspective, the mind/body connection, is much easier for us now that we can see through the lens of the MRI. For decades, critics have pejoratively referred to play-based and creative therapies as "touchy-feely" approaches that lacked any scientific support. However, the latest developments in neuroscience have revealed that a safe and empathic relationship provides the ideal conditions to promote neural plasticity. Moreover, therapeutic interventions can actually help survivors of trauma to change their neural networks (Cozolino, 2010).

The fourth perspective is ecology—a wide-angle lens that broadens our perspective. The authors address such ecological issues as family dynamics, institutional environment, and cultural concerns. In particular, they offer a uniquely helpful chapter on designing the ideal therapeutic environment for the successful treatment of trauma. The chapter sensitized me to the therapeutic opportunities of the entire environment of our Beirut program, including experiences that were not on the schedule. For example, when our participants rode the bus together, they often broke into lively Arabic songs, clapping to the beat, swaying together, gesturing broadly, and cheering. I clapped along to these wonderful examples of emotional regulation, touched and inspired by the sheer joy in life that these land mine survivors expressed.

Many professional trade books begin with an introductory chapter that describes a conceptual framework and summarizes the relevant research literature. Then, in the remaining chapters, these books concentrate only on clinical practices. Other books on trauma focus entirely on techniques without any serious consideration at all of theory and research. Of course, we want interventions that are effective, but techniques ultimately must be based on meaningful concepts and empirical studies. Theory and research without application are only an interesting light show, while technique without any conceptual framework and supportive evidence is just a shot in the dark. What I especially liked about *Trauma-Informed Practices With Children and Adolescents* is that every single chapter offers a great integration of concepts, evidence and practice. Each chapter includes detailed case examples, sidebar theoretical discussions, summaries of related studies, and countless examples of trauma-informed practice in action.

Of course, the contributors to this book would be the first to point out that creative interventions are powerful therapeutic tools for adult survivors, too. For example, one of our Beirut activities, "Out of the Ashes," started with describing the trauma on a small piece of paper. Then, each participant burnt the paper and put the ashes into modeling clay. Finally, the person used the clay to create a sculpture that is a symbol of hope. One young woman who had lost her leg to a land mine created a beautiful sculpture. It was a flower growing in the ground that no longer hides a deadly killer.

I am certain that reading *Trauma-Informed Practices With Children and Adolescents* will be a valuable experience for any student or practitioner in the field. You will come away with not only an appreciation for the current best practices, but also with a deeper appreciation for the potential in all children of trauma to become survivors who can go on to become thrivers in their lives.

As for myself, I did not need a translator to appreciate the resilience of the land mine survivors in our training program. They may have been missing hands, arms, feet, and legs, but their hearts were ever present through their courage, compassion, hope, and joy. When I said good-bye to them at the end of the workshop, I kept replying with the one Arabic word that I can say without mangling—"Shukran," which means "thank you." I was so grateful to them for the countless ways in which they had enriched my life during our time together. So, to Bill Steele, Cathy Malchiodi, and the other contributors to *Trauma-Informed Practices With Children and Adolescents*, I also say, "Shukran!"

Lennis G. Echterling
Harrisonburg, Virginia

Reference

Cozolino, L. (2010). *The neuroscience of psychotherapy: Healing the social brain* (2nd ed.). New York: W. W. Norton.

Acknowledgments

William Steele: Over the past 20 years as founder and past director of the National Institute for Trauma and Loss in Children (TLC), I have been privileged to work with and learn from the wisdom of thousands of practitioners in schools and agencies across the country. Their support, contributions, and expertise are at work throughout this text. The vision and support of Dr. Martin Mitchell, president of Starr Commonwealth, has ensured a long life for TLC and the services we provide to traumatized children, families, schools, and organizations. He and the staff at Starr Commonwealth have significantly broadened my understanding and appreciation of what constitutes trauma-informed resilience-focused environments where children can flourish.

Additional appreciation goes to my colleague, Caelan Kuban, TLC director, who over the past several years has done so much to assist practitioners and their work with traumatized children, and has also transformed my thoughts and experiences into useful practical resources and programs now benefitting practitioners across the country. Over the past 15 years, Deva Ludwig's expertise in information technology has allowed us to connect with and learn so much from practitioners throughout the world. Because of her, their wisdom and expertise encouraged us to write this book. And without Diane Cusmano, I would still be hacking away at the keyboard. Her uncanny ability to make sense of all my side notes, inserts, and sometimes shaky scribbles while maintaining patience and a sense of humor made it so much easier to meet our deadlines while still attending to our daily responsibilities.

Cathy Malchiodi: It has been both a privilege and an ongoing learning experience to interact with thousands of helping professionals associated with the National Institute for Trauma and Loss in Children and numerous universities, agencies, hospitals, and schools over the past 25 years. In retrospect, I am humbled by encounters with so many practitioners and students and all that I have learned from them. Above all, I want to acknowledge the children, adults, and families I have met through my work as an art therapist and mental health counselor because they have repeatedly taught me how sensory-based methods make a difference in recovery and wellness. It is their resilience, wisdom, and courage in times of trauma that made writing this book possible and that continue to inspire me each and every day.

No book comes together without the help of editorial staff. We thank Anna Moore, associate editor at Routledge for her expertise, patience, and guidance during the process of writing this volume. Finally, we express our gratitude for our collaboration with other practitioners and their expertise in the field of trauma that allow us to present many valuable trauma-informed practices to help children and adolescents. We gratefully acknowledge them for their generous contributions to this book.

Introduction

The Experience Matters

Marie is 10 years old, and has experienced two divorces and three long-term separations from her mother from the ages of 1 to 3. There were several reports to child protective services concerning abuse and domestic violence; as a result, Marie spent a short amount of time in foster care. When she was 8 years old, she was hospitalized for a short time for a stomach ulcer (Figure 0.1) and needed special dietary restrictions to prevent a recurrence. She is now living with her biological mother, Anna, and recently placed on medications for attention deficit disorder (ADD) because of her erratic and disruptive behavior in school. Her teacher is frustrated because Marie is not able to pay attention during class; she also gets into fights with other children on the playground. Her mother has asked the school counselor to intervene because Marie is oppositional at home and her behavior is creating tension between Anna and her new husband, Marie's stepfather.

Jenny is 12 years old and living at a residential treatment center after four failed foster care placements and the termination of her mother's parental rights 3 years earlier due to child abuse and neglect. Like many children with similar experiences, she has been diagnosed with several different disorders—attention deficit disorder (ADD), oppositional defiant disorder (ODD), bipolar disorder (BPD), and reactive attachment disorder (RAD). Labeled as a "biter" and a "runner," multiple medications have little impact on her behavior. Her fine and gross motor skills are that of a much younger child; as a result, other children bully Jenny frequently. Jenny's overall reasoning abilities are only better than 2% of children her age and her vocabulary and comprehension are that of a 6-year-old. Despite a history of disruptive events and abuse, a diagnosis of posttraumatic stress disorder (PTSD) has never been assigned.

Figure 0.1 Drawing of my "stomachache" by Marie, age 10 years. (Reproduced with permission of C. Malchiodi.)

After years of witnessing his father, stepfather, and other men "beat on" his mother, 16-year-old Sam found his way into the juvenile justice system. Sam's truancy, school suspensions, fighting, and rule-breaking behavior challenge the best of school counselors, probation officers, and foster care parents. Although it appears that being a long time witness to physical abuse is the major contributor to his current struggles, when asked to draw a picture of what he remembers most, he draws eight different very troubling experiences other than witnessing the abuse of his mother. Described in reports as noncompliant, unwilling to accept help, unable to form significant attachments, and quick to react physically, Sam received several mental disorder diagnoses with a very poor prognosis (Figure 0.2).

Cassie, age 4 years, was separated at birth from her mother, due to her mother's addictions and hospitalization. She was returned to her mother at age 6 months, but was again removed from her mother's care at age 18 months due to sexual and physical abuse by her grandfather. Cassie has been in three foster care placements and is currently being placed in a fourth home; caretakers reported being unable to manage her tantrums and violence toward family members. She briefly attended a therapeutic preschool, but she was unable to use the toilet appropriately and often became socially isolated and withdrawn in response to the environment. While at preschool,

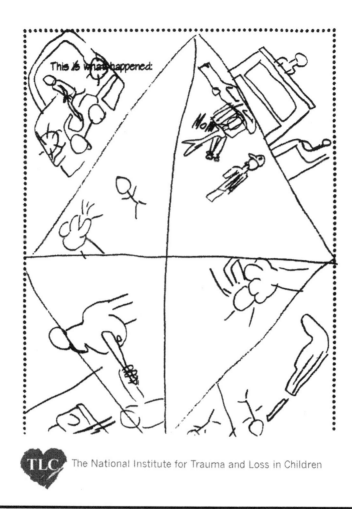

The National Institute for Trauma and Loss in Children

Figure 0.2 Sam's drawing of "what happened." (Reproduced with permission of W. Steele.)

her teachers observed that her play activities and behaviors were more like those of a 2-year-old; she enjoyed drawing, but her inability to draw basic forms or rudimentary figures (Figure 0.3) reflects the development level of a much younger child.

At age 2, James saw his father shoot and kill his mother (Figure 0.4). For several months he stayed with his aunt until the grandparents were awarded custody for unknown reasons. The past several years James has frequently fallen asleep on the floor. Attempts to get him to sleep in bed meet with more resistance than his grandparents can manage. At times his grandmother also reports that James will follow her into the bathroom. Given a diagnosis of reactive attachment disorder (RAD), inhibited type, he is very quiet at school, bullied, and labeled a sissy. When he tells his story of what happened to his

Figure 0.3 Four-year-old Cassie's scribble drawing showing developmental delays. (Reproduced with permission of C. Malchiodi.)

Figure 0.4 James' picture of his father shooting his mother. (Reproduced with permission of C. Malchiodi.)

mother he states, "my mother got up to leave the house because my daddy be mean to her and when she got out to the car she forgot me and came back to get me and that's when my daddy shot her."

These examples describe behaviors and scenarios that practitioners face all too often in their work with children. In each case, these children have been given one or more diagnoses in an attempt to explain their symptoms and guide treatment. What all these children have in common is exposure to multiple traumas including child abuse, exposure to violence, separations, and other stressful events; these traumas have seriously impacted emotional, cognitive, and psychosocial development.

Advances in neuroscience clearly demonstrate and dictate that helping professionals must reframe their understanding of trauma not so much through diagnostic criteria, but as a series of experiences that have been so disruptive that the brain and the body are unable to complete normal developmental functions. At the same time, these experiences have shaped personal logic, worldviews, and ultimately trauma-related behaviors in response to others and the environment.

About Trauma-Informed Practices (TIPs)

Trauma-Informed Practices (TIPs) With Children and Adolescents is intended for all helping professionals who work with traumatized children and adolescents. Mental health counselors; psychologists; social workers; marriage and family therapists; art, play, and expressive therapists; case managers; residential treatment staff; school counselors; and others will benefit from the recommended practices. New professionals as well as seasoned practitioners who work in schools, clinics, guidance centers, child welfare agencies, shelters, juvenile justice, residential care, and healthcare settings will benefit from the practical, structured approach to assisting traumatized children and adolescents. *TIPs* uses strategies, policies, and procedures that meet the criteria supported by the National Center for Trauma-Informed Care (NCTIC) and approaches from recognized leaders in the trauma field. In brief, the strategies detailed in this book are based on best practices and are designed to be reparative, restorative, and resilience enhancing.

So what does being trauma-informed mean? In brief, it means that trauma is a predominately sensory process for many children and adolescents that cannot be altered by cognitive interventions alone. Because the experience of trauma is often one of terror, and being vulnerable and powerless to do anything about one's situation, trauma-informed care must engage children and adolescents in sensory, neurosequential experiences to help restore a sense of safety and bring about a renewed sense of empowerment. Practices that address individuals' "survival brains" through sensory and somatic (body-oriented) experiences, and enhance self-regulation, trauma integration, and healthy relationships and environments are central to trauma-informed care. *TIPs* focuses on practices that communicate and connect with traumatized individuals' experiences with themselves, others, and the world as a result of exposure to trauma-inducing incidents. In brief, approaches presented in this text are designed to help children and adolescents move from victim thinking to survivor thinking and eventually "thriver" status.

Because there is no one intervention that fits every situation, *TIPs* provides multiple strategies for achieving each of the trauma-informed criteria listed. Readers will learn the following:

1. What constitutes trauma-informed care and the guiding principles of practice as defined by leaders in the field
2. What constitutes developmental trauma and chronic trauma with an emphasis on how the body responds to traumatic events over time
3. What constitutes trauma-informed assessment and its critical importance in treatment planning and the validation of practices assigned to support assessment-driven outcomes
4. How to establish and maintain safe relationships and environments and apply interventions that support safety, trust, and respect for the traumatized individual
5. How to apply practices to help young clients learn to self-regulate their responses to perceived threats and activated trauma memories
6. How to develop trauma-informed environments
7. How to create trauma-informed relationships between practitioner and child and between parent/caretaker and child
8. What allows some individuals to do better than others who are exposed to trauma, and the practices that can enhance resilience and posttraumatic growth
9. Specific strategies using sensory integration, somatic techniques, art, play, and expressive arts therapies approaches, and other trauma-informed best practice methods appropriate for children and adolescents

There are several aspects that make *TIPs* unique. First, it is a practical sourcebook of information and approaches on trauma-informed care. Second, it brings together valued practices used by trauma experts, thereby giving the reader a view of the wide range of approaches available. Each chapter contains short excerpts, case examples, and commentary relevant to the chapter topic from recognized leaders in the field of trauma intervention with children and adolescents. This exposes readers to other trauma-informed practitioners who have established currently accepted best practices and research, and supplements the foundational and pragmatic information provided by the authors.

Most importantly, *TIPs* translates theory into actual practice. As trauma specialists with more than 30 years of experience with children, adolescents, and families, we have experienced the challenges of working with chronically traumatized individuals firsthand and are committed to providing other practitioners with strategies that they can immediately apply to intervention. Therefore, chapters contain easily applied activities, methods, and specific recommendations for assessment, self-regulation, trauma integration, and resilience building. We are convinced that a structured yet comprehensive trauma-informed approach can improve the lives of traumatized children and capitalize on the strengths and resources of victims of multiple traumas so that all professionals can help them move from being survivors to thrivers.

William Steele, PsyD, MSW

Cathy Malchiodi, PhD, LPAT, LPCC

About the Authors

William Steele, PsyD, MSW, is the founder of the National Institute for Trauma and Loss in Children (TLC), established in 1990. In 2009, TLC joined Starr Commonwealth where Dr. Steele continues to practice. Starr is an international leader in transformational programs for children, families, schools, and communities established in 1913. Dr. Steele began his work in the field of trauma by taking the lead in helping schools across the country develop crisis response teams in response to the epidemic of suicide among young people in the early 1980s followed by the epidemic of violence in the late 1980s. He has assisted professionals over the years following such tragedies as the bombing of the Federal Building in Oklahoma, 9/11 in New York and Washington D.C., Hurricanes Katrina and Rita, and the 2009 killings (while in school in the presence of students) of a coach in Iowa and a teacher in Texas, to name but a few. He was one of the first Americans selected by the Kuwaiti government to assist them in the aftermath of the Gulf War and continues to consult with agencies and schools across the country.

Dr. Steele has had numerous publications in such journals as the *School Social Work Journal, Children and Schools, Residential Treatment for Children and Youth, National Social Sciences Associations, Reclaiming Children and Youth,* and publications with Guilford Press, American Counseling Association, and Allyn & Bacon.

Today there are over 6,000 TLC Certified Trauma and Loss School and Clinical Specialists who Dr. Steele has personally trained. Insistent that intervention for traumatized children be outcome driven, he developed and conducted evidenced-based research on TLC's intervention model—Structured Sensory Interventions for Traumatized Children, Adolescents and Parents (SITCAP™)—including trauma-specific school and agency intervention for children 6 through 18 years of age. With its focus on early intervention, TLC's I Feel Better Now Program for children 6 to 12 years is, for example, one of the very few school-based, evidence-based program of its kind in the country. Of the numerous honors Dr. Steele has received over the years, he is most proud of the 6,000 Certified Trauma Specialists who are providing TLC SITCAP interventions and resources to thousands of children daily whose exposure never receives national media attention.

Since 1990 Dr. Steele has consistently trained professionals to relate to childhood trauma not as a diagnostic category (posttraumatic stress disorder [PTSD]), which is deficit focused as well as inadequate, but as a series of sensory experiences, the elements of which are experienced by traumatized children regardless of their culture. "Terror is terror," he explains. "Symptoms only define the ways the child's neurological, biological, emotional, and behavioral systems are struggling to survive." Dr. Steele states, "Provide new experiences, and symptoms diminish as TLC's research documents." The proposed 2009 developmental trauma disorder (DTD) category supports TLC's long-standing approach to trauma intervention as detailed in the 2001 publication *Structured Sensory Interventions for Traumatized Children, Adolescents and Parents* (SITCAP), authored by Dr. Steele.

Cathy Malchiodi, PhD, LPCC, LPAT, is an art therapist, counselor, and research psychologist and author in the fields of art therapy and art in healthcare. She has published numerous books including *The Art Therapy Sourcebook* (2006), *The Soul's Palette: Drawing on Art's Transformative Powers* (2002), *Breaking the Silence: Art Therapy with Children from Violent Homes* (1997), *Handbook of Art Therapy* (2011), *Expressive Therapies* (2005), *Creative Interventions with Traumatized Children* (2008), *and Understanding Children's Drawings* (1998), all of which are standards in the field. Cathy has given over 300 invited keynotes, workshops, and courses throughout the United States, Canada, Asia, and Europe. She has been an adjunct professor at Lesley University's Expressive Therapies Department for more than 20 years and has been a visiting professor at numerous universities throughout the United States.

Cathy is a recognized advocate and innovator of art therapy programs for children, adolescents, adults, and families, particularly those who are survivors of trauma. She has been involved in a wide variety of community, national, and international agencies, including the National Institute for Trauma and Loss in Children, Issues Deliberation America/Australia, American Art Therapy Association, and Save the Children Foundation, helping to create global art therapy initiatives for children around the world. Cathy has also served on the boards of the American Counseling Association (ACA), serving as the first representative from the Association for Creativity in Counseling (ACC); Association for Humanistic Counseling (AHC); American Art Therapy Association (AATA); and on numerous national and international boards in mental health, counseling, arts, and public service. In honor of her clinical and academic contributions, Cathy is the only person to have received all three of the American Art Therapy Association's highest honors: the Distinguished Service Award, the Clinician Award, and the Honorary Life Member Award. She has also received national honors from the Kennedy Center and Very Special Arts (VSA) and is the 2011 recipient of the Bill Steele Award, National Institute of Trauma and Loss in Children.

About the Contributors

Jeffrey A. Allen, M.Ed., is the cofounder of Inner Coaching.

Michael A. Bayda, DCSW, is in private practice and a TLC Certified Trauma Specialist with expertise in the diagnostic assessment of autism spectrum disorders and developmental assessment and treatment of infants and toddlers.

Sandra L. Bloom, MD, is an associate professor and codirector of Health Management and Policy for the Center for Nonviolence and Social Justice, School of Public Health, Drexel University, Philadelphia, Pennsylvania.

Larry K. Brendtro, PhD, is the founder of the Circle of Courage Institute, a program of Starr Commonwealth, and editor of *Reclaiming Children and Youth*.

Lisa Conradi, PsyD, is an associate professor at the California School of Professional Psychology, Alliant International University, and oversees the Trauma Assessment Pathway (TAP) Model within the Chadwick Center, Cady's Children Hospital and Health Center in San Diego, California, and at National Child Traumatic Stress Networks across the country.

Kiaras Gharabaghi, PhD, is a professor at the School of Child and Youth Care, Ryerson University, Toronto, Canada.

Eliana Gil, PhD, ATR, RPT-S, is the director of Clinical Services for Childhelp, Inc. in Fairfax, Virginia.

Deanne Ginns-Gruenberg, MA, RPT-S, is in private practice and owner of the Self-Esteem Shop in Royal Oaks, Michigan.

Eric J. Green, PhD, LMFT, PRT-S, is an assistant professor of counseling at the University of North Texas in Dallas, Texas, and the director of the university's community counseling clinic.

Richard Jones, MD, is the network medical director, Aetna US Healthcare, Las Vegas, Nevada.

Roger Klein, PsyD, is the cofounder and director of Family Resources Associates, cofounder of Inner Coaching, and is a TLC Certified Trauma Specialist.

Nicole T. Kletzka, PhD, is a consulting forensic examiner for the state of Michigan.

Maggie Kline, MS, MFT, is in private practice and senior instructor of Somatic Experiencing®, teaching Peter Levine's methods to professionals internationally.

P. "Gussie" Klorer, PhD, ATR-BC, LCSW, is the director of the graduate Art Therapy Counseling program at Southern Illinois University, Edwardsville.

Caelan Kuban, LMSW, is the program director and clinical coordinator for the National Institute for Trauma and Loss in Children (TLC).

Peter A. Levine, PhD, is the originator of Somatic Experiencing® and founder of the Somatic Experiencing Trauma Institute.

John Micsak, MA, is the clinical director and founder of the National Institute for Resilience and Wellness, LLC, and is a TLC-Certified Trauma Specialist.

Linda Peterson-St. Pierre, PhD, a tenured associate professor of pediatrics and psychiatry at University of Nevada School of Medicine from 1978 to 2004, she now conducts a clinical practice in Reno, Nevada.

John R. Seita, EdD, is an associate professor at the School of Social Work, Michigan State University, Lansing, Michigan.

The following are co-contributors to the CTAC Assessment submission found in Chapter 2.

Ben Atchinson, PhD, is a professor in the Department of Occupational Therapy at Western Michigan University (WMU) and consultant to the Children's Trauma Assessment Center (CTAC).

Connie Black-Pond, MA, is the cofounder and the clinical director of the Children's Trauma Assessment Center (CTAC), Western Michigan University (WMU) School of Social Work.

Jim Henry, PhD, is the cofounder and director of the Children's Trauma Assessment Center (CTAC) and associate professor at Western Michigan University (WMU) School of Social Work.

Yvette Hyter, PhD, is an associate professor in the Department of Speech Pathology and Audiology at Western Michigan University (WMU) and a consultant to the Children's Trauma Assessment Center (CTAC).

Amy B. Mack, MSW, assists with assessments at the Children's Trauma Assessment Center (CTAC) and is currently training manager for a Substance Abuse and Mental Health Services Administration (SAMSHA) grant supporting trauma infusion in school districts.

Margaret Richardson, PhD, currently provides comprehensive assessments and consultations at the Children's Trauma Assessment Center (CTAC) and overall evaluation of CTAC programs.

Mark Sloan, DO, is the medical director of the Center for Behavioral Pediatrics, Western Michigan University (WMU) and manages the medication and treatment of traumatized, drug- and alcohol-exposed children and adolescents at the Children's Trauma Assessment Center (CTAC).

Chapter 1

What Is Trauma-Informed Practice?

Each day children and adolescents are exposed to traumatic events including abuse, domestic violence, accidents, witness to homicide, divorce and separation, loss, disasters, and war. They may encounter these events from early childhood through teenage years; some experience multiple traumas or live in situations that include chronic neglect, abandonment, and abuse. Given the complexity and variability in the severity of young people's exposure and responses to trauma, it is not surprising that the identification of effective treatment has only recently materialized.

This chapter reviews the previous and current theories about trauma intervention with children and adolescents and how these approaches have enhanced understanding of trauma-informed approaches. It also presents contemporary findings in neuroscience, psychology, and medicine that have influenced trauma intervention, including cognitive-behavioral, somatic, sensory integration, and expressive arts therapies. Finally, a comprehensive definition of trauma-informed practice is presented with an emphasis on the key factors necessary in developing effective assessment, environments, relationships, and treatment.

Traumatic Stress Reactions in Children and Adolescents

Over previous decades, researchers have conducted extensive investigations examining trauma reactions in children and adolescents. The recognition of societal, domestic, and interpersonal violence against children during the mid-1980s precipitated significant research on its impact and revealed strong evidence that "acute posttraumatic stress symptoms result from violent life threat, and that severity is related to the extent of exposure to the threat or witnessing of injury or death" (Pynoos, Nader, Arroyo et al., 1987 p. 1057). In the 1990s, numerous authors described trauma reactions in children induced by physical and sexual abuse, (Famularo, Kinscherff, & Fenton, 1992), witness to parental homicide and violence (Trickett & Putnam, 1993; Deblinger, Lippman, & Steer, 1996), and exposure to living in violent communities (Terr, 1990; Saigh & Bremner, 1999; Garbarino, 1992; Wallen, 1993). During the same time, trauma specialists realized that trauma and PTSD were not only specific to exposure to violence, but also to other traumatic events such as natural disasters, for example, fires (McFarlane, Policansky, & Irwin, 1987; March Jackson, Costanzo, & Terry, 1993), hurricanes (Lonigan, Shannon, Finch, Daugherty, & Taylor, 1991; Vernberg, LaGreca, Silverman, & Prinstein, 1996), boating incidents (Yule, 1992), burns and other serious accidents, and medical procedures such as bone marrow transplants (Stubner, Nader, Yasuda, Pynoos, & Cohen, 1991). Living with a terminally ill adult or sibling, drowning, house fires, car fatalities, living with substance-abusing parents and divorce were also identified as events that preceded the onset of PTSD in children (Raider, Steele, & Santiago, 1999).

While PTSD was recognized as a diagnostic category in 1984, it was not until 1994 that children were included in this category by the American Psychiatric Association (APA, 1994). The description of the disorder, however, was not conclusive or comprehensive in its coverage of childhood trauma. The category failed to capture what Herman (1992) and van der Kolk, Roth, Pelcovitz, and Mandel (1993) described as the outcomes of those who experienced chronic, multiple, long-standing, repeated events and atrocities of human design and intent. In 1992 Herman wrote, "while the victim of a single acute trauma may feel after the incident that she is not herself, the victim of chronic trauma may feel herself to be changed irrevocably or she may lose the sense that she has any self at all" (p. 86).

The Adverse Child Experiences (ACE) supported by the Centers for Disease Control (CDC) is advancing understanding of the relationship between multiple childhood traumatic events and adverse outcomes later in life. The initial phase of the ACE study began in 1995 with more than 17,000 participants whose exposure to childhood maltreatment and family dysfunction are being tracked along with current health status and behaviors. Almost two-thirds of participants reported at least one adverse childhood experience, and more than one of five reported three or more ACEs. The short- and long-term outcomes of these childhood exposures include a multitude of health and social problems including heart and liver disease, alcoholism, drug abuse, fetal death, and interpersonal violence (CDC, 2011). The ACE study underscores that childhood trauma does not only impact psychosocial outcome, but also physical well-being and overall health (Corso et al., 2008; Chapman et al., 2007).

Neuroscience: Enhancing Understanding of Trauma Memory and Reactions

During the 1990s and early 21st century, neuroscience research enhanced our understanding of the effects of trauma on the mind and body. In *Traumatic Stress,* van der Kolk, McFarlane, and Weisaeth (1996) observe that when a terrifying incident such as trauma is experienced and does not fit into a contextual memory, a new memory or dissociation is established and memories are "stored initially as sensory fragments that have no linguistic components" and furthermore, "that intrusive sensations, even after the construction of a narrative, contradict the notion that learning to put the traumatic experience into words will reliably abolish the occurrence of flashbacks (and other reactions)" (p. 289). Michaesu and Baeltig (1996) also explain that memories of trauma are not stored "explicitly" (cognitively) or within a contextual framework, but "implicitly" in iconic and sensory forms. In essence, trauma memories are experienced and remembered through images and sensations. Terr (1994) reports that memories of traumatized individuals are far more emotional and perceptual in content than declarative components. Steele (2003) also notes that when memory cannot be linked linguistically in a contextual framework, it remains at a symbolic (iconic) level and there are no words to describe it, only sensations and images. Before traumatic memory can be encoded, expressed through language, and successfully integrated, it must be retrieved and implicitly externalized in its symbolic (iconic) sensory forms (p. 142). The trauma experience, therefore, is more easily communicated through imagery and activities associated with the sensory experiences of those incidents than through cognitive processes (Malchiodi, 2001, 2008).

Other authors underscore the mind–body connection in trauma reactions and PTSD. Levine (1997) suggests that trauma is experienced primarily in the nervous system and that it is a physiological phenomenon as much as a purely psychological one. He indicates that when children's physiological survival systems are activated by threat, the excess energy used to defend oneself must be expended. If that energy is not fully discharged and metabolized, it does not simply disappear. Instead it remains as a kind of highly charged body memory creating the potential for repeated traumatic symptoms.

In *The Body Remembers*, Rothschild (2000) observes that the sensations experienced at the time of trauma are contained in the body rather than stored solely as cognitive memories; these sensations are activated when similar events are experienced after the actual trauma passes. Bessel van der Kolk (2006) echoes Rothschild's observations, saying, "For therapy to be effective it might be useful to focus on the patient's physical self-experience and increase their self-awareness, rather than focusing exclusively on the *meaning* that people make of their experience ..." (p. 13).

Perry (2006) provides a neurosequential model of therapeutics (NMT), a developmentally informed, biologically respectful approach to working with at-risk children. NMT is not a specific therapeutic technique or intervention; it is a way to organize the children's history and current functioning to optimally inform the therapeutic process. It integrates several core principles of neurodevelopment and traumatology into a comprehensive approach to the child, family, and the community. The NMT process helps match the nature and timing of specific therapeutic techniques to the developmental stage of the child, and to the brain region and neural networks that are likely mediating the neuropsychiatric problems. This approach structures assessment of the child, articulates primary problems, identifies key strengths, and applies educational and therapeutic interventions that will help family, educators, therapists, and related professionals best meet the needs of the child (Perry & Hambrick, 2008).

Developmental Trauma

NMT reflects the recent recognition of the importance of developmental factors in the evaluation and treatment of trauma in children and adolescents. Many practitioners today appreciate that the current PTSD category does not reflect the actual experiences of traumatized children. It also does not integrate developmental factors that contribute to the complexity of exposure to trauma during childhood.

THE ROOTS OF TRAUMA
Peter Levine and Maggie Kline

A child's brain/body develops and is shaped through the experiences s/he has, both traumatic and reparative. Fortunately, because of the brain's plasticity and the biological imperative to move toward self-regulation, with a little understanding and skill of how to engage a child's instinctual resources, clinicians (and parents) can help transform symptoms of fear to robust self-confidence and resilience.

A method called Somatic Experiencing® (SE) is currently being employed successfully in the prevention and healing of trauma. The premise of SE is that *trauma is a fact of life; but so is resilience*. Trauma can result from events that are clearly extraordinary, such as violence and molestation, but it can also result from everyday "ordinary" events. In fact, common occurrences such as accidents, falls, invasive medical procedures, and divorce can cause children to withdraw, lose confidence, or develop anxiety and phobias. Traumatized children may also display behavioral problems including aggression, hyperactivity, and as they grow older, addictions of various sorts and dysfunctional relationships.

In order to help children feel secure and balanced, it is necessary to recognize the underlying roots of trauma, how the trauma response is held in the body as implicit/procedural memory, and how it disturbs the child's self-regulatory capacities. In other words *trauma is a physiological phenomenon*, rather than a purely psychological one. As such, psychologists, psychiatrists, and other helping professionals need to understand the core mechanisms of how to stabilize the body's reactions to traumatic stress on the *physical* level in order to help children and teens regulate their sensations and emotions.

TRAUMA IS NOT ONLY IN THE EVENT

Trauma happens when an intense experience stuns a child like a bolt out of the blue; it overwhelms the child, leaving him or her altered and disconnected from his body, mind, and spirit. Coping mechanisms are undermined and he feels utterly helpless. It is as if his legs were knocked out from under him. Trauma can also be the result of ongoing fear and nervous tension. Long-term stress responses wear down a child, causing an erosion of health, vitality, and confidence.

While the magnitude of the stressor is clearly an important factor, it does not define trauma. Here the child's capacity for resilience is paramount. In addition, trauma resides not in the event itself; but rather [its effect] in the nervous system. The basis of single-event trauma (as contrasted to ongoing neglect and abuse) is primarily *physiological* rather than psychological. What we mean by "physiological" is that there is no time to think when facing a threat; therefore, our primary responses are instinctual. Our brain's main function is survival! We are wired for it. At the root of a traumatic reaction is our 500-million-year heritage—a heritage that resides in the oldest and deepest structures of the brain.

THE RECIPE FOR TRAUMA

When these primitive parts of the brain perceive danger, they automatically activate an extraordinary amount of energy—like the adrenaline rush that allows a mother to lift an auto to pull her trapped child to safety. This fathomless *survival energy* that we all share elicits a pounding heart along with more than 20 other physiological responses designed to prepare us to defend and protect ourselves. These rapid involuntary shifts include the redirection of blood flow away from the digestive and skin organs and into the large motor muscles of flight, along with rapid respiration and a decrease in the normal output of saliva. Pupils dilate to increase the ability of the eyes to take in more information. Blood-clotting ability increases, while verbal ability decreases. Muscles become highly excited, stiffening in preparation for action with a vast expenditure of energy. Alternatively, when faced with inescapable threat or prolonged stress, certain muscles collapse in fear as the body shuts down in an overwhelmed frozen state as the last-ditch default response.

While the body may *look* inert in this state of freeze/collapse, those physiological mechanisms that prepare the body to escape may still be prepared for "full charge." Muscles that were poised for action at the time of threat are thrown into a state of immobility or shock. When in shock, the skin is pale and the eyes vacant, the pupils may be small pinpoints. Breathing is shallow and rapid, or just shallow. The sense of time is distorted. However, underlying this situation of helplessness is an enormous vital energy. This potential energy lies in wait to complete whatever action had been initiated. In addition, young children (this can happen with older children, too, especially girls) tend to bypass active responses, becoming motionless instead. Later, even though the danger is over, a simple reminder can send the exact same alarm signals racing once again through the body until it becomes hyperaroused and/or shuts down. When this happens we may see the child becoming agitated, sullen, depressed, whiny, clingy, and withdrawn.

Whether a youngster is still fully charged or has shut down and resigned, the guidance of a therapist or other adult is imperative to alleviate their traumatic stress response and to build up their resilience and confidence. Furthermore, younger children generally protect themselves not by running away, but by running toward (and attaching to) the protective adult. Hence, to help children resolve a trauma, *there must be a safe adult to support them.* The adult who has the skills of emotional first aid can help them literally "shake things off" and breathe freely again as their nervous system "resets."

How does the outpouring of survival energy and multiple changes in physiology affect children and teens over time? The answer to this question is an important one in understanding the consequences of trauma. This depends on what happens during and after the threat. The catch is that to avoid being traumatized, the excess energy mobilized to defend oneself must be used up. When the activation is not fully discharged and metabolized, it does not simply go away; instead it remains as a kind of highly charged "body memory" creating the potential for repeated traumatic symptoms. This type of imprint is not primarily conscious but is registered unconsciously as implicit procedural (i.e., motoric) memory. Children who are guided with consistent, patient support to release this highly charged state can easily return to healthy, flexible functioning. When a child is overwhelmed, whether from a traumatic event or cumulative stress, his or her self-protective reflexes and fight-or-flight mechanisms become unavailable. With physical shutdown, children develop feelings of helplessness and hopelessness. The recipe for recovery lies in restoring these bodily resources, which lead to self-regulation.

If these same children had been cheetah cubs, they wouldn't need our help. After withstanding terrifying exposure to danger (such as from a hunting lion), the frisky pack mates might be found playing, rough-housing, and shaking it off. Documentaries have filmed this reenactment mirroring the drama they witnessed by playing through the actions their parents took to battle off the intruder. Excess adrenaline, cortisol, and other chemical and hormonal releases in the wake of survival get channeled into use, or discharged as the siblings practice the skills of healthy aggression that they will use, in turn, to protect themselves and their young when they grow up.

The National Child Traumatic Stress Network (NCTSN) (2009) supports the inclusion of a new, more comprehensive PTSD category for children and adolescents called developmental trauma disorder (DTD). Van der Kolk, Pynoos et al. (2009) explain, "Whether or not they exhibit symptoms of PTSD, children who have developed in the context of ongoing danger, maltreatment, and inadequate care-giving systems are ill served by the current diagnostic system, as it frequently leads to no diagnosis, multiple unrelated diagnoses, an emphasis on behavioral control without recognition of interpersonal trauma and lack of safety in the etiology of symptoms, and a lack of attention to ameliorating the developmental disruptions that underlie the symptoms." Traumatic events have their most pervasive and significant influence during the first 10 years of children's lives, although the current PTSD category does not adequately describe these children's behavior and symptoms. As a result, children may be given a wide range of co-morbid diagnoses that imply that symptoms occur independently from PTSD symptoms. Essentially, helping professionals may miss important opportunities for trauma-informed intervention if only co-morbid diagnoses are the focus and the impact of DTD is left unaddressed.

According to van der Kolk, Pynoos et al. (2009), DTD includes the following criteria:

■ **Exposure.** There are multiple or chronic exposures to one or more forms of developmentally adverse interpersonal trauma (abandonment, betrayal, physical assaults, sexual assaults, threats to bodily integrity, coercive practices, emotional abuse, witnessing violence, and death) and subjective experience (rage, betrayal, fear, resignation, defeat, and shame).

■ **Repeated Dysregulation.** Trauma responses persistently include dysregulation in affective functioning; somatic functioning (motoric, medical, physiological); behavior (reenactment); cognition (confusion, dissociation, repetitive thoughts about trauma events); relationships (oppositional, mistrust, overly compliant); and self-attributions such as self-hate or blame.

■ **Persistently Altered Attributions and Expectancies.** These may include negative self-attribution, loss of expectation of safety or protection by others and social agencies, lack of belief in retribution or social justice, expectation of future victimization, and general distrust of caregivers.

■ **Functional Impairment.** Functional impairments may occur in any of the following areas: educational, familial or social relationships, vocational, and self-efficacy.

Trauma Versus Grief Reactions

Many practitioners confuse trauma and grief reactions in children and adolescents. In brief, grief is an emotional response that accompanies loss; when experiencing a trauma, there is often grieving about what is lost whether it is a significant person, possessions, home, or even the loss of innocence when betrayed by abuse or abandonment. Reactions to grief and trauma are different and it is important to distinguish these reactions in traumatized children and adolescents; for this purpose, Table 1.1 is provided to summarize the differences and underscore the common reactions found in those who are traumatized versus those who are grieving.

A Brief History of Trauma Intervention With Children and Adolescents

It was not that long ago when practitioners concurred that addressing traumatic events with children and adolescents was detrimental and even counterproductive to their emotional reparation and recovery. Several decades ago, children were not believed to be capable of even experiencing trauma symptoms. In fact, when 26 children were buried alive and survived the Chowchilla School Bus kidnapping in California in 1976, doctors pronounced the children to be in good physical condition

Table 1.1   Grief Reactions Versus Trauma Reactions

Grief Versus Trauma	
GRIEF	*TRAUMA*
Grief generally does not attack or "disfigure" our identity.	Trauma generally attacks, distorts, and "disfigures" our identity.
In grief, guilt says, "I wish I would or would not have …"	Trauma guilt says, "It was my fault. I could have prevented it. It should have been me."
In grief, dreams tend to be of the person who died.	In trauma, dreams are about the child himself dying or being hurt.
Generalized reaction … SADNESS	Generalized reaction … TERROR
Grief reactions can stand alone.	Trauma reactions generally also include grief reactions.
Grief reactions are generally known to the public and the professional.	Trauma reactions, especially in children, are largely unknown to the public and often to professional counselors as well.
In grief, pain is related to the loss.	In trauma, pain is related to the tremendous terror and an overwhelming sense of powerlessness and fear for safety.
In grief, a child's anger is generally not destructive.	In trauma, a child's anger often becomes assaultive (even after nonviolent trauma, fighting often increases).
Trauma Reactions are DIFFERENT from Grief Reactions	
Trauma Reactions OVERPOWER Grief Reactions	
Children can be traumatized by violent or nonviolent incidents. Separation from a parent through divorce or foster care, a family member's terminal illness or sudden death, exposure to physical or sexual abuse, witnessing drug use, house fire, tornado, flood, earthquakes, or hurricanes, as well as drowning, murder, suicide, and school violence can all be traumatizing incidents.	

Copyright TLC 2011. http://www.starrtraining.org/tlc.

and did not request any further mental health intervention. Fortunately, Lenore Terr, a psychiatrist, was invited to study the children some 5 months later. Terr evaluated children at different developmental stages and was the first to study children's trauma reactions over time. The Chowchilla findings described in *Too Scared to Cry* (1990) eventually became a landmark study, creating new avenues of research into children's reactions to trauma and suggesting that they could indeed experience clinically significant mind/body reactions following exposure to terrifying events.

In response to the acceptance that children do indeed experience trauma reactions and posttraumatic stress, a variety of methods have been used to address and ameliorate symptoms. Psychodynamic therapy has a long tradition in addressing childhood trauma and has had some success. When successful, it includes two factors: (1) a consistent relationship between therapist and child and involvement of parents or caretakers during treatment, and (2) longer, more intensive intervention to support change, growth, and improvement in developmental achievements. It is also more effective with younger children than with older children and adolescents (Lieberman & Horn, 2005). Evidence from psychodynamic therapy tells us that traumatized children do benefit from stable, consistent relationships with adult caretakers; that trauma recovery takes time; and that early intervention is key to establishing positive attachment and normal developmental gains.

Psychopharmacological interventions have been used with children and adolescents, but knowledge of how these treatments can help young people lags behind that for adults (Foa, Keane, Friedman, & Cohen, 2000). The consensus is that medications may help those who have symptoms so debilitating that confrontation of traumatic memories is difficult. The ongoing study of these treatments with children and adolescents underscores that trauma, particularly repeated events, increases arousal and other reactions. In brief, it supports the fact that the body's reactions to trauma must be addressed in order to attend to normal developmental functions such as learning and social interaction.

More recently, cognitive behavioral interventions have been applied to the treatment of traumatized children and adolescents. Foa and Kozak (1986) observe that trauma reactions involve a *fear network*—a set of responses to threatening stimuli and situations that produce a fight, flight, or freeze reaction. In exploring fear reactions, they cite that what differentiates PTSD from anxiety disorders is that trauma is a psychological and physiological state that destabilizes a sense of safety. As a result, experiences that previously felt safe become associated with danger and subsequent fear and terror. This discovery led to increased interest in how intervention could be used to change thinking in individuals with trauma reactions and reduce PTSD through cognitive-behavioral therapy (CBT).

In brief, CBT focuses on the interactions among affect, cognition, and behaviors through identifying errors in thinking and how thoughts influence behavior. CBT has been validated as a treatment of choice for adult victims of trauma (Foa, Rothbaum et al., 1991) and child sexual abuse (Cohen, Mannarino, & Deblinger, 2006; Deblinger, Stauffer, & Steer, 2001). Cohen, Mannarino, and Deblinger (2006) developed trauma-focused cognitive-behavioral therapy (TF-CBT) to address trauma's impact on cognitive functioning.

Many practitioners see limitations in a purely cognitive-behavioral approach to trauma intervention with children and adolescents because of developmental, cognitive, and verbal challenges. Gil (2006) notes that "traumatic events are experienced and stored in the right hemisphere of the brain" and that "this suggests that allowing children a period of time to access and stimulate the right hemisphere of the brain could eventually activate the necessary (explicit) functions of the left hemisphere, which appears to shut down during traumatic experiences" (p. 102). Gil underscores that for many children, forms of CBT may not always be the treatment of choice and may even be counterproductive to the healing process when the dominant processing of trauma experiences is more right brain than left brain.

Sensory-Based Trauma Intervention

In response to the challenges of applying CBT in work with children, a variety of approaches have emerged that address the sensory response to trauma rather than only cognitive areas. These include, but are not limited to, somatic experiencing, neurodevelopmental approaches, and experiential therapies such as expressive arts therapies and play therapy.

Levine and Kline (2008) adapt somatic experiencing, a body-awareness approach to alleviating trauma symptoms by restoring self-regulation, to work with children. In brief, it involves "felt-sense experiences" to promote the awareness and release of physical tension. Levine's approach focuses on fight, flight, or freeze responses that occur during traumatic situations. Techniques include successive titration (slowly helping the individual to release uncomfortable emotions) and pendulation (the movement between regulation and dysregulation (aroused or frozen).

As previously mentioned, Perry and Hambrick (2008) describe the neurosequential therapeutic model (NTM), which also underscores the importance of sensory-based interventions in work with children and adolescents.

In addition to addressing brain development from early childhood through teenage years, this model provides an important structure for choice and application of treatments based on the developmental needs of traumatized individuals. Like Levine's and similar approaches, NTM highlights the need for experiential interventions and the importance of improving attachments among children and caretakers, empathy, resilience, and self-regulation.

Steele and Raider (2001) describe an evidence-based, sensory integration model called structured sensory interventions for traumatized children, adolescents, and parents (SITCAP™). This approach, according to Gil (2010), is "congruent with trauma-focused play in which children are encouraged to utilize play (primarily drawing in this model) in order to externalize their areas of distress (exposure); to learn to tolerate and release affect (abreaction); and to compensate for injuries and create feelings of mastery (management and restoration of power)" (p. 57). According to this model, trauma is the result of exposure to experiences that are terrifying and leave individuals feeling unsafe and powerless. By introducing traumatized individuals to new experiences that are safe and empowering, trauma reactions can be diminished. The SITCAP model in schools and agencies has demonstrated its efficiency in reducing not only trauma-specific symptoms but also mental health–related reactions (Steele & Raider, 2003; Steele, Raider, Kuban et al., 2008; Raider, 2010).

Finally, expressive arts therapies involving art, music, dance, drama, play, and sand play tray are considered trauma-informed because of their ability to allow for processing of the trauma narrative through nonverbal expressions (Malchiodi, 2005, 2008). The use of art in trauma-related work goes back to the early 1990s when Nader, Pynoos et al. (1990) used drawing to interview children to "identify traumatic imagery and avoidance, to introduce discussion of the child's individual traumatic experience and to assess the embedded perceptual aspects of the trauma" (p. 379). More recently, art therapies have been most often used to address child abuse (Coulter, 2000; Pifalo, 2002; Klorer, 2008; Malchiodi, 2010) and war and terrorism (Yehidia & Itzhaky, 2004).

According to the International Society for Traumatic Stress Studies (Foa, Keane, Friedman, & Cohen, 2008), these therapies are accepted ways to access nonverbal material and are suited to work with children who have experienced trauma. The main benefit of expressive approaches is their sensory quality—kinesthetic, auditory, and visual—and their relationship to neurological functioning and neurodevelopment (Malchiodi, 2011a). To date, only one small, randomized controlled art therapy study has been conducted (Chapman et al., 2001); this study did

PTSD IN CHILDREN—A HEALTHCARE PERSPECTIVE

Richard Jones and Linda W. Peterson

Physicians should be aware that PTSD can occur at any age and can result from a broad spectrum of traumatic experiences. What most physicians would regard as "relatively minor" trauma, such as an eye injury, a single episode of sexual abuse, or an automobile accident, can produce emotional sequelae that may be just as disabling as those produced by experiencing wartime atrocities or being buried alive in a school bus as in the case of the Chowchilla incident described by Lenore Terr (1990).

Although a family physician may not be involved in the immediate treatment of one who has had a traumatic experience, he or she may be the first to detect emotional trauma. The most common symptoms of PTSD are described in an article by Terr. According to Terr, children most often "re-see" their trauma during leisure times, when they are resting, daydreaming, or trying to fall asleep, rather than in nightmares or the characteristic flashback of adult PTSD. Furthermore, children engage in repetitive posttraumatic play that can consist of reenacting a specific aspect of the traumatic event or simply reenacting the violence they experienced, as in this case.

Children exhibit specific fears, which are easier to identify if the traumatic event is known. However, when a child presents with intense fear toward specific objects, individuals, or situations, the physician should carefully obtain a thorough history, even if emotional trauma is not suspected initially. Even fear of mundane things such as the dark, strangers, being alone, being outside, food, animals, and vehicles should be investigated. Traumatic experiences can also change a child's attitudes about people, life, and the future. Most children possess a great deal of trust and optimism. Phrases such as "Mommy gets mad when I'm bad" or "Daddy can't always protect me" should alert physicians to the possibility of emotional trauma.

Studies have demonstrated that although most family practice and pediatric residents provide opportunities for parents or children to voice their psychosocial concerns, the residents often respond with information, reassurance, guidance, or referral less than half of the time. Many parents have never heard of PTSD, yet a simple intervention can reduce parents' anxiety regarding their children's condition and also can help parents begin to abate children's symptoms.

Understanding PTSD symptomatology in children provides a framework for physicians to organize their thinking about childhood trauma, and can help them avoid overlooking the condition. Studies have shown that the optimal time for intervention is during the first few weeks following the trauma. The effects of emotional trauma in children can last for decades, influencing the child's development of trust, initiative, interpersonal relations, self-esteem, and impulse control. The symptoms can be effectively treated, and developmental difficulties can be avoided if the child is promptly referred for appropriate therapy.

PTSD is more common in children than most physicians believe; therefore, the diagnosis can often be missed. Children being treated for "behavioral problems" may actually be suffering from PTSD. Physicians can prevent more serious sequelae that might otherwise interfere with psychosocial development if they are mindful of PTSD in children, elicit a careful history, take time to explain the disorder, refer the patient to an appropriate mental health professional as soon as possible, and take steps to ensure that the appointment with the mental health professional is kept.

not show significance for art therapy as a method to reduce PTSD over time. Although there is very little empirical evidence to support efficacy of the arts therapies, they have been successfully integrated within CBT sessions with children and in other sensory-based models such as SITCAP (Steele & Raider, 2001).

Finally, play therapy is a sensory-based approach that has, for several decades, been widely applied to the amelioration of trauma in children (Gil, 2006; James, 1989). Approaches emphasize attachment (Booth & Jernberg, 2009; Klorer & Malchiodi, 2003), communication of the trauma narrative (McMahon, 2009), crisis intervention (Webb, 2007), and emotional reparation and recovery (Gil, 2006). Overall, play therapy provides a method of communication and imaginal exposure similar to the expressive arts therapies by capitalizing on props, toys, and self-expression to assist in trauma recovery in children (Malchiodi, 2005).

Emergence of Trauma-Informed Practice

What has been learned from neurodevelopmental findings and sensory-based, somatic, cognitive-behavioral, and expressive therapies over the preceding decade has led to the development of a trauma-informed approach to work with children and adolescents. Recognition that trauma is a central factor in many mental health challenges and disorders is a common denominator in defining current best practices. While individuals react to trauma in idiosyncratic ways depending on the nature of the incidents and a variety of circumstances, trauma often becomes a defining characteristic that affects psychological, social, physical, and cognitive aspects of life, even for its youngest survivors. In fact, trauma reactions in children may be inaccurately identified as depression, attention deficit problems, oppositional defiant disorder (ODD), conduct disorder, anxiety disorders, separation anxiety, or reactive attachment disorder (Cook, Blaustein, Spinazzola, & van der Kolk, 2003). As previously mentioned, it is widely accepted that long-standing, untreated trauma reactions may result in a variety of medical conditions later in life including heart disease, cancer, and respiratory problems, and social conditions such as homelessness, prostitution, or delinquency (WISQARS, 2010).

Trauma-informed care is an approach to engaging people with histories of trauma that recognizes the presence of trauma symptoms and acknowledges the role that trauma has played in their lives. The development of the National Center for Trauma-Informed Care (NCTIC) in 2005 is a turning point in understanding trauma's impact on children and adolescents. NCTIC is funded by the Center for Mental Health Services (CMHS), Substance Abuse and Mental Health Services Administration (SAMHSA) and has brought national attention to the prevalence of trauma and the need to create trauma-specific interventions and trauma-informed environments. Its presence brings to light that traditional service delivery may actually exacerbate traumatized individuals and that a comprehensive approach addressing the individual, environment, and service providers is fundamental to trauma recovery. According to NCTIC (2011), the principles of trauma-informed care include:

1. **Understanding Trauma and Its Impact:** Understanding traumatic stress and how it impacts people and recognizing that many behaviors and responses that may seem ineffective and unhealthy in the present represent adaptive responses to past traumatic experiences.

2. **Promoting Safety:** Establishing a safe physical and emotional environment where basic needs are met, safety measures are in place, and provider responses are consistent, predictable, and respectful.

3. **Ensuring Cultural Competence:** Understanding how cultural context influences one's perception of and response to traumatic events and the recovery process, respecting diversity within the program, providing opportunities for consumers to engage in cultural rituals, and using interventions respectful of and specific to cultural backgrounds.

4. **Supporting Consumer Control, Choice, and Autonomy:** Helping consumers regain a sense of control over their daily lives and build competencies that will strengthen their sense of autonomy; keeping consumers well informed about all aspects of the system, outlining clear expectations, providing opportunities for consumers to make daily decisions and participate in the creation of personal goals, and maintaining awareness and respect for basic human rights and freedoms.

5. **Sharing Power and Governance:** Promoting democracy and equalization of the power differentials across the program; sharing power and decision making across all levels of an organization, whether related to daily decisions or in the review and creation of policies and procedures.

6. **Integrating Care:** Maintaining a holistic view of consumers and their process of healing and facilitating communication within and among service providers and systems.

7. **Healing Happens in Relationships:** Believing that establishing safe, authentic, and positive relationships can be corrective and restorative to survivors of trauma.

8. **Recovery Is Possible:** Understanding that recovery is possible for everyone, regardless of how vulnerable they may appear. Providing opportunities for consumer and former consumer involvement at all levels of the system, facilitating peer support, focusing on strength and resiliency, and establishing future-oriented goals.

Trauma-specific interventions are designed specifically to address the consequences of trauma in the individual and to facilitate healing. Treatment programs using a trauma-informed approach generally: recognize that survivors need to be respected, informed, connected, and empowered; help to reinforce hope in the recovery process; emphasize the interrelation between trauma and symptoms of trauma (e.g., substance abuse, eating disorders, depression, and anxiety); and encourage collaborative work with survivors, their family and friends, and other human services agencies.

In work with children and adolescents who experience sexual abuse, physical abuse or neglect, or are witnesses to interpersonal violence, Malchiodi (2011b) notes that trauma-informed practice integrates neurodevelopmental knowledge and sensory intervention, such as art and play therapy and other experiential approaches, in trauma intervention. In general, a trauma-informed approach must take into consideration, but is not limited to, the following: (1) how the mind and body respond to traumatic events, (2) recognition that symptoms are adaptive coping strategies rather than pathology, (3) emphasis on cultural sensitivity and empowerment, and (4) helping to move individuals from being not only survivors, but ultimately to becoming thrivers through skill building, support networks, and resilience enhancement. In regard to the latter, trauma-informed practice also clearly dictates that treatment be individualized and supported by comprehensive trauma assessment to determine the impact on all aspects of functioning. This includes specific, strength-based aspects of not only the child, but the family, community, and culture/environment in order to design a comprehensive action plan to address the effects of trauma (Malchiodi, 2011b).

In brief, a great deal of research has recently emerged to support the development of interventions that address mind–body and cognitive responses to trauma as well as enhance strengths and needs of traumatized children and adolescents. Witness Justice, a resource for victims (2010), summarizes (in their health and wellness section under the title, *Trauma Is the Common Denominator: New Discoveries in the Science of Traumatic Behavior*, http://www.witnessjustice.org) the impact of trauma as follows:

> When experienced in childhood, trauma produces neurobiological impacts on the brain, causing dysfunction in the hippocampus, amygdala, medial frontal cortex and other limbic structures. When confronted with danger, the brain moves from a normal information-processing state to a survival-oriented, reactive alarm state. Trauma causes the body's nervous system to experience: an extreme adrenaline rush; intense fear; information processing problems; and a severe reduction or shutdown of cognitive capacities, leading to confusion and defeat. … The healing journey is now seen to include biological as well as psychological transformation.

Trauma-Informed Care: Best Practices

There is no one intervention that fits every situation. At first glance, the numerous variables practitioners face when providing intervention seem overwhelming because successful care must address the biological, physiological, neurological, and psychological aspects of trauma. Developmental differences, age, gender, settings, medications, diversity, socioeconomic conditions, and social support all affect outcomes. Interpersonal trauma, medical illness, disasters, and early attachment disruption are significant factors that challenge intervention. Some children do better with individual interventions while others flourish within group settings; some will require long-term care while others may experience rapid posttraumatic growth due to personality and resiliency. Additionally, practitioners' education, commitment, and understanding of trauma reactions as well as their own vulnerability to secondary trauma reactions can make a difference in successful trauma-informed care.

If there are multiple interventions and practice variables to consider, what should guide the development and application of treatment? To be trauma-informed means that assessment and intervention are based on principles that are supported by best practices and research in trauma-informed care. There is general agreement that these principles include, but are not limited to, the following:

1. Restore a sense of safety, empowerment, and self-regulation (Bath, 2008; Briere & Scott, 2006; Perry & Szalavitz, 2006; Greenwald, 2005).
2. Apply trauma-informed assessment through an understanding of neurosequential development and sensory-based trauma reactions.
3. Capitalize on interventions that address the right hemisphere of the brain (Gil, 2006).
4. Develop trauma-informed relationships between child clients and therapists, parents/caretakers, teachers, and other helping professionals and significant adults to establish positive attachment and improve interpersonal skills.
5. Create trauma-informed environments that support internal locus of control, positive social interaction, safety, and empowerment.
6. Promote trauma integration to help individuals reach a new meaning for trauma events and capability to manage trauma reactions (Steele & Raider, 2001).

7. Encourage posttraumatic growth and resiliency (Malchiodi, Steele, & Kuban, 2008) and positive affective enhancement (Cook, Spinazzola, Ford et al. 2005).
8. Recognize that no one intervention fits every situation and that in the course of intervention, trauma integration results from the timely and developmentally appropriate application of sensory-based, somatic, cognitive, and behavioral approaches and practices.
9. Develop and include interventions that respect and support cultural diversity.
10. Empower children and adolescents and their families/caretakers to become active participants in intervention and programming.

Cultural Implications for Trauma-Informed Practice

In terms of cultural sensitivity and competence, best practices and research data on applications is still emerging. The following is a list of recommendations based on the current literature and best practices on effective intervention across cultures:

1. Intervene earlier rather than later to achieve greater and more sustainable gains (Cicchetti, Rogosch, & Toth, 2006).
2. Apply psychoeducational parenting interventions to improve social and family relationships and educational achievement (Boden, Horwood, & Fergusson, 2007).
3. Ethnically match the professional to the client whenever possible and when not possible, use and supervise ethnically matched paraprofessionals to assist with intervention (Snowden, Hu, & Jerrell, 1995).
4. Provide support services to children to assist with acculturation in school.
5. Avoid using children to interpret for parents.
6. Facilitate connections to ethnically matched support groups during intervention.
7. Always determine what is and is not culturally acceptable regarding recommendations and/or expectations you present.
8. Determine the expectations all clients (adults, families, and children) have regarding service and outcome.
9. Attempt to assess what change will mean in that individual's or family's cultural context and evaluate their cultural acceptability.

10. Obtain the intergenerational history of trauma and its impact on behavior and psychological factors. Understand that even within a specific culture, trauma experiences may differ and call for a different intervention focus.

Conclusion

Trauma-informed practice with children and adolescents requires the integration of the principles presented in this chapter along with best practices in the field. This chapter has underscored the importance of not only how trauma influences mind and body, self-regulation, and trauma integration, but also the impact of relationships, environment, and development throughout childhood and adolescence. Each of these aspects is critical to creating individualized and comprehensive trauma-informed care that addresses the sensory experiences of young clients who are traumatized.

Because any effective intervention requires an accurate evaluation of trauma and its effects, the next two chapters provide overviews of trauma-informed assessment. While evaluation often involves determining the deleterious effects of trauma on individuals, a trauma-informed approach dictates that helping professionals identify survivors' adaptive coping strategies rather than a pathology-only viewpoint. It also includes an understanding of developmental, cultural, relational, and environmental factors affecting traumatized children and adolescents, with the ultimate goal of helping them move from survivors to thrivers.

Chapter 2

Trauma-Informed Assessment

Before defining what constitutes a comprehensive trauma-informed assessment, the following example is important to consider. Think about two children exposed to the same traumatic event. Each will respond differently because they experienced that exposure in different ways. Ask one child what worries him the most since this happened and he might say, "Is my mother going to die, too?" Ask the other child and his reply might be, "Does this mean we can't go on our field trip?" This response might be misinterpreted as a denial or avoidant behavior. This child is making it clear that he is experiencing the situation differently than the other child and is going to need a different response from helping professionals and caretakers.

Any discussion related to conducting a comprehensive trauma-informed assessment must address the importance and validity of evaluating children's reactions, behaviors, and thought patterns that preceded traumatic events. Trauma-informed practices also dictate a multidimensional approach to assessment in order to adequately evaluate children's reports of how they have survived their traumatic ordeals and what kind of relationships and circumstances gave them the strength to survive. In addition, the roles the environment and interpersonal relationships play are key to understanding young clients' responses to trauma.

This chapter defines trauma-informed assessment and provides several standardized models for assessment including developmental, ecological, and trauma histories. Additionally, Chapter 3 provides sensory-based models for evaluation using play- and art-based methods. Both chapters underscore the need for continual assessment and sensitivity to cultural aspects that impact evaluation with traumatized children and adolescents. Overall, strength-based trauma-informed assessment is highlighted over deficit-focused methods.

What Is Trauma-Informed Assessment?

As previously mentioned, there is wide agreement that early childhood trauma presents with symptoms that have often been confused with other disorders including bipolar disorder (BPD), attention deficit hyperactive disorder (ADHD), oppositional defiant disorder (ODD), severe mood dysregulation (SMD), and many others (van der Kolk, Pynoos et al., 2009). Furthermore, numerous complex disturbances are often observed with multiple traumatized children such as eating disorders, metabolic, and sexual disorders. Trauma-informed assessment reflects the growing knowledge of how trauma impacts the brain in multiple ways to clarify why behaviors and reactions are occurring. For this reason, it is essential that trauma assessment incorporates ecological and developmental approaches that include the various biological, physiological, neurological, behavioral, and affective processes throughout early childhood and throughout adolescence.

As Bayda notes ("Ecological Assessment"), the pressure of time and money unfortunately often compromises the provision of the most appropriate and efficacious treatment to traumatized youth. The purpose of conducting an assessment is to formulate an appropriate individualized treatment plan. If that assessment fails to evaluate all aspects, it is not possible to arrive at an appropriate individualized treatment plan. For example, Janeela, a 12-year-old child who has experienced multiple sexual abuse events and who has been placed in a residential program may receive a psychiatric assessment, but usually does not receive a detailed evaluation of cognitive deficits and strengths. Although research has clearly substantiated trauma's impact on cognitive processes, this particular childcare-governing agency often denied the request for a cognitive assessment citing budget restrictions. The agency knew that Janeela's multiple sexual abuse incidents during early childhood had likely caused cognitive problems that were addressed in previous placements. Janeela presented with multiple diagnoses and medications, and each previous placement reported that she was "oppositional and would not listen;" she was also reported to be an assaultive and consistently disruptive child who did not respond to behavioral rewards.

When a cognitive assessment was completed, it revealed that this 12-year-old was primarily functioning at a 6-year-old level. She had significant

ECOLOGICAL ASSESSMENT
Michael Bayda

Ecological assessment of children in their family, peer, and school contexts is challenging, to say the least. Many of us were trained to focus on the pathological aspects of a client's presentation, and to devote much less if any time to understanding other important aspects of a child's functioning. In the field of traumatic stress, the need for a more comprehensive approach to the initial and ongoing assessment is necessary and gaining more support (Cook et al., 2005). More and more we are coming to understand that a focus on the topological features of a behavior or a category of behaviors (disorders) often leads to inadequate understanding of the individual and the development of an individualized approach to treatment, which is warranted even when the treatment involves an evidence-based protocol approach. In describing this need for a comprehensive and functionally based evaluation and intervention, Greenspan and Lewis (2000) writes that ultimately, a behavioral health assessment should "enable clinicians to individualize … intervention approaches in response to the child-and-family-specific question: 'what is the best approach for a given child and family?' Answering the child- and family-specific question makes it possible for clinicians to tailor the approach to the child, rather than fit the child to the program" (p. 3).

Sometimes, focusing assessment only on "what's wrong" may appear to simplify the assessment process. Compounding this reality is the fact that mental health consumers often present with urgent service requests for help in reducing their level of distress or impairment, thereby shifting focus from assessment to immediate crisis intervention. Furthermore, the additional pressure of time and fiscal constraints in many practice settings has unfortunately, over the years, lessened the emphasis on comprehensive assessments.

short-term memory problems and difficulty understanding verbal communications. In short, she could not process written or verbal information or retain even the simplest directions. She certainly was not oppositional, but instead was responding with adaptive coping to a hostile environment that activated her primal survival responses. Once the staff realized that this was a 12-year-old trapped in the brain of a 6-year-old, they also realized that her earlier traumatic experiences likely caused other delays. Following a more complete workup, the environment made significant adjustments and the treatment plan was changed; Janeela's responses changed dramatically. The assessment additionally identified that her visual memory was quite strong and that she could arrive at appropriate meanings to visual cues. For example, storyboards were recommended as a more effective way to communicate with this youngster; seven months later she was successfully placed with a relative.

This brief example demonstrates that trauma-informed assessments must include attention to strengths as well as deficits and the full range of developmental variables associated with trauma—biology, physiology, neurology, ecology, behavioral, affective, and cognitive processes. Furthermore, trauma-informed care must be developed and governed by the outcomes of trauma-informed assessment, that today go beyond traditional psychiatric evaluations. Given these considerations, what constitutes a comprehensive trauma-informed assessment? In the rest of this chapter, specific trauma-informed assessment approaches are described along with observations from experts in the areas of development, neuroscience, behavior, and sensory-based methods.

The Trauma Assessment Pathway (TAP) Model

The Trauma Assessment Pathway (TAP) (Taylor, Gilbert, Ryan, & Mann, 2005) model was developed at the Chadwick Center for Children and Families, part of Rady Children's Hospital in San Diego, California, and with funding from the Substance Abuse and Mental Health Services Administration. It standardizes the assessment, triage, and treatment process using clinical pathways with a goal of reducing arbitrary selection of the treatment intervention and makes best practice everyday practice (see Figure 2.1). The term *pathway* refers to a sequence that clinicians follow in making assessment, triage, and clinical decisions. The TAP model provides a framework to increase the capacity for mental health agencies to build and sustain an assessment-based trauma treatment program. It helps agencies incorporate and integrate existing appropriate evidence-based treatment services into their programs. Additionally, for children with complicated and complex trauma histories, the TAP model provides a guide for individualized trauma treatment (Conradi, Kletzka, & Oliver, 2010).

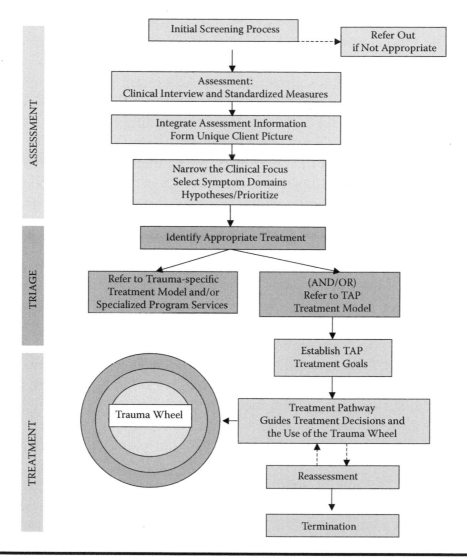

Figure 2.1 Assessment-based treatment for traumatized children: A Trauma Assessment Pathway (TAP). Developed by Chadwick Center for Children and Families, 2009.

The TAP model is designed for children 2 to 18 years of age who have experienced any type of trauma. It can be used by any clinician who works with traumatized children, from interns to experienced clinicians. The TAP model is individualized to meet the needs of each child. Depending on the needs of the particular child and family requesting treatment, the duration and type of treatment may vary, as will the inclusion of additional family members. Clinical pathways are used to help make decisions regarding assessment and treatment at each stage of intervention. The clinical components of these pathways are based upon research on complex trauma, and the current research on efficacious treatment modalities (Cook, Blaustein, Spinazzola, & van der Kolk, 2003; Taylor et al., 2005).

The TAP model defines a multifaceted assessment process to enable clinicians to appropriately screen clients and then, if appropriate for the treatment setting, to gain an in-depth understanding of the child; developmental level; traumatic experiences; and the family, community, and cultural system in which the child lives. Assessment-based treatment programs systematically incorporate standardized assessment measures into treatment to improve the effectiveness of the assessment process and to track client outcomes. The type of data collected within an assessment program must be specific to the goals of the program. Within a mental health treatment setting, the assessment data typically includes a combination of measures that assess symptoms and behaviors commonly exhibited by the targeted population as well as systemic or environmental influences. A complete assessment often includes using both standardized (validated paper-and-pencil measures) and nonstandardized (clinical interview and observation) methods. Standardized assessments allow clinicians to gather information in a more efficient and time-effective manner, while nonstandardized methods can be more individualized. The combination of standardized measures and clinical judgment increases the thoroughness and accuracy of the treatment planning process (Taylor et al., 2005).

Within the TAP model, strategies are presented to help the clinician make sense of the information gathered during the assessment process. Information is organized into four general domains: (1) trauma history, (2) symptom presentation, (3) relevant contextual history, and (4) developmental history. Trauma history includes information on the specific traumatic events experienced by the child, as well as their duration, and the age at which they occurred. Symptom presentation includes internalizing or externalizing behavior problems, problems in school, or problems with peers. Relevant contextual history includes family dynamics and structure (i.e., is the child in foster care?) and the child's individual culture. Developmental history includes the child's age, developmental issues, and the child's attachment to his or her primary caregiver. Each domain is assessed using a combination of behavioral observation, caregiver report, collateral report (i.e., teachers, child welfare workers, etc.), and standardized measures completed by the caregiver and/or child, as applicable. These domains are combined to create the *Unique Client Picture*. The

Unique Client Picture plays a critical role in determining how the clinician may best work with the child and the family.

Clients are then placed in the most appropriate form of treatment based upon their Unique Client Picture. Whenever possible, these treatment models have strong evidence supporting their efficacy for certain problems and populations. The TAP manual and the TAP Web-based training (http://www.taptraining.net) provide some "triage trees," to several common evidence-based modalities. They were developed in consultation with various treatment developers for treatments such as parent–child interaction therapy* (PCIT; Eyberg, 1988) and trauma-focused cognitive-behavioral therapy† (TF CBT, Cohen, Mannarino, & Deblinger, 2006). These triage trees guide clinicians through the decision-making process to determine whether or not certain evidence-based practices are appropriate for the child. The triage trees are updated on an ongoing basis as new evidence emerges for these and other modalities. Clinicians and agencies are encouraged to create and update their own triage trees depending on the treatments available in their agency or community. Internet resources such as the California Evidence-Based Clearinghouse for Child Welfare (CEBC) are available to help agencies determine which practices are the most efficacious and relevant for the children and families they serve. Children might also be referred to adjunct programs to address needs that are not addressed through therapy.

If children have complex trauma and do not fit into one of the established evidence-based practices, there is also a treatment component of the TAP model.‡ The TAP treatment component includes a series of interventions that have empirical support and guides the clinician through a series of questions to determine which interventions to use and in which order.

---

* Parent Child Interaction Therapy (PCIT) is an empirically supported treatment for conduct-disordered young children that emphasizes improving the quality of the parent–child relationship and changing parent–child interaction patterns.

† Trauma-focused cognitive behavioral therapy (TF-CBT) is a manualized model of psychotherapy that combines trauma-sensitive interventions with cognitive-behavioral therapy. Children and parents are provided knowledge and skills related to processing the trauma; managing distressing thoughts, feelings, and behaviors; and enhancing safety, parenting skills, and family communication.

‡ Due to space issues, information on the treatment component of the TAP model is not presented here. Readers are encouraged to see Taylor et al., 2005 or go online to http://www.taptraining.net for more information about the treatment component.

THE TRAUMA ASSESSMENT PATHWAY
(TAP) MODEL IN PRACTICE

Lisa Conradi and Nicole Taylor Kletzka

Sonia was a 10-year-old Hispanic girl who was referred for treatment by Child Protective Services due to an allegation of one-time sexual abuse by her uncle. Sonia's mother complained that she was sad and withdrawn at times, while at other times she would throw temper tantrums. She was also highly anxious about going into her room (where the abuse allegedly occurred), and had difficulty sleeping.

Every day children like Sonia present for treatment at mental health clinics across the country. Each child comes to treatment with a unique history, a unique family system, and a unique level of developmental, cognitive, and emotional functioning that influences how they respond to trauma and how the trauma can most effectively be resolved. Understanding the child through the use of a comprehensive assessment that incorporates a clinical interview, observation, and standardized measures completed by the caregiver and/or child is the first step in effectively treating the child. This solid understanding becomes the basis for identifying an effective individualized treatment intervention for the child.

So how would the TAP model be used to direct treatment for Sonia, the 10-year-old girl discussed earlier in this text box? For Sonia, the therapist conducted an assessment utilizing the TAP format. Sonia's mother completed the Child Behavior Checklist (Achenbach & Rescorla, 2001), the UCLA Posttraumatic Stress Disorder Reaction Index (Steinberg et al., 2004), and the Trauma Symptom Checklist for Children (TSCC; Briere, 1996). The results from these objective assessment measures indicated that Sonia was experiencing a lot of sadness, fears of going into her room (where the abuse allegedly occurred), throwing temper tantrums, and having general anxiety, and sleep problems. This assessment was consistent with information obtained through the clinical interview and behavior observations. Based on the assessment results, the incident of sexual abuse, and the presence of a supportive caregiver who agreed to participate in the sessions, it was determined that Sonia was appropriate for trauma-focused cognitive behavioral therapy (TF-CBT) and she was triaged into that modality using the TAP model.

A manual-driven treatment intervention was completed that included a trauma narrative, a psychoeducational component involving Sonia and her mother, and use of cognitive strategies to confront thinking errors that were contributing to her emotional distress. She was in treatment for over a year for a total of 55 sessions due to the complexity of her family dynamics. At the conclusion of treatment, her assessment results indicated that she was no longer anxious and depressed and appeared to have resolved the trauma.

Reassessment

Assessment within the TAP model is an ongoing process. Reassessment occurs through clinical interviews, questions, and observations incorporated into each session with a child or the child's caretakers. Additionally, standardized measures are periodically readministered. By monitoring progress in treatment, the clinician is able to respond to changing client needs, to assess efficacy of current treatment approaches, and to update or modify working clinical hypotheses and interventions.

In summary, the TAP model is a helpful method for clinicians, supervisors, and mental health agencies striving to become more trauma focused. The model helps individual clinicians become more strategic and organized in their assessment, triage, and treatment procedures. Central to the model is gaining a comprehensive understanding of the client as a unique individual, with a unique culture, developmental level, and support system, and a unique symptom presentation. This model also helps supervisors guide and oversee clinical work. At the agencywide level, the model provides a framework for program administrators who are creating a trauma-informed mental health treatment program and for those who want to evaluate an existing program. It provides step-by-step, detailed information on how to assess the needs of a treatment center based on the client population, reviewing the available assessment measures and integrating those that are the most parsimonious for a given client population, instituting an assessment-based treatment program, and ascertaining which evidence-based treatment practices should be institutionalized at a given agency. With future research, the TAP model shows promise in helping clinicians and mental health agencies become more trauma-informed in the services they provide.

Child Trauma Assessment Center (CTAC) Comprehensive Transdisciplinary Trauma Assessment Model

The Southwest Michigan Children's Trauma Assessment Center (CTAC) at Western Michigan University presents a unique transdisciplinary model for the assessment and treatment of traumatized children and youth and uses a trauma-informed brain-based framework to determine treatment strategies. The treatment recommendations resulting from their comprehensive assessment focuses on the integration of five domains through a trauma-informed lens. Medicine, social work, speech-language pathology, psychology, and occupational therapy are the primary disciplines utilized in assessments. CTAC was created in 2000 when a diverse professional group (social work professor, clinical social worker, behavioral pediatrician, occupational therapy professor, and speech-language professor) with collective experience assessing and treating maltreated traumatized children collaborated to develop a unique transdisciplinary assessment to enhance understanding of and intervention with maltreated children. The basic components of a transdisciplinary model require joint functioning, continuous staff development, and role extension and release (McCormick & Schiefelbusch, 1990; Hyter, Atchison, Henry, Sloane, & Black-Pond, 2001). The development of the CTAC transdisciplinary assessment model combined diverse professional expertise with current research on complex trauma, attachment, and brain development. It has been used extensively to evaluate children who have been maltreated, in foster care, and in residential and home-based settings.

The CTAC assessment process addresses five primary domains: physical/medical, developmental, social/family, emotional/behavioral, and trauma. Ethnographic interviewing, standardized instruments, CTAC-developed tools, behavioral questionnaires, and a psychosocial interview provide a wealth of information on the children's current status/functioning within each of the domains (see Table 2.1). Within each domain, findings are integrated using a trauma-informed brain-based paradigm (Henry, Sloane, & Black-Pond, 2007) to provide a comprehensive understanding of the potential traumatic impact on children's internal and external functioning. The CTAC assessment process begins with a referral, which most often comes from a child welfare agency. Required referral information includes an initial services plan (completed by the child welfare caseworker), the most recent updated services report, and other professional reports or assessments that have been

Table 2.1   CTAC Assessment Protocol Tools

Children's Ages	< 3.0	3–5.11	6–8.11	9–15
Medical Examination				
• General Physical Examination	X	X	X	X
• Facial Dysmorphology Measurements for Fetal Alcohol Spectrum Disorder	X	X	X	X
Ethnographic Interview	X	X	X	X
Neurodevelopmental Assessments				
• Sensory Profile	X	X	X	X
• Early Intervention Developmental Profile (EIDP)	X			
• Preschool Development Profile (PDP)		X		
• Pediatric Early Elementary Examination (PEEX)		X		
• Pediatric Examination of Educational Readiness (PEER)			X	
• Pediatric Examination of Educational Readiness at Middle Childhood (PEERAMID)				X
• ADHD Rating Scale		X	X	X
Kaufman Brief Intelligence Test		X	X	X
Emotional/Behavioral/Social				
• Attachment Behavior Observations	X			
• Marschak Interaction Method	X	X	X	X
• Psychosocial Interview		X	X	X
• Draw-A-Person (DAP)		X	X	X
• CBCL Parent/Teacher Rating Scale	X	X	X	X
• Vineland Adaptive Behavior Scales		X	X	X
• In-home and/or Classroom Observations	X	X	X	X
• Alexithymia Scale for Children		X	X	X
• Children's Depression Inventory (CDI)			X	X

(continued)

Table 2.1 CTAC Assessment Protocol Tools (continued)

Children's Ages	< 3.0	3–5.11	6–8.11	9–15
• Multidimensional Anxiety Scale for Children (MASC)			X	X
• Child Behavior Checklist				X
• Child Dissociative Checklist	X	X	X	X
• Adolescent Dissociative Experience Scale II Child Disssociative Checklist			X	
• Adolescent Dissociative Experience Scale II				
Pragmatic Language Protocol				
• Grice's Conversational Maxims		X	X	X
• Narrative Assessment: Story Retelling				
• Narrative Assessment: Story Regeneration		X	X	X
• Social Cognitive Skills: First-Order Belief Attribution			X	X
• Social Cognitive Skills: Second-Order Belief Attribution		X		
• Social Cognitive Skills: Third-Order Belief Attribution			X	X
Trauma Assessment				
• Trauma Symptom Checklist for Children (TSCC)			X	X
• Child Behavior Sexual Inventory	X	X	X	X
• Traumagenic Impact of Maltreatment Scale	X	X	X	X
• UCLA PTSD Index for DSM-IV			X	X

Source: Used with permission. Children's Trauma Assessment Center (CTAC), 2011, chhs-ctac@wmich.edu.

previously completed (psychological, school information, therapist reports), especially those within the last year.

Prior to the assessment, caregivers complete a series of rating scales (see Table 2.1). Additionally, in order to gather more in-depth and updated historical information on the child, an ethnographic caregiver interview is completed before the assessment by using a semistructured format to encourage caregiver conversation about the child. This style elicits detailed information, but more importantly, caregiver perception of the child and a snapshot of the environment in which the child functions on a day-to-day basis. This more interactive interview style taps into the caregiver's emotional impression of the child through their choice of language used to describe the child, as well as avoiding a way to observe the quality of the child–caregiver attachment relationship.

On the day of evaluation, a preassessment transdisciplinary team meeting is conducted and the caregiver ethnographic interview is reviewed. Team members offer suggestions regarding potential assessment challenges and unique child-specific areas of concern, and the specific instruments and tools to be used. The assessment process typically requires approximately four contact hours (preschool children typically take less time). Two clinicians from different disciplines conduct the assessment, administering tests for cognitive/neurodevelopmental functioning, and social communication/cognition. These clinicians remain with the child during the morning session with nonparticipating team members observing through one-way mirrors. The team reconvenes during lunch to revisit assessment strategies, make adjustments, and discuss psychosocial interview approaches. Medical evaluations and audiological screenings are accomplished throughout the day. An observation and/or attachment evaluation with the child and caregiver is conducted near the end of the assessment. The psychosocial interview (conducted by social work staff) is the final component and provides an understanding of the child's perceptions of himself/herself and the familial environment. Age-appropriate arrays of techniques are employed: play, projective drawings, physical activity, and an alternative semistructured interview.

At the postassessment meeting, preliminary assessment results are reported and processed by the transdisciplinary team utilizing an integrated trauma-informed, brain-based framework. Conclusions and specific recommendations are documented for eventual inclusion in the final report. Note: Children in foster care/kinship care are observed by CTAC staff (including a formal attachment evaluation) at a later time during the child's regularly scheduled visitations with the biological parent(s). Upon completion of the assessment report, the family and caregivers are invited to review the final report with the lead clinician and meet (if appropriate) with the behavioral pediatrician for a psychopharmacological consultation.

Data entry into a statistical database follows completion of the report. Unpublished research on a sampling of the statistical analysis on approximately 2000 assessed children reveals:

- 71% have moderate to major receptive language delays
- 82% have moderate to major memory delays
- 70% have moderate to major visual processing delays
- 85% have moderate to major attention deficits
- 60% have probable to definite sensory processing problems
- The mean of rule-breaking, aggression, and externalizing behaviors are at statistically elevated levels

These findings document the need for comprehensive assessments to identify the likely pervasive harmful impact that results from exposure to trauma. In the conclusion of the report, CTAC clinicians focus on integration of all the domains through a complex trauma lens. Diagnosis is secondary, as the current diagnoses in the *Diagnostic and Statistical Manual of Mental Disorders* (*DSM-IV*; American Psychiatric Association, 1994) are not fully adequate for CTAC-assessed children. Armed with a global trauma/brain-based understanding, recommendations can be formulated that address not only the identified neurodevelopmental and neurobehavioral delays and deficits, but also provide professionals and caregivers with a specific action plan designed to mitigate the deleterious effects of trauma.

THE CTAC IN ACTION

James Henry

Mike is 8 years old. His foster mother expressed concern with his cognitive, social, and emotional development, as well as his speech and language abilities. She also reported that he has sensory and fine motor issues. Mike is overly sensitive to touch (e.g., sometimes he reacts painfully to even a light touch) and he has some extreme reactions to noise. He is also unable to keep himself clean while eating and does not seem to notice when food is on his face. His foster mother's primary concerns are Mike's emotional well-being and developmental delays. He often vacillates from being clingy to explosive and emotionally disengaged from others. She describes him as "an active, busy, unfocused little boy."

Mike's mother and father have a documented history of drug use. Mike was frequently passed off to numerous friends of his parents, who were neglectful of him (physical and emotional needs not met). Mike was exposed to domestic violence and to neglect prior to age 3. He was first removed from his mother's home for approximately 1 year when he was 3 years of age, then returned to his father, and then removed after 10 months with his father for both neglect and physical abuse, which included bruises on his face and back from his father. Note: This is a typical history for a child referred to CTAC. The vast majority of the children have histories of complex traumatization and exhibit concerns in multiple areas.

ASSESSMENT

The previously explained CTAC assessment protocol was utilized to assess Mike. For Mike this included:

- A review of the Department of Human Services reports and other previous testing
- An ethnographic interview with the foster mother prior to the assessment
- A transdisciplinary team review of his records and ethnographic history on the day of the assessment
- Neurodevelopmental testing utilizing the Pediatric Early Elementary Examination (PEEX)
- Intelligence testing using the Kaufman Brief Intelligence Test (KBIT)
- Pragmatics testing
- Psychosocial interview
- Physical examination and measurement of facial features for prenatal alcohol exposure
- Review of parent behavioral questionnaires, which includes the Sensory Profile
- Transdisciplinary team meeting immediately following Mike's assessment
- Comprehensive report integrating all the testing and interviews

SUMMARY

A physical exam was completed and found Mike to be in generally good health with growth patterns within the normal ranges. Facial characteristics associated with fetal alcohol exposure are mildly present. Neurodevelopmental delays for Mike were global. Major concerns were noted in fine motor, language, memory, sequencing, and visual processing. All of these identified delays prevent Mike from functioning successfully. The significant attention deficits noted compromise him from realizing his full potential. Mike's performance was noted to improve slightly during the assessment when visual cues were present. Additionally, Mike was noted to attempt to use various strategies to support his performance, though these strategies proved ineffective. An area in which some strengths were noted is the area of gross motor development. This area of development can provide some means for Mike to experience success and support his resiliency in overcoming other identified areas of delay.

Mike's intelligence potential (KBIT-2) indicates that he is in the low average range for his verbal reasoning as well as his nonverbal reasoning (Composite, 89, 23rd percentile). He exhibits difficulty with abstract reasoning skills and is likely to be very concrete in his thinking. Mike has social communication deficits that affect his perceptions of what other people are thinking about a particular situation and understanding the needs of the listener when trying to communicate his own perspective. He will perceive others as making the same meaning out of experiences that he does, and he has difficulty knowing how to change his own communication to be better understood. This will compromise his ability to communicate and reciprocate in interactions with others. The combination of deficits found in Mike's intellectual reasoning, his information processing, and his social/emotional delays all contribute to his difficulty interpreting and responding to others. His delays also contribute to impulsivity, frustration intolerance, and displays of aggression.

Observations during the assessment and the Sensory Profile completed by the foster mother revealed a number of problems concerning sensory processing delays. In any situation, difficulty with sensory input can interfere with the child's ability to complete important activities in daily life as successfully as other children do. Further, his sensory problems contribute to his explosiveness as sensory input overstimulates his brain. He does not currently have the skills to modulate his sensory and affective responses.

Research indicates that children who have been exposed to complex traumatization are often in a perpetual state of alarm and scan their environment for cues that may indicate danger. Mike's difficulty attending for prolonged periods of time may be related to hypervigilance and reactivity to changes in the environment. Hypervigilance compounded with poor social communication skills contributes to more confusion and fear as Mike will be prone to misinterpret facial expressions and body language as potentially threatening or rejecting. Mike will benefit from caregivers articulating their thoughts and feelings, and discussing with Mike their intentions when expressing their own emotions. The more concrete caregivers can be in communicating the intention in their communications, the more he will be able to learn to understand other peoples' intentions.

Mike scored high on the alexithymia scale. *Alexithymia* is the inability to identify emotions or the lack of awareness of emotions. Although Mike may regularly experience strong emotions, he has difficulty identifying what he is feeling and/or discriminating between feelings such as sadness and anger. This compounds his identified expressive language deficits because he is not only unable to clearly identify his feelings for himself, but even if he could identify his feelings, he cannot express and communicate them adequately to others. In order for Mike to be able to identify his feelings, it is important for adults in his life to identify and reflect his feelings back to him. He is apt to often describe himself as mad, when in reality it is likely sadness. Children most often express their sadness and underlying depression through anger.

Information provided with the referral describes Mike's history of exposure to home conditions that were chronically dangerous and neglectful. In an environment that involved drug use and domestic violence, Mike was likely exposed to chronic chaos, lack of predictable care, physical harm, and inadequate nurturance. His exposure to this environment along with emotionally unavailable parents and multiple disruptions to his primary relationships are consistent with the formation of insecure attachment. It is important to provide Mike with consistency, routine, and emotional attunement as a way to help him build feelings of safety and trust. Permanency is critical to his continuing development of skills necessary for emotional/behavioral regulation and attachment.

Mike's history, his current behaviors, and the testing results all strongly indicate serious executive functioning difficulties, which is consistent with children with trauma histories due to brain changes in the prefrontal cortex areas of the brain. He cannot consistently monitor his thoughts, feelings, and actions, especially when experiencing stress. His brain, due to his early experiences, is wired for danger, and he is likely to quickly exhibit fight/flight behaviors, which to adults are inappropriate and unacceptable, but for him are primitive survival responses to a perceived unsafe environment.

Mike is at high risk for future academic, relational, and behavioral problems. His early relational trauma, along with his subsequent traumas, has seriously compromised his development. His hyperarousal, emotional and behavioral dysregulation, and his aggressive reenactments are consistent with his complex traumatization. His brain requires simple repetitions of praise, attunement to his underlying needs and feelings, which he cannot express, and caregivers who are willing to absorb his affect and aggression. To build resiliency he needs relatedness with safe and permanent caregivers, the development of mastery through positive experiences of success and affect regulation skills to emotionally and behaviorally regulate.

CTAC FIVE PRIMARY RECOMMENDATIONS

1. Attachment activities that promote calming routines with caregivers are recommended. Caregiver modeling of emotional expression, including the identification of his emotional states and strategies for regulating (i.e., "you look angry, let's sit down, look at a book, and calm down"), are recommended. Learning to read his body responses and identifying feeling states associated with them is the first step. Traditional talk therapy will not be successful for him until he learns to modulate affect and experiences safety. This will take significant time, intensive effort, and will produce small gains.
2. Occupational therapy to address ongoing sensory processing concerns; intensive services within the home.
3. Specific expressive language tasks.
4. Therapy that utilizes the core elements of trauma treatment including psychoeducation, affect regulation skill building, creating a narrative, managing triggers, and building relatedness.
5. A medical consult to explore the benefits of pharmacological interventions.

DEVELOPMENTAL AUDIT

Larry Brendtro

Brendtro and Shahbazian (2004) developed the Developmental Audit, an assessment process that is based on resilience, neuroscience, and ecological research. The Developmental Audit provides strength-based assessment with children and youth in conflict in their ecologies: school, family, and community. The audit examines how children cope with challenging life events and identifies significant interpersonal connections in the social ecology. It addresses two key questions: What has happened to bring this young person to this point in his or her life, and where should we go from here to foster healing, growth, and resilience? The young person then participates in developing their individualized restorative plan (Brendtro, Brokenleg, & Van Bockern, 2002). The Developmental Audit proceeds in three stages: Challenges, Connections, and Courage.

CHALLENGES: EVENT TIMELINES

Initially, the young client is engaged in exploring *timelines of challenging events*. The human brain stores significant life experiences in autobiographical memory, selectively archiving emotionally charged events. When children share these experiences, practitioners have a window into their thinking, emotions, and behavior (Long, Wood, & Fecser, 2001).

CONNECTIONS: THE ECOLOGICAL SCAN™

The Developmental Audit identifies sources of strain and support in interpersonal relationships (Bronfenbrenner, 2005). In a healthy ecology, children live in harmony. But a disrupted ecology produces conflict and maladjustment. Since thousands of factors impact the social ecology, the Ecological Scan targets those forces that most directly impact learning and development (Morse, 2008). These come from interactions in the child's immediate life space of family, school, peers, and community.

The Developmental Audit proposes that the universal needs of every child are belonging, mastery, independence, and generosity. Since young people are the real experts on their lives, practitioners ask them to describe the ways they experience themselves in different situations to determine their needs. For example, "I was always afraid of messing up, which is why I didn't participate" helps us understand the need for *mastery* that can be developed with that youth into a restorative plan and a set of new experiences. Once initiated, the assessment process turns to the youth as the real expert and asks him to describe the changes these new experiences have created. When mastery is being experienced, a child often realizes, "Here if I make mistakes, people help me and teach me how to do it right. Nobody makes bad comments or calls me dumb. My parents can see a difference in me. I think I carry myself in a successful 'yes, I'm worth it' way."

Most will agree that it is unlikely that individuals, especially children and adolescents, will accurately identify their behaviors, thoughts, and feelings by checking answers presented in assessment tools. How children experience life often tells us far more than formal assessment tools. Social intelligence is individually constructed based on life events, and it guides interpersonal behavior. These experiences create what Alfred Adler (1930) called "private logic," a unique view of self, others, and the world. It is this private logic that drives behavior. As we come to know the private logic of a traumatized youth, we can better appreciate the strengths of that youth as well as his or her needs. The vital balance is created when we present new experiences that address the basic biological and social needs of that youth (Menninger, 1963).

THE DEVELOPMENTAL AUDIT IN PRACTICE

In a healthy ecology, children live in harmony. But a disrupted ecology produces conflict and maladjustment. Since thousands of factors impact the social ecology, the Ecological Scan™ targets those forces and experiences that most directly impact learning and development (Morse, 2008). These come from interactions in the child's immediate life space of family, school, peers, and community. The human brain stores significant life experiences in autobiographical memory, selectively archiving emotionally charged events. When children share these experiences, we have a window into their thinking, emotions, and behavior (Long, Wood, & Fecser, 2001). Furthermore, the large brains of humans are designed for complex interpersonal relationships (Szalavitz & Perry, 2010). Traditional assessment employs tests and checklists to measure deviation from an external norm. But it is more useful to know how a life event is understood by the person who lived it than to use the "distorted optics" of various disciplines" (Csikszentmihalyi, 1990, p. 26).

Brief Assessments

Because practitioners and many centers may not have the capacity or resources to conduct a comprehensive assessment, several brief assessment tools are listed here that may yield helpful information to establish a baseline for intervention. This is not an endorsement or recommendation of these tools. Practitioners should understand that the real value of any tool is not necessarily the information it yields, but the interpretation of that information within a trauma-informed context. The less comprehensive the assessment, the greater the risk for developmentally inappropriate use of interventions and outcome expectations that do not reflect the neurological functioning of traumatized children. This said, some assessment is better than no assessment.

Many trauma-informed readers are familiar with four of the more common instruments used to measure PTSD and other mental health–related symptoms:

1. *Trauma Symptom Checklist for Children* (TSCC-A) (Briere, 1996) is a standardized self-report measure of posttraumatic and related symptoms for children 8 to 16 years of age. The instrument can be used with children as young as 7 and adolescents as old as 17 years. This instrument evaluates children's responses in five symptom domains: anxiety, depression, anger, posttraumatic stress, and dissociation.
2. *Youth Self-Report* (YSR) (Achenbach & Rescoria, 2001) is a standardized self-report measure that assesses problem behaviors in two summary domains: internalizing and externalizing. These summary domains are composed of eight symptom scales: anxious/depressed, withdrawal/depressed, somatic complaints, social problems, thought problems, attention problems, rule-breaking behavior, and aggressive behavior. The YSR is designed to assess problem behaviors of children and adolescents 11 to 18 years of age.
3. *University of California PTSD Reaction Index for DSM-VI* (UCLA-PTSD-RI) (Steinberg et al., 2004) is a 48-item semistructured interview that assesses a child's exposure to 26 types of traumatic events and

RECOMMENDATIONS FOR TRAUMA ASSESSMENT

Michael Bayda

Clinicians may also find helpful the *Behavior Assessment System for Children, Second Edition®* (BASC-2), a multidimensional system used to evaluate the behavior and self-perceptions of children and young adults aged 2 through 25 years. The BASC-2 consists of five components, which can be used separately or in various combinations. These components include Parent and Teacher Rating scales for various age groups; a Self-Report scale for children as young as 8 years, adolescents, and young adults; a Structured Developmental History Form; and a form for recording and classifying behavior observed in a school setting.

A recently developed tool for evaluating sensory functioning is the Sensory Processing Measure (SPM) (Miller Kunaneck, Henry, & Glennon, 2007) designed to assess children in kindergarten through sixth grade (ages 5–12). The SPM is "an integrated system of rating scales that enables assessment of sensory processing issues, praxis, and social participation in elementary school children" (p. 3). The SPM is composed of the following scales: Social Participation, Vision, Hearing, Touch, Taste and Smell, Body Awareness, Balance and Motion, and Planning and Ideas.

assesses *DSM-IV* PTSD diagnostic criteria. It includes 19 items to assess the 17 symptoms of PTSD as well as 2 associated symptoms (guilt and fear of the event recurring).

4. *Child and Adolescent Questionnaire* (CAQ) was developed by the authors (Steele & Raider, 2001) and is a modification of the UCLA PTSD Reaction Index (Frederick, Pynoos, & Nader, 1992). The CAQ consists of 35 Likert-type questions comprising three scales. Scale I evaluates the re-experiencing of the traumatic event, Scale II evaluates avoidance of stimuli associated with the traumatic event, and Scale III evaluates the symptoms of increased arousal due to the traumatic event.

Finally, the Behavioral Emotional Rating Scale (BERS-2) (Epstein et al., 2004) is a widely used instrument to evaluate strengths. It includes five subscales: interpersonal strengths, intrapersonal strengths, family involvement, school functioning, and affective strength. It is very easy to score and assist in the inclusion of a strength-based focus in planning treatment. Obviously, the standard achievement and intelligence tools can yield information regarding cognitive functions that ought to be included in the assessment process.

This is not meant to be an inclusive listing of the many available tools, but does represent the more frequently used instruments. There is one additional caution—traumatized children and adolescents can present significant challenges in response to the use of these assessment tools. The real skill is being attuned to the concerns of children and adolescents as well as their capacity to attend and focus long enough to complete an assessment in one session. Furthermore, with multiply traumatized individuals it is very important to use instruments that record the observations of others as the traumatized child's self-report will be skewed by the neurological impact of trauma. Basically, the assessment of traumatized children takes patience, a good understanding of the limitations of each tool, and the realization that outcome data must be interpreted within the context of the child's history, environment, and experiences.

Cultural Aspects of Trauma-Informed Assessment

Trauma-informed assessment dictates that helping professionals be sensitive to diversity (ethnic, gender, socioeconomic, and religious) and worldviews of their young clients and their parents or caretakers. For example, while it is commonly believed that disclosure of distressing experiences will make an individual feel better, asking certain questions may actually make some children or their parents feel worse, or at best, confused. In other cases, disclosure may make some clients feel uncomfortable, that they have revealed a family secret, or have divulged something personally shameful. Additionally, some youngsters or caretakers may perceive an evaluation to be deceptive and designed to trick them into telling or revealing things about themselves.

Helping professionals are cautioned that there is still relatively little data on cultural aspects of trauma-informed assessment and procedures are based on Western models of evaluation and appraisal. In contrast to other forms of assessment, however, it changes the traditional question of "what is wrong with you?" to "what has happened to you?" adjusting the focus to strength building over deficit finding. For individuals from non-U.S. cultures who have been exposed to war, political upheaval, and disasters, this viewpoint underscores acceptance that trauma may have happened and that it may be a significant factor in any current challenges or problems in

THE NEED TO BECOME TRAUMA-INFORMED ABOUT ASSESSMENT

William Steele

Every year for the past 25 years I have had the privilege of interacting with thousands of professionals in schools, clinics, child and family agencies, and statewide service systems. Their collective experience and wisdom has always been phenomenal and their long-term dedication to servicing challenging children even more amazing. They have taught me a great deal because of what they have learned or do not practice. This is by no means a criticism, as there is no one person who can possibly meet all the needs traumatized children present today. Their openness about their efforts, experience, and knowledge has always led to helpful "teachable moments" for all of us.

A recent example that supports the rationale for devoting two chapters to assessment occurred shortly before and during our writing of this book. Given the opportunity to interact with so many frontline practitioners, I will frequently conduct informal surveys. One such survey presented to several groups asked each participant to write down the five most important bits of information they felt were critical to determining an effective treatment plan before actually beginning intervention.

Somewhat surprising and yet understandable were the areas rarely identified. The following were rarely mentioned:

- Assessment of cognitive processes, strengths as well as limitations
- Assessment of sensory integration development
- Identification of activation (arousal) triggers and what actions and/or resources the child uses to calm, deactivate, or self-regulate
- Developmental assessment history
- Identification of strengths

How can we possibly determine the most appropriate interventions without this neurodevelopmental information given the well-established impact trauma has on the brain (the body as well)? We simply cannot.

These are only a few of the areas of functioning that the neuroscience of trauma clearly demands that we evaluate. Putting this in the perspective of what constitutes the most beneficial trauma-informed treatment for children, we must advocate strongly for comprehensive assessment if we are truly committed to giving traumatized children the resources to flourish. Yes, the neuroscience data on trauma is relatively new. Yes, such evaluations can be costly. Yes, very few are trained to provide the kind of comprehensive trauma assessment that will be presented in this text. Yes, many childcare systems are not informed sufficiently to support a mind-set shift to the long-term mental health issues and costs that are involved by failure to provide traumatized children today with a comprehensive assessment. And yet, we must advocate for such assessments as this is in the best interest of the child, his family, and his community.

Providing comprehensive assessments within a trauma-informed context does present challenges for all of us and yet, knowing what we know today about trauma's impact on learning, behavior, and health, trauma-informed care dictates that intervention be supported by and match the neurodevelopmental needs of traumatized children today.

As much of a challenge as this presents, it is extremely exciting to know that our ability to actually see how the brain and body react to traumas, as well as treatment, is providing new and more effective approaches to treatment. The benefits we can now bring to traumatized children and their families when we provide a comprehensive trauma-informed assessment certainly makes the challenge more than worthwhile.

contrast to personal shortcomings. Ultimately, trauma-informed assessment's goal is to provide comprehensive information on children and adolescents based on a variety of factors, not just emotional disorders, allowing for evaluation of a wide range of responses to physical, emotional, cognitive, and social domains.

Finally, a trauma-informed approach to assessment underscores the need to establish a strong relationship where possible with parents or caretakers; identifying any cultural values and preferences for evaluation is key to successful assessment. First and foremost, the trust of children and adolescents in the procedures that are administered is essential, not only to encourage participation, but also to obtain enough information to fully understand these young clients' histories, challenges, and trauma responses.

Conclusion

This chapter provides a sampling of best practices in standardized trauma-informed assessment that address multidimensional aspects of children and adolescents. Any comprehensive evaluation should reach beyond psychiatric tools to gather information on trauma histories, environment, interpersonal skills, and developmental aspects. Just as there is no one intervention that fits every child, there is no one assessment style or protocol that fits every child. For this reason, the next chapter addresses alternative ways to evaluate children and adolescents through activity-based protocols that include the sensory benefits of play and art to provide additional information on psychosocial and developmental aspects of trauma on young clients.*

---

* The authors wish to thank the following individuals for their contributions to this chapter: The Trauma Assessment Pathway (TAP) Model prepared by Lisa Conradi and Nicole Taylor Kletzka and the Comprehensive Transdisciplinary Trauma Assessment Model prepared by Jim Henry, Ben Atchison, Connie Black-Pond, Yvette Hyter, Mark Sloan, Margaret Richardson, and Amy Mack.

Chapter 3

Sensory-Based, Trauma-Informed Assessment

The trauma-informed assessments described in the previous chapter are essential and comprehensive instruments and protocols for gathering data on children and adolescents. However, traumatized individuals are sometimes hesitant to talk about their experiences during standardized assessments for many reasons. First, they may find it difficult to explain events verbally because of cognitive and emotional challenges that interfere with conceptualization and perception. As described in previous chapters, experiences of terror affect language areas of the brain, including Broca's area, leaving children with "speechless terror" that limits communication via words. Self-reports may even stir up feelings of extreme fear, worry, and confusion when flight, fight, or freeze responses surface if children are confronted with exhaustive, multiple interviews.

For example, consider 9-year-old Tasha, who has been repeatedly sexually abused since the age of 3 years by a stepfather and other family members. She has been interviewed by almost a dozen professionals including law enforcement, social workers, child protective service workers, a residential counselor, a psychologist, and a pediatrician. Some of the professionals were as nervous as Tasha herself because of the types of questions they had to ask her and the lengthy paper-and-pencil assessments they had to conduct. While all of these evaluations were necessary to determine a course of action for Tasha, not all may have been trauma-informed protocols as described in Chapter 2. Even when well-constructed trauma-informed protocols are used, they may not have provided Tasha with child-oriented, developmentally appropriate, and activity-driven procedures to allow her to relate the sensory experiences of her multiple traumas.

This chapter covers a series of sensory-based assessments that can be applied to evaluation of children who have experienced a variety of traumas. Practical play and art-based assessments are described to help the reader understand how these protocols may complement other types of trauma-informed assessments and interviews. Several models for applying art and play in evaluation are provided, ending with a summary of best practices for sensory-based, trauma-informed assessment with traumatized children and adolescents.

Trauma-Informed Art and Play Assessment

Sensory-based, trauma-informed assessment is based on the principles of trauma-informed art therapy (Malchiodi, 2010) and includes, but is not limited to, art-based and play-based approaches. The overall goal is to more clearly identify an individual's developmental functioning and the impact of trauma and other events during the child's lifespan in order to determine what interventions, adjustments to environment, and resilience-building strategies will be most effective. In particular, it is important to evaluate *neurosequential development*, a hierarchy described by Perry (2006) (Figure 3.1); as discussed earlier in this volume, trauma changes how the brain functions and traumatized individuals may have problems in one or more areas of the brain as a result. For example, an inability to focus, lack of attunement to others, and attachment problems may reflect difficulties at the lowest level,

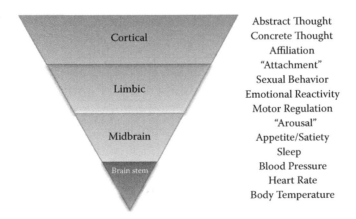

Figure 3.1   Neurosequential development. (From B.D. Perry. (2002). *Brain and Mind,* **3(1), 79–100. Used with permission.)**

the brain stem; challenges involving hyperarousal and the ability to have satisfying productive relationships may indicate limbic system dysfunction. In normal individuals, the brain develops in an age-related sequential fashion over the course of childhood into adolescence; in traumatized children, one or more areas may be impacted by events such as abuse, neglect, or other disruptive experiences.

Goals of trauma-informed art and play assessment are similar to observational and interviews and include the following:

1. Evaluation of children's overall functioning, including patterns of communication and attachment and attunement to others
2. Identification of the impact of traumatic events
3. Evaluation of the child's developmental level, including physical, emotional, and relational aspects
4. Evaluation of the child's perceptions of parental/caretaker support
5. Evaluation of the child's internal support (resilience and posttraumatic growth)
6. Observation of the child's level of enjoyment, curiosity, spontaneity, and creativity

In brief, art- and play-based assessment is meant to help practitioners meet children and adolescents at the individual's own level and in a way that addresses their interests and preferences for self-expression and disclosure. Both products (creative expressions in play, art expression, and sand tray) and the process (the unique way children and adolescents approach the activities and how they relate to the helping professional and environment) are equally important. In order to provide a foundation for applying sensory-based, trauma-informed assessment in practice, two major approaches are described: (1) a play-based assessment that is carried out over many sessions, and (2) art-based assessments that may be applied as part of a comprehensive assessment or used in single-session evaluations. Finally, examples of protocols combining both art- and play-based methods are provided for one- or three-session evaluations.

Extended Developmental Assessment

Gil (2003b, 2006; Gil & Green, n.d.) describes an *extended developmental assessment* (EDA) that reflects a trauma-informed approach and uses sensory-based approaches including play therapy and art therapy. This 10- to 12-session assessment includes an intake meeting with parents or care-takers and initial collection of historical and behavioral data similar to the assessments noted in the previous chapter. Originally designed to evaluate abused children, this assessment is useful in work with children because of its developmental focus. While many assessments focus on brevity in observation, this protocol favors multiple sessions in order to get a more complete understanding of children, developmental functioning, and possible impact of traumatic events. Extended meetings over time allow anxious children to feel more relaxed in sharing experiences through spontaneous play and increase the comfort level between children and helping professionals. Like other sensory-based assessments, it underscores children's natural mode of communication (play) as a form of nonverbal narrative and symbolic language.

EDA can be broken down into three major phases:

1. **Early phase**. The goal of the first three to four sessions is to help children feel safe and comfortable with the practitioner and play-based work. These sessions may involve free, nondirected play and art expression.
2. **Middle phase**. These sessions are designed to facilitate disclosure in indirect ways if children are uncomfortable with direct discussion; if children have openly discussed or revealed sensitive events or issues, these sessions may be used to continue talking about trauma experiences. Sessions may include family play genogram (see section "Family Play Genogram" in this chapter), directed sand tray work, self-portraits, family drawings, and using art to express feelings.
3. **Final phase**. The last three to four sessions include preparation for termination of the assessment or discussion with children and/or parents or caretakers about goals for future intervention and treatment.

While practitioners who use EDA may note observations about physical functioning, relational interactions, themes in play and art, and other areas, the protocol is designed with the following goals in mind (Gil, 2003, 2006; Gil & Green, n.d.):

1. Determination of developmental functioning
2. Identification of symptoms and problems
3. Determination of impact of traumatic events

4. Identification of children's coping strategies and internal strengths
5. Clarification of children's perceptions of social support from parents or other sources
6. Facilitation of appropriate parental or caretaker support of children

EDA is trauma-informed because it capitalizes on nondirective approaches and the relationship between the helping professional and the child. To the extent possible, the child is able to control decision making about activities; in response, the helping professional provides unconditional acceptance and avoids symptom-focused, pathology-driven evaluations. The objective is to encourage the child to externalize worldviews, lessen expectations, and allow engagement at one's own pace; for the traumatized child, it tends to be less threatening because it holds the view that the child has individual needs and interests (Gil & Green, n.d.). EDA also stresses the importance of having specific toys and props to stimulate children to talk about or play out scenarios related to traumatic events or fears and anxieties about traumatic experiences. For example, having a toy replica of a courtroom can be essential during initial sessions with an abused child who will be going to court to testify; having miniatures and props that represent medical equipment, doctors, nurses, and first responders are important in work with young clients who have been traumatized by surgeries, accidents, or physical violence. A basic list of play materials, toys, and props is found in Tables 3.1 and 3.2.

Family Play Genogram

Gil originated the family play genogram based on the widely used pencil-and-paper genogram (McGoldrick, Gerson, & Petry, 2008) and sand tray therapy. In brief, this activity is designed to gather information about children's perception of families and social support networks. Because it is visual and three-dimensional, it allows the helping professional to see what the family looks like through the child's lens and obtain demographic information in a creative, child-centered fashion.

For this session, the following materials are needed: large sheet of white paper, marking pens, miniatures (see Table 3.2), child-safe modeling clay (to create figures that are not in the selection of miniatures), and a digital camera to take pictures of the genogram. For some children it is preferable for the helping professional to make a drawing of a genogram of the family ahead of time; optionally, the practitioner can create this drawing with

Table 3.1   Play Therapy Materials[a]

Wood doll furniture	Popsicle sticks
Bendable doll family	Truck, car, airplane, tractor, and boat
Bendable Gumby	Toy bus
Dolls	Toy bench and hammer
Doll bed, clothes, etc.	Xylophone
Pacifier	Cymbals
Plastic nursing bottle	Drum
Purse and jewelry	Toy soldiers and army equipment
Chalkboard and chalk	Hats
Colored chalk and eraser	Toy pine log, hammer, nails
Wood refrigerator	Sandbox, large spoon,
Wood stove	Funnel, sieve, and pail
Plastic or tin dishes	Zoo animals and farm animals
Pans and silverware	Rubber snake, alligator
Pitcher	Bobo (bop bag)
Dishpan	Suction throwing darts
Plastic food	Target board
Empty fruit and vegetable cans	Rubber knife
Egg cartons	Handcuffs
Sponge and towel	Dart gun
Broom and dust pan	Toy machine gun
Soap, brush, and comb	Balls, various sizes
Crayons, pencils, and paper	Telephone
Transparent tape and paste	Blunt scissors
Toy watch	Construction paper, various colors
Building blocks (different shapes and sizes)	Toy medical kit
Paints, easel, newsprint, and brushes	Play money and cash register

(continued)

Table 3.1 Play Therapy Materials[a] (continued)

Play-Doh or clay	Tissues
Pipe cleaners	Rags or old towels
Tongs	Rope
Hand puppets	
Suggested Art Supplies[b]	
Colored markers, thick and thin points	Magazine pictures [precut] and construction paper [full color range]
Oil pastels, colored pencils	Scissors, white glue and glue sticks, tape and stapler
Watercolor tray, watercolor paint brushes	Modeling clay such as Model Magic; cookie cutters, child-safe modeling tools and rolling pin.

Sources: [a] Copyright (2002) from *Play therapy: The art of the relationship* by Garry L. Landreth, p. 126. Reproduced by permission of Taylor & Francis Group, LLC, a division of Informa plc.
[b] Malchiodi, C. A. (1998). *Understanding children's drawings.* New York: Guilford Press; Malchiodi, C. A. (2008). Creative interventions and childhood trauma. In C. Malchiodi (Ed.), *Creative interventions with traumatized children* (pp. 3–21). New York: Guilford Press.

children during the session (Figure 3.2). In all cases, be sure to ask children to include all relationships such as grandparents, foster parents and foster siblings, friends, teachers or mentors, and pets. In other words, children should be encouraged to add anyone of importance to them to the genogram drawing; a trauma-informed approach underscores identification of social supports and resiliency-building networks.

Once the drawing is complete, miniatures are chosen by the child to "best show your thoughts and feelings about everyone in the family, including yourself" (Gil, 2006, p. 80). These miniatures are placed on the square or circle representing that person on the drawing (Figure 3.3); some children will choose one figure for each spot while others may choose more than one to place on the drawing. When this activity is completed, the practitioner and child look at the completed genogram together. Take the child's lead in conversation and allow a narrative to unfold about the figures. If the child is hesitant to speak or cannot think of anything to say, you can encourage the child with any or all of the following questions/prompts:

Table 3.2   Miniatures for Family Play Genograms and Sand Tray Therapy

People	Family sets of different ages, sizes; children (nude and dressed), infants, adolescents; brides and grooms (separate and together); ethnic diversity in all figures
Professions	Police, judge, physician, nurse, firemen, sports figures
Armed forces	Tanks and equipment, soldiers, wounded with stretchers, different military branches
Historical	Cave people, aborigines, knights and royalty, cowboys, modern figures
Fantasy	Wizard, castle, fairy godmother, dragons, angels, fairies, space aliens
Spiritual	Minister, priest, rabbi, nun, bible, crosses, devil, Buddha, "wise" men and women
Animals	Zoo animals, farm animals, dinosaurs, domestic and wild animals, insects and butterflies
Nature	Water, trees, bushes, rocks, volcano, cave, sea shells, twigs
Vehicles	Cars, trucks, airplanes, boats, motorcycles, ambulance, school bus, police car
Structures	Buildings, churches, schools, bridges, wells, caves, fences; and items to make structures and boundaries such as popsicle sticks, string, cardboard
Miscellaneous	Scary and weird characters, cross-cultural items and figures, culture symbols, containers

Source: Based on Gil, E. (2000). *Family play therapy: Rational and techniques.* Fairfax, VA: Starbright Training Institute for Family and Child Play Therapy.

1. Tell me about your figures (or genogram).
2. Tell me about this (figure) (pointing to the miniature).
3. Tell me about the figure you used to represent you.
4. If that figure could talk, what would that figure say? (This question can refer to any of the figures.)
5. What is the figure doing, thinking, feeling, and/or wishing?
6. What would this figure (miniature) say to that figure (miniature)?
7. Do this figure and that figure get along?

In sensory-based, trauma-informed assessment it is important to refrain from judgments or guesses about the child's interpretation of the figures and relationships. The advantage of this approach is that the practitioner uses the

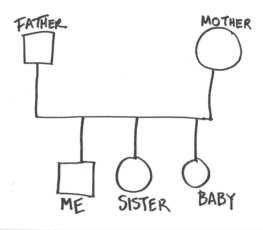

Figure 3.2 Family play genogram drawing.

Figure 3.3 Family play genogram with miniatures placed on genogram drawing. (Reproduced with permission of C. Malchiodi.)

characteristics of the figures to enter into a conversation with the child. For example, if the child picks a roaring lion to represent a sibling, the helping professional can say, "I see you picked the lion that is roaring. Can you tell me more about that lion? What do you think that lion is thinking and/ or feeling?" The goal is to get the child to express as much as possible about the figures, particularly any sensory characteristics that will help the child relate feelings and experiences with family members and relationships.

In ending the session, it is helpful to take photos of the genogram as a record of the activity to compare at a later date and to include in the child's file. In some cases, this activity may tell the professional more about family and extended relationships than noted by the child and parents or caretakers because of the tactile, visual nature of the experience.

Trauma-Informed Art-Based Assessment

Assessment strategies that include child-friendly activities are helpful not only because they can diffuse fears and anxieties about working with a counselor or therapist, but can also be a way for many young clients to "talk without talking" (Malchiodi, 2008). Drawing is one way to help children communicate difficulties when words are difficult or impossible; it also can be a useful, practical way to evaluate cognitive development and the impact of trauma. Because trauma is a sensory-based experience, the hands-on nature of art expression is now widely accepted as a method of tapping implicit memories of traumatic experiences (Hass-Cohen & Carr, 2008; Malchiodi, 2001, 2008; Steele & Raider, 2001) and can facilitate language and storytelling (Gross & Haynes, 1998; Lev-Weisel, 2007).

However, not all traumatized children and adolescents express their experiences through drawing in the same way. Some children will depict the horror of their experiences while others may prefer to relate as few details as possible. Because trauma affects development in children, the content, style, and characteristics in traumatized children's drawings often appears different from those children who have grown up in less-distressing circumstances. Therefore, any art-based assessment involving children's drawings should begin with an understanding of the normal developmental characteristics of drawings by age and stage. The following is a synopsis of these stages and serves as a basic guideline for evaluating developmental levels of drawings (adapted from Lowenfeld & Brittain, 1987; Golumb, 1990; Malchiodi, 1998, 2011a) (see Table 3.3 for a visual synopsis):

■ **Stage 0: Attunement, attachment, and kinesthetic development (0–18 months).** At this earliest stage, children have visual perception and can see colors and shapes, are attuned to picture books, images and people, begin to form attachments to caretakers as well as objects, and will grasp objects with hands (Malchiodi, 2011). Toward the end of this stage a child may be able to hold a crayon and make marks or

THE FAMILY PLAY GENOGRAM
Eliana Gil

We overemphasize verbal communication, especially in the field of child trauma. When children come to therapy, they are tongue-tied, ambivalent, uncertain, and often haven't made sense of their experiences. The ability to be reflective and develop insight may occur over time in young verbal children, especially when they learn to trust the clinician and the environment. I learned early on to make many invitations to children, not just to speak but to show. The play genogram was born from an interest in learning about children's perceptions of their world and their important relationships, as well as an interest in giving them another language they could use: symbol language. (I personally think of myself as trilingual: I speak Spanish, English, and Symbol languages). When working with play genograms, children have a "safe enough distance" to speak volumes about their thoughts and feelings about people in their lives. When an 8-year-old chooses a brick wall to show the relationship between her parents, the meaning is clear. When a child picks (and labels) a sleeping deer for a parent and a scary two-headed dragon for a sibling, this is an interesting combination and the parent may be perceived as sleeping through the danger the child perceives. Even the youngest child of 5 can select amazing symbols for family members: A 5-year-old child I worked with picked a fire-breathing dragon for her mother, who had been diagnosed with schizophrenia and had violent outbursts. For her father she chose a cake with fruit on the top. It was remarkable to see her turn the fire onto the cake because the implication she made was understood. Her mother was capable of destroying her father (melting him away). This child loved her mother very much and verbally she said her mother was "nice" and "pretty." However, when asked to choose among hundreds of symbols, her choice was less defended and much more on target of her true feelings.

uncontrolled scribbles on paper, but may not know that he or she made those marks. There is an enjoyment of movement, repetition, sensory activities, and gross motor skills.

■ **Stage 1: Scribbling and motor skills (18 months to 3 years).** Children can hold a drawing tool (crayon or marker) and use it to

Table 3.3 Stages of Development in Visual Arts

Stage	Age	Developmental Norms	Art Expression
0	0–18 mths	Attunement Attachment Early grasping of objects Toward end, uncontrolled mark-making	
I	18 mths–3 yrs	Scribbles of various types, including horizontal, vertical, and circular	
II	3–4 yrs	Naming scribbles Circles, crosses, rectangles Mandala	
III	4–6 yrs	Pre-schematic Subjective use of color First human figures	
IV	6–9 yrs	Schematic Baselines/skylines X-ray pictures Objective use of color	
V	9–12 yrs	Differentiation of sexes Detail/design Attempts at perspective Notice color in nature Caricatures/cartooning	
VI	12 yrs and onward	Greater detail/mastery Color in nature Abstraction Not everyone reaches this stage	

Source: Reproduced with permission of C. Malchiodi.

make marks on paper and uncontrolled scribbles; they can also pat and grasp clay. Children start to make the association between moving a crayon or marker on the paper and seeing a result appear. At first there is little control of the motions that are used to make the scribble; accidental results occur and the line quality of these early drawings varies greatly. As motor skills improve, scribbles include repeated motions, making horizontal or longitudinal lines, circular shapes, and assorted dots, marks, and other forms. At this stage there is also not much conscious use of color (i.e., the color is used for enjoyment without specific intentions) and drawing is enjoyed for the kinesthetic experience it provides.

■ **Stage 2: Basic forms and naming (3 to 4 years).** Children may still make scribbles at this age, but they also become more involved in naming and inventing stories about them. The connection of one's marks on paper to the world around him or her occurs. Children want to talk about their drawings, even if they appear to adults as unidentifiable scribbles. Attention span is still limited and concentration is restricted. Meanings for images change; a child may start a scribble drawing by saying, "This is my mommy," only to quickly label it as something else soon after. Other configurations emerge at this time, including the mandala—a circular shape, design, or pattern—and combinations of basic forms and shapes such as triangles, circles, crosses, squares, and rectangles. These forms are the precursors of human figures and other objects, the milestone in the next stage.

■ **Stage 3: Human forms, beginning schema, and symbols (4 to 6 years).** The major milestone of this stage is the emergence of rudimentary human figures, often called tadpoles. There is a subjective use of color at this stage, although some children may begin to associate color in their drawings with what they perceive to be in the environment (e.g., leaves are green). Children of this age are more interested in drawing the figure or object than the color of it. Also, there is no conscious approach to composition or design, and children may place objects throughout a page without concern for a ground-line or relationships to size. A figure may float freely across the page, at the top or sides, and some things may be appear upside down because children are not concerned with direction or relationship of objects.

■ **Stage 4: Development of visual schema and repetitive symbols (6 to 9 years).** Children rapidly progress in their artistic abilities during this stage. First and foremost is the development of visual symbols or schema for human figures, animals, houses, trees, and other objects in the environment. Many of these symbols are fairly standard, such as a particular way to depict a head with a circle, hairstyles, arms and legs, a tree with a brown trunk and green top; a yellow sun in the upper corner of the page; and a house with a triangular, pitched roof. Color is used objectively and sometimes rigidly (e.g., all leaves must be the same color green). There is the development of a baseline (a ground-line upon which objects sit) and often a skyline (a blue line across the top of the drawing to indicate the sky). During these years children also draw see-through or X-ray pictures (such as cutaway images of a house, where one can see everything inside) and attempt beginning perspective by placing more distant objects higher on the drawing page.

■ **Stage 5: Realism (9 to 12 years).** At this stage, children become interested in depicting what they perceive to be realistic elements in their drawings. This includes the first attempts at perspective; children no longer draw a simple baseline but instead draw the ground meeting the sky to create depth. There is a more accurate depiction of color in nature (e.g., leaves can be many different colors rather than just one shade of green), and the human figure is more detailed and differentiated in gender characteristics (e.g., more details in hair, clothing, and build).

■ **Stage 6: Adolescence (12 years and onward).** Many children (and adults) never reach this stage of artistic development because they may discontinue drawing or making art at around the age of 10 or 11 due to other interests. However, by the age of 13, children who have continued to make art or have art training will be able to use perspective more accurately and effectively in their drawings, will include greater detail in their work, will have increasing mastery of materials, will be more attentive to color and design, and will be able to create abstract images.

In brief, these stages are guidelines for benchmarks that normal children reach at each approximate age range. In cases of chronic trauma and other challenges that cause developmental problems, helping professionals will see delays in the content and style of drawings at expected chronological age ranges. Applying these stages can be helpful in understanding young clients, supplementing existing developmental information from other instruments; in particular, this stage model can be applied to drawing tasks described throughout this chapter and in particular those activities outlined in the final section on brief sensory-based, trauma-informed assessment.

Developmental Art-Based Assessments

There are specific art-based assessments that are developmental in nature and were designed with the belief that practitioners may underestimate the intelligence of certain children and adults when verbal skills are compromised. The Silver Drawing Test (SDT) (Silver, 2007) includes two particularly useful instruments that can help practitioners evaluate cognitive development based on Piaget's work (Piaget & Inhelder, 1969) and also observe artistic development, problem-solving skills, emotional challenges, and capacity for imagination in children ages 6 years and older.

Silver devised a set of three tasks to measure children's predictive abilities: (1) drawing how liquid sequentially disappears from a series of soda glasses, (2) showing how water would look if a bottle is tilted, and (3) drawing a house on a steep slope. Children with cognitive difficulties may perform below accepted age levels on these three drawing tasks for a variety of reasons including developmental trauma during early years (Figure 3.4). Silver also created sets of drawings of people, animals, objects, and environmental items (houses, trees, landscapes) called *stimulus drawings*. Stimulus drawings were originally developed for use with children with hearing impairments, but have been widely applied to individuals with a wide range of challenges including learning disabilities, communication problems, and emotional disorders. As their name implies, stimulus drawings are meant to stimulate the imagination to create stories about the images in the various drawings. In brief, the child or adolescent is asked to choose two drawings from a specific set of images and to "draw a story" using the two cards as the inspiration (Figure 3.5); the images do not have to be copied exactly and can be changed or altered in any way the client determines. After the drawing is completed, the individual writes a story about the drawing and determines a title for the picture (the practitioner can also take dictation for the child if writing is difficult). Silver provides a specific worksheet and protocol for this activity, but 8½ × 11-inch drawing paper, markers, crayons, and pencils can also be used to complete it.

While Silver established a scoring system to screen for depression and aggression for the draw-a-story task, helping professionals can use the draw-a-story activity as an informal assessment by considering the following questions:

1. Using the developmental stage model presented in this chapter, what stage of the model does the drawing most closely represent?

SDT Predictive Drawing

Suppose you took a few sips of a soda, then a few more, and more, until your glass was empty. Can you draw lines in the glasses to show how the soda would look if you gradually drank it all?

Suppose you tilted a bottle half filled with water. Can you draw lines in the bottles to show how the water would look?

Suppose you put the house on the spot marked x. Can you draw the way it would look?

Figure 3.4   Example of Silver test for cognitive abilities. (From Rawley Silver, *The Silver Drawing Test and Draw a Story: Assessing Depression, Aggression, and Cognitive Skills.* **Copyright 2007. Reproduced by permission of Taylor & Francis Group, LLC, a division of Informa plc.)**

2. Is the child able to select and combine two images in a single drawing?
3. Can the child tell you a story about the drawing?
4. What is the underlying theme of the story about the drawing?
5. What is the underlying effect of story and drawing? For example, is it positive, neutral, or negative? Does it contain violence or aggression? Are the characters passive or active? Does it present more than one emotion or contradictory emotions?

Draw a Story

Drawing

Story:_____
_____
_____
_____
_____

Please fill in the blanks below:
First name D Sex F Age 10 Location (state): _____ Date:_____
Just now I'm feeling ____very happy X O.K. ____angry ____frightened ____sad

Figure 3.5 Example of Silver draw-a-story. (From Rawley Silver, *The Silver Drawing Test and Draw a Story: Assessing Depression, Aggression, and Cognitive Skills*. Copyright 2007. Reproduced by permission of Taylor & Francis Group, LLC, a division of Informa plc.)

6. How does the child relate to the helping professional during the activity (attuned, attached, detaching, withdrawn, dissociated)?

In a trauma-informed capacity, activities like the Silver Drawing Test allow and encourage children and adolescents to communicate through metaphors rather than direct disclosure. This type of task can be particularly important early in intervention because it provides an opportunity to convey uncomfortable, confusing, or unresolved concerns nonverbally through drawing and imaginative storytelling.

Screening for Posttraumatic Stress and Human Figure Drawings

Requesting a human figure drawing (HFD) is a simple procedure and one that most children and adolescents are eager to do; it is also one of the most widely used standard drawing tasks with children (Cox & Catte, 2000; Malchiodi, 1998). Using a standard HFD instrument based on developmental factors, Malchiodi (2009) found that the HFDs of school-age children with posttraumatic stress disorder (PTSD) as measured by the University of California Los Angeles (UCLA) Reaction Index (Steinberg et al., 2004) were significantly different from those of children without measurable PTSD. While these findings could be attributable to other causes or circumstances, the study underscored the fact that developmental characteristics in children's drawings of people may point to the impact of trauma on cognitive and other areas of functioning. Differences in HFDs were derived by measurement on a modified form of the Koppitz (1968) HFD test, which uses a set of possible emotional indicators found in children's HFDs. The list of indicators that Koppitz created are based on developmental features found in normal children's HFDs and characteristics and omissions found in HFDs by children with a variety of emotional disorders.

For this task, the child is asked to use a pencil to draw a person, a whole person, on a piece of white paper (8½ by 11 inches). In brief, the total number of items yields a total score; by Koppitz's original estimates, two or more items are indicative of an emotional problem (unspecified). The 2009 study concluded that there was a high degree of inter-rater reliability for the instrumentation for the measurement of both groups and a strong positive relationship between child participants' scores on the drawing test and the UCLA PTSD Reaction Index for DSM-IV (UCLA-PTSD-RI). Because this study and subsequent research data have only been collected from children between 6 and 12 years, these guidelines cannot be applied to younger children or adolescents.

Body Scan or "Show Me the Color of Your Feelings"

Since 1994, the National Institute for Trauma and Loss in Children has been using what many practitioners call a "body scan" activity (Malchiodi, 2008; Steele & Raider, 2001) with traumatized children and adolescents. In brief, it

HUMAN FIGURE DRAWINGS AND PTSD IN CHILDREN—TWO CASE EXAMPLES

Cathy Malchiodi

Case 1. Janet is a 7-year-old girl who attends an outpatient trauma intervention program at a mental health clinic. When she was 4 years old, she recalls the police coming to her home because of domestic violence between her mother and father. Over the next several years, she witnessed more domestic violence between her parents and began to become anxious when she saw police in her neighborhood. Recently, there was a police raid on her home to arrest a family member for drug possession. After this incident, Janet became increasingly anxious and fearful, began to have insomnia, complained about "bad dreams," and reported that she could not stop thinking about the police breaking into her home. In Janet's situation, traumatic incidents occurred suddenly and unexpectedly, were visually disturbing, and could not be controlled or avoided.

Janet's total score on the UCLA-PTSD-RI was 27. Her most troublesome PTSD symptom as measured on the UCLA-PTSD-RI was reexperiencing the traumatic event and feelings associated with it. Janet's HFD (Figure 3.6) received a score of 3 on the Koppitz instrument because it included the following characteristics: shading of body, asymmetry of limbs, and no feet. A score of 2 or higher is indicative of emotional

Figure 3.6   Janet's human figure drawing. (Reproduced with permission of C. Malchiodi.)

Figure 3.7   Angelo's human figure drawing. (Reproduced with permission of C. Malchiodi.)

disorders according to the Koppitz rating system. Although Janet's HFD included no neck, this item is adjusted for age and is only scored for children 10 years and older who do not include the feature.

Case 2. Angelo is a 12-year-old boy who attends a public school in an urban area. When interviewed with the UCLA-PTSD-RI, he reported that he had recently witnessed violence in his neighborhood and had been bullied by a classmate at school occasionally. He received a score of 12 on the UCLA-PTSD-RI, a score well below the cutoff for significant symptoms of PTSD. His school counselor reported that although Angelo was initially agitated after witnessing a violent event, he did not exhibit any lasting symptoms indicative of posttraumatic stress.

Angelo's HFD (Figure 3.7) received a score of 1 on the Koppitz test. His figure drawing was less than 2 inches in height and otherwise included appropriate features.

consists of an outline of a gingerbread figure or body image and the individual is asked to use colors, lines, shapes, and images to show where in the body a "hurt, worry, or fear" is experienced or felt. This mind–body technique is a helpful tool in assisting young clients in communicating to helping professionals how they experience traumatic feelings. For example, 10-year-old Ben, at the request of his therapist, was able to indicate how he experienced his trauma as a "hurt in his head" and the fear (hyperarousal and flight reaction) as primarily located in his belly (Figure 3.8). When helping professionals can begin to understand how children and adolescents actually experience trauma on a sensory level, it is easier to subsequently design

Figure 3.8 Ben's body scan showing his headache and stomachaches. (Reproduced with permission of C. Malchiodi.)

trauma-informed interventions to reduce these reactions and help clients start to feel better.

A second variation of this activity is described by Gil (2006), who asks children to "color your feelings." The child, with the help of the therapist, makes a list of different feelings and then chooses a color to represent each of these feelings. Finally, the child is given an outline of a gingerbread figure on paper to then use these color codes to "show the feelings you have" about a worry, situation, or a person, and where these feelings (colors) are in the child's body. For children who cannot think of names for their feelings, a set of feelings cards or images can be helpful to facilitate this activity.

While neither of these activities constitutes a formal, standardized assessment, the fact that each taps the sensory experiences of young clients assists practitioners as a form of clinical, trauma-informed interview. Because the children in particular may not have the language to tell a therapist or counselor how trauma is affecting their bodies, these activities can stimulate a conversation about fear and worry while giving individuals a trauma-informed way to communicate it.

Brief Sensory-Based, Trauma-Informed Assessment

In many environments, practitioners do not have the luxury of providing lengthy assessments over the course of 10 or more meetings. While undoubtedly more sessions provide a more complete evaluation, there is a substantial amount that a professional can learn during one to three sessions of sensory-based, trauma-informed assessment.

If you are limited to one session, it is important to provide structured activities to get the most information possible from child clients. Free play or drawing may work with some children, but with others, directed activities may be necessary. While a single session can provide a significant amount of information, seeing children's responses over several sessions is preferable. For example, drawing styles or play responses may change as clients become more comfortable with helping professionals and the environment in which the assessment is conducted. The following section provides guidelines for single-session or three-session assessments:

Single Session

1. A human figure drawing (as previously described)
2. A drawing of a house, tree, and person on the same piece of paper (colored markers, colored pencils, and pencil and eraser)
3. Choice of one of the following:
   A. A free drawing (colored markers, colored pencils, and pencil and eraser)
   B. Use modeling clay (Model Magic in various colors) to create something (client's choice)
   C. Using images from the Silver Drawing Test to "draw a story" and create a narrative about the story (as previously described)
   D. Invite the client to create a "world" using miniatures in a sand tray (as previously described in EDA)

Three Sessions

1. Session 1: Same activities and choices presented in the single-session protocol
2. Session 2: Any of the activities in the single-session protocol that were not used in session 1; body scan activity or "color your feelings" (previously mentioned)

3. Session 3: Family play genogram (as previously described); if time permits, include any of the activities in the single-session protocol that were not used in session 1

Overall Recommendations

In providing sensory-based assessments such as art and play, keep in mind the following:

1. Traumatized children have a critical need for safety; while most art- and play-based assessments may be perceived as nonthreatening, there is potential for retraumatizing events to occur when tapping sensory-based memories via sensory means. Practitioners should watch children for signs of distress such as increased anxiety, withdrawal, or dissociation during implementation of any of these assessments.

2. Approach assessment as a witness to children's experiences and stories and be curious about every aspect of what they do; if young clients are comfortable with you, ask them about all parts of their drawings and art expressions, including what is not included. For example, if children do not include themselves in a drawing, ask "Where are you?" or "If you were in this picture, where would you be?" Simple questions will help stimulate children to talk about images or play. For additional questions, please see Table 3.4.

3. Keep track of your own projections and impressions about children's creative expressions. *Projection* means applying your own point of view, which can get in the way of understanding the child's perspective; in contrast, your impressions about the content of art and play can be very helpful in understanding how your young clients feel. Note your own reactions to their creations in a nonjudgmental way rather than interpreting any particular symbol or response to have a specific meaning. In sensory-based, trauma-informed assessment, your goal is not to take a pathology-oriented stance, but to try to determine children's responses from a neurodevelopmental perspective in terms of flight, fight, or freeze reactions, trauma responses, and personal worldviews.

4. Finally, as in all trauma-informed practice, it is important to be culturally sensitive to clients' art and play responses. Gil and Drewes (2006) provide an excellent resource for understanding cross-cultural play therapy

Table 3.4   Children's Drawings: Suggestions for Observations

Process-Related Observations
• Does the child wait for directions or instruction, or is s/he impulsive about materials and beginning the drawing activity?
• Does the child seem calm and focused or restless and agitated? Active or withdrawn? Is the child able to concentrate, or does she or he appear distracted?
• Does the child seem to be unaware of the environment or you during the drawing activity?
• Does this change during the session, with the art activity, or with any particular intervention or interaction?
• Is the child able to follow instructions, or is s/he easily frustrated or unable to follow simple instructions?
• Does the child seem confident in drawing or is s/he overly concerned about mistakes?
• Does the child seem to work independently or does s/he seem overly dependent on the therapist?
• To what degree does the child require structure or assistance in drawing?
• Can the child share materials and maintain appropriate boundaries?
• Does the child have difficulty leaving the session?
• How does the child respond to leaving his or her work if requested?
• Does the child seem excited to take the work with her or with him?
• Does the child specifically want the therapist to keep the drawing?
Product-Related Observations
• Is the child proud of the finished product, or does s/he devalue the drawing?
• Does the drawing contain unique expressive imagery, or does it contain stereotypic images?
• How does the child respond to questions about the drawing?
• Does the child associate image in the drawing with her- or himself, or does s/he not seem to self-associate with the drawing?
• If asked "Where are you in the drawing?" is the child able to give an answer or show you where he or she is in the drawing or in relation to the drawing?

(continued)

Table 3.4 Children's Drawings: Suggestions for Observations (continued)

• Can the child discuss the drawing metaphorically or in relationship to the self, or is discussion or describing the drawing difficult?
• Is the drawing developmentally appropriate for the child's age?
• What developmental stage best describes the child's drawing? Is this developmental stage consistent with the child's age?
• Are there any elements in the drawing that seem to be emphasized more than others? Is this emphasis consistent over several sessions?

Source: Based on Malchiodi, 1997; 1998; 2008. © 2011 Cathy Malchiodi; reproduced with permission of the author.

that includes an explanation of cultural sensitivity in applying art therapy to work with traumatized children (Malchiodi, 2005). Additionally, art and play materials used in trauma-informed work should include multicultural dolls, miniatures, and toy animals; paints, crayons, and markers that represent diverse skin tones; and culturally relevant religious/spiritual or ethnic symbols and items. Understand that with some children and adolescents, there are certain toys and props that might be considered "bad luck" or even "evil" by certain cultures (Gil & Drewes, 2006).

5. Before applying any of the procedures described in this chapter, practitioners should try each activity firsthand to learn what the procedure entails and to gain an understanding of the materials involved. Additionally, it is important to have the recommended media, toys, and props available in an appropriate, trauma-informed physical environment (see Chapter 5) so that clients will feel as safe and comfortable as possible in engaging in any of these tasks.

6. Finally, practitioners may need additional training or supervision to conduct art- and play-based assessment if they have not had coursework in these areas. Like any trauma-informed work, it is important to practice within the scope of skill, knowledge, and experience.

Conclusion

This chapter presents a very brief overview of possibilities for sensory-based protocols for trauma-informed assessment. While these instruments and procedures are more like clinical interviews than quantifiable assessments, they offer an additional window into young clients' worlds, including how trauma reactions have impacted psychosocial patterns and developmental skills. Most of all, they are child-friendly and provide activity-oriented ways for self-expression that are often empowering for children and adolescents as well as enlightening to practitioners.

Chapter 4

Establishing Safety Through Self-Regulation

Within a trauma-informed context, in order to discuss safety and self-regulation we first must revisit the developmentally appropriate use of the body to restore and regulate the brain's response to stress; sensory responses; implicit memories; self-protective reflexes; and fight, flight, survival responses. This discussion briefly repeats some of the Chapter 1 mind–body references, but also elaborates on their significance to and relationship with achieving safety and self-regulation. Therefore, this chapter addresses (1) the body's responses to trauma, (2) methods to help individuals achieve self-regulation, (3) examples of self-regulation processes, (4) safety and its relationship to self-regulation and trauma-informed intervention, (5) key elements of safe interventions, and (6) what constitutes a safe environment for traumatized children and adolescents.

The Body Remembers

The idea that the body *remembers* traumatic experiences is widely accepted in the 21st century, but it is really a concept that is several decades old. In 1967, Alexander Lowen wrote *Betrayal of the Body* to describe the ways the body shapes itself, moves itself, and numbs itself to manage anxiety and terror. He indicates, for example, that children learn early to hold their breath to cut off unpleasant sensations and feelings. Lowen and others (Kruger, 2002; Reich, 1972) underscore that traumatized individuals make somatic adaptations and that in turn result in how they respond to future environmental stresses (Ogden, Minton, & Pain, 2006).

In the 1990s and early 21st century, the field of trauma began to fully embrace the connection between mind and body in the understanding of not only the experience of trauma, but also as a best practice in trauma-informed intervention. Bessel van der Kolk (1994) wrote an article for the *Harvard Review of Psychiatry* titled: "The Body Keeps the Score: Memory and the Evolving Psychobiology of Posttraumatic Stress." He noted that the body retains a memory of that traumatic event as much as does our brain, and that memory forms in response to the body's efforts to escape that trauma. Inevitably, somatic conditions result when escape from threat is impossible or the body is not allowed to complete its survival response. Similarly, in *The Body Remembers* (2000), Rothschild observed the ways the body contains traumatic memories and strongly recommends that trauma resolution cannot be completed without learning to use the body as a resource in the healing process. These and many other authors have provided abundant documentation as to the important role the body plays in self-regulation.

Trauma-informed care dictates that intervention includes working with the body. Traumatized children and adolescents frequently present with delayed or impaired cognitive processes because trauma is not experienced in the frontal cortex where explicit cognitive processes take place, but in the midbrain where there is no language and memories are stored implicitly (Stien & Kendall, 2004; Levine & Kline, 2006). When multiple traumas occur, the midbrain region becomes the dominant sensory processor of day-to-day events, preventing the normal expression of cognitive processes. An imbalance between left (explicit) and right (implicit) brain hemispheres is the result.

Melillo (2009) details what happens to children when their left and right brain are out of balance. He proposes that an overdeveloped right brain is believed to be at the source of many disorders affecting children, including attention deficit hyperactivity disorder (ADHD), autism spectrum disorders, dyslexia, and other neurological conditions. Melillo's intervention has been used in over 1,000 individuals to engage the body in a variety of activities to increase functions in the nondominant brain to restore a normal balance of functioning between hemispheres. His research demonstrates that significant progress is associated with left and right brain functions including improved cognitive processes such as attending, focusing, retaining, recalling, linear thinking, and making meaning as well as improved self-regulation, affect, and attachments. Melillo's work underscores that cross-hemisphere activity goes hand in hand with the development of cognitive capacities (Ratey, 2000).

Self-Regulation: The Body as a Resource

Trauma-informed care proposes that traumatized children and adolescents learn to use their bodies to decrease unpleasant sensations induced by their trauma experiences or day-to-day situations that lead to distressful reactions. Stien and Kendall (2004) recommend that the body be used to involve new implicit memories in direct contrast to the traumatic experiences of the past, Seigel, Ogden, Minton, and Pain (2006) write, "In a psychotherapeutic setting, focusing primarily on word-based thinking and narratives can keep therapy at a surface level and trauma may be unresolved. ... Within an interpersonal neurobiology view of therapy, as we 'sift' the mind, we attempt to integrate the sensations, images, feelings and thoughts that compromise the flow of energy and information that defines our mental lives" (p. XI). In work with chronically traumatized children in a residential setting, Ziegler (2002) finds that these individuals present with persistently activated arousal. By teaching the children to raise and lower arousal levels by inducing arousal reactions and then returning to a calm state, the children learned what to do with their bodies when faced with a threatening situation, and in so doing Ziegler notes that children became much better at self-regulation. Basically, when practitioners help children become aware of their sensory experiences, an integrated healing process begins.

Ogden "blends techniques from both cognitive and psychodynamic therapies (such as attention to cognitive schemata and putting language to felt experience) with somatically based interventions (such as learning to track bodily sensations and working with movements)" (Ogden, Minton, & Pain, 2006, p. 189). For example, a child's body might become tense and breathe shallowly when talking about school and just the opposite when talking about home. In this situation, asking children to experiment with breathing (shallow and abdominal) or with different body postures or actions when talking about "school" (a stressful sensory memory) until they feel sensations similar to those associated with "home" (a calming experience), teaches them that they can empower themselves to regulate their reactions to stressful events. From a safety perspective, we can suggest another activity: "Let's see if we can find something you can do that lets you feels safer (not be as afraid) when talking about school. How about we just draw or color as you talk. Let's see what that is like."

By redirecting children to sensations in their bodies, practitioners can help children to identify and express the intensity and scope of the body's reactions. This is accomplished by being as curious as possible about their sensations and asking them to describe what each sensation is like; for example, is it heavy, warm, cold, soft and fuzzy, or prickly? Children can also be encouraged to "draw a picture of what it might look like" or use other references like music or movement by identifying what might best describe what the sensation is like. It is widely recognized that experiential processes activate both left and right hemispheres and further stimulate an integrative balance between the two, ultimately resulting in an experience of self-regulation (Malchiodi, 2011a). For example, music has an extensive track record as a self-regulator for survivors of catastrophic incidents. In an emerging technique called Music Entertainment Desensitization and Reprocessing (MEDR) (Gao, 2008) directs individuals to visualize the worst part of what they have witnessed during a catastrophic event. While visualizing the event, the music is altered between scary or sad to peaceful and relaxing. By repeating this rhythm back and forth, individuals are able to learn to self-regulate through music that is calming and uplifting. Research has demonstrated that music allows individuals to express feelings, redefine their identity, and rebuild inter- and intrapersonal relationships (Davis, 2010; Else, 2009). Art has been used as a form of gradual exposure therapy with individuals with posttraumatic stress disorder and as a method to reduce trauma reactions through relaxation and repetitive activity (Malchiodi, 2011b).

Mindfulness as Self-Regulation

The concept of *mindfulness* is defined by science as a practice that self-regulates both mind and body (Cahn & Polich, 2006); it is also a technique that may increase relaxation and reduction of stress (Kabat-Zinn, 1994). Rothschild (2009) suggests a *mindful* approach for achieving self-regulation that focuses on the body, its sensations, moods, and feelings to identify what it is we are doing, thinking, or being exposed to that is stressful and what brings us calm. Rothschild writes, "Damasio concluded that body awareness and emotional awareness are necessary to decision making (engaging safe, self-regulatory activities when needed). He identified that the experiences we encounter in our lives leave pleasant and unpleasant traces inscribed in our bodies—somatic markers—that help guide our future decision making as to what to avoid, what to embrace" (p. 13). Lazar, Kerr, and Wasserman (2005) find that meditation, the experience of mindful attention, stimulates the brain regions associated with sensory processing. By identifying the body's sensations, moods, and feelings associated with other people, events, situations, and environments, traumatized individuals can begin to feel safe and learn to regulate responses by selecting those environments, events, activities, and people that bring a somatic sensation of safety, control, and calm.

Most of the literature and research on mindfulness focuses on adults, but with adaptation, mindfulness can be an important part of the self-regulation learning process for traumatized children and adolescents. As previously mentioned, creative activities involving drawing, music, play, and movement can be used to teach the basic principles of mindfulness to young clients. To teach children the power that deep breathing has to relax the body, they can be asked to imagine "breathing a cloud." Willard (2010) offers this adaptation for relaxation, imagination, and mindful awareness: "Pick out a cloud; you may want to start with a small one. Focus on that cloud and just breathe into that cloud. With each breath, watch and see that cloud change shape or start to get smaller or larger. If your mind wanders, just try to bring your attention back to the cloud. Just remain focused on the cloud, watching and breathing until it gradually fades away" (p. 36). Repetitive rewarding activities that involve creating with one's hands can also direct awareness or redirect focus from anxious feelings to sensations that are soothing and absorbing (Malchiodi, 2008, 2011a).

Finally, it is equally important that helping professionals who work with traumatized children and parents/caretakers practice mindfulness, too. Siegel and Hartzell (2003) underscore that mindfulness is at the core of attuned and nurturing relationships with children. When helping professionals, parents, and caretakers are able to maintain a mindful presence with children and adolescents during experiences of connection and communication, children and adolescents are more likely to increase emotional well-being and attachment to others and help young clients thrive. In turn, they also develop a greater capacity for relating and empathy for others, key factors in resilience (see Chapter 7 on resilience for more information).

Structured Sensory Interventions

Steele and Raider (2001) approach trauma as a series of experiences. This model addresses fear and terror, worry, hurt, anger, revenge, accountability, and feeling unsafe and powerless "victim" thinking versus survivor/thriver thinking. It integrates sensory, implicit processes with cognitive, explicit processes. For example, "being hurt" is a common experience in traumatized children; in a structured sensory approach, the child is asked to draw

READY, SET, RELAX

Roger Klein and Jeffrey Allen

The use of relaxation, imagery, and self-talk are powerful tools to help children and teens self-regulate. Imagery is the language that the mind uses to communicate with the body. Unfortunately, many of the images and self-talk typical of children and teens do more harm than good. In fact, the most common type of imagery is related to worry. Images are influenced by a child's thoughts and internal language. Thus, the use of techniques that help young people develop skill in using positive self-talk will help them influence and regulate their internal world. This skill set is an essential component in helping our young clients develop an internal locus of control and overcoming victim thinking.

The first step after the therapist has established a relationship that feels safe to the child is to teach progressive muscle relaxation. The relaxation in and of itself is a healing experience and allows the child easier access to changing imagery and self-talk. The relaxation experience is followed by a series of stories. Each script instructs the child/teen to imagine being in a present-tense story. The client is asked to personalize the experience, visualize solving a problem or issue related to the experience, and finally to repeat a positive self-statement in the present tense. Participants are cued to visualize stressful situations in rich detail while remaining calm and resolving the source of the stress. They are asked to see themselves handling the situation with confidence, power, and self-control. This helps teach them about the power of their thoughts and how those thoughts can lead them into positive, goal-directed behaviors. It is clear from both research and clinical practice that changes in behavior result from the practice of positive, problem-solving self-talk, regardless of the age of the participant.

The following case study presents compelling examples of the efficacy of using relaxation and positive self-talk.

Julie came to see me at age 19 suffering from depression and drug abuse, which led to a suicide attempt. Like others, she found the task of generating a positive self-talk sheet very difficult. Her thoughts about herself had always been negative. Julie had always been her own worst critic. She tended to see her faults and not her strengths.

Her parents were good people who were happily married, but very stressed by the behavioral difficulties of Julie's younger brother. Much of their attention and energy was directed toward the brother, as well as Julie's physically handicapped sister.

Julie, as the oldest, had taken a great deal of responsibility in caring for her sister. She found leaving home and being on her own as a college freshman very difficult. Although a good athlete and student in high school, she found the rigors of college somewhat overwhelming. She had started smoking pot and drinking alcohol while in her senior year in high school and found herself using daily near the end of her first year in college. She was finding it increasingly difficult to sleep at night and eventually began to think about suicide as an option. She told me that thinking about suicide actually calmed her down and helped her to eventually fall asleep. She found her thoughts continuing to return to the option of suicide. Shortly after she found out that her boyfriend was going out with someone else behind her back, she decided to kill herself. She took an overdose of aspirin, but fortunately was found by her roommate in time to be saved.

Julie was a perfect candidate for cognitive-behavioral therapy, as she understood immediately the implication of how her thinking contributed to her near death. Julie was also seen by a psychiatrist and was started on an antidepressant medication. I taught her progressive relaxation and used specific scripts. Several sessions into her treatment she told me that she never knew how good it felt to be relaxed and said, "It feels just like smoking some really good pot." She began using relaxation and listened to the CD, *Relaxation & Success Imagery* (Klein & Klein, 2011) daily. Julie posted her positive self-statements on her bedroom door and put them on her MP3 player so that she could listen to them when she drove her car. Near the end of our 10th session, four months after our first session, she told me that initially she didn't think she would ever really believe the positive things she was saying to herself, but that she indeed believed them now. She discontinued medication after 12 months. I received an e-mail from her two years post-treatment.

Since treatment, she entered a new college and ended up on the Dean's List. She has had some relationship crises, but has been able to stay positive minded and upbeat. She still has her original positive thought sheet and has added many more and returns to reading them aloud when she finds her mind drifting toward negative thoughts.

a picture of what that hurt might look like as a way to reflect the iconic, implicit sensory memory of that hurt as experienced by the child. This is followed by a comprehensive set of questions as to what that hurt is like. The child's responses provide the lead-in for subsequent curiosity from the interviewer.

For example, a practitioner might ask, "How big or small is your hurt? Show me by making a drawing of it or fill in the box that best shows me" (Figure 4.1). A 7-year-old girl who witnessed the traumatic death of her mother was asked one year later what her biggest worry was since her mother died. She wrote, "When my dog runs away I'm afraid she'll get hit by a car but she comes back." Children often displace their anxieties on pets, when really she may fear that her father or other significant people in her

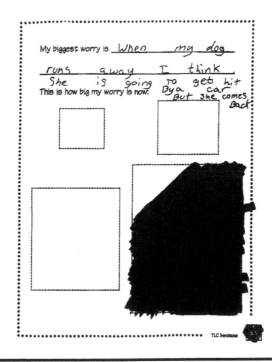

Figure 4.1   A 7-year-old girl's drawing of her worry. (Copyright TLC 2011, http://www.starrtraining.org/tlc. Used with permission.)

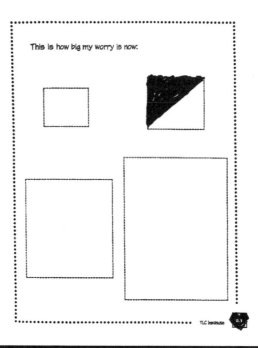

This is how big my worry is now.

Figure 4.2   Girl's worry after intervention. (Copyright TLC 2011, http://www.starr training.org/tlc. Used with permission.)

life would die, too. In order to understand how small or big her worry was at that time, she was asked to fill in the box that best showed how small or big her worry was. As it turned out, it is a "big worry," which was also supported by the clinically significant anxiety serving on the formal assessment tool used. Obviously, a practitioner would then want to see a significant reduction of that worry (anxiety) through appropriate, trauma-informed intervention; in this girl's case, she shows us how much her worry was reduced in Figure 4.2.

This activity could be followed by additional questions like, "If your hurt could talk, what do you think it would say?" Or, "If it could listen, what would you say to it?" This process allows the child to act as an observer of the body's sensations. It also helps make that hurt something tangible and gives it a voice for the child to say what is needed to feel better. By calling upon the body in a mindful way through activities that use both right and left hemispheres of the brain, children learn what they can do with their bodies and minds to react in a less stressful manner when trauma-inducing situations occur.

WHAT IF ...?

William Steele

What if a child is given one or two verbal requests or directives and five minutes later it appears he never listened or did not take the request seriously? When this happens repeatedly we might begin to think he is being oppositionally defiant, when in fact early trauma has limited short-term memory capacity and other cognitive processes. Without this information, our responses are likely to become even more frustrating and agitate the child and ourselves.

What if we are asked to help a child who is continually scapegoated and bullied by his peers, but we never complete a sensory integration evaluation that, if completed, would show sensory delays in several areas? Without this information we are likely to focus interventions on emotional processing with little success when we ought to have engaged the child in sensory-focused occupational therapy.

What if we never ask a child what really gets him going, but also never ask what really calms him down? What if we never determine the actual duration of his meltdowns as well as their frequency? How can we support his efforts to self-regulate? How can we determine that intervention is making a difference?

What we do *not* know about a child's neurodevelopment and associated neurobehavioral patterns within a trauma-informed context seriously limits the efficacy of our interventions and in some cases may actually bring about secondary trauma through attempting interventions that simply do not match the "faulty wiring" of that child's brain induced by trauma.

Expressive, Self-Regulating Interventions

Unfortunately, many treatment approaches often ignore the mind–body connection. Expressive interventions like art, music, dance, and play are gaining recognition, yet are slow to be accepted as powerful self-regulating agents (Malchiodi, 2008). We believe that practitioners have been so convinced to believe that talking is the only healer that somatically based interventions have been defined as less than scientifically sound approaches. However, everything known about the neuroscience of trauma clearly illustrates that implicit, sensory (body-oriented) activities are as critical to recovery as cognitive behavioral interventions. Bessel van der Kolk's Trauma Center also provides a variety of nontraditional approaches—theater groups, yoga, sensorimotor psychotherapy, expressive art therapy, and neurofeedback. These activities help to promote the integration of psychology and biology to reconnect minds and bodies affected by trauma.

The International Society for Traumatic Stress Studies (ISTSS) acknowledges in Principle 17 that creative arts therapies (art, music, dance/movement, and drama) are emerging approaches to the treatment of posttraumatic stress disorder in children and adolescents and that they are unique methods of gaining access to traumatic content and of enhancing self-regulation (Foa, Keane, & Cohen, 2008). Many art-making activities can be self-soothing and self-regulating experiences for children; for example, making a "worry doll" out of a clothespin and yarn is not only an engrossing activity for some children, but also becomes a tangible product for learning about how to manage worries. For other children and adolescents, focusing excess energy into making something from clay or learning a new craft skill can become an experience of self-regulation and relaxation (Malchiodi, 2008). While single-session art therapy interventions have not proven to reduce PTSD in children (Schierer et al., 2005), there is evidence that using drawing and other creative experiences over time is helpful in reducing stress and helping children identify experiences that trigger trauma reactions (Steele & Raider, 2001; Malchiodi, 2008; Gil, 2006). Creative activities may also be combined with cognitive-behavioral therapy (CBT) to support self-regulation in some older children and adolescents who can also tap executive functions through drama activities such as role-play (Foa, Keane, & Cohen, 2008).

Developmentally Appropriate Self-Regulation

In *The Boy Raised as a Dog* (2006), Perry and Szalavits use several cases to illustrate trauma's impact on the brain and the developmental implications with self-regulation. They describe Tina, whose symptoms from early traumatic experiences implied abnormalities throughout her brain; she experienced sleep and attention problems (brain stem), lack of fine motor control (diencephalon and cortex), social and relationship dysfunction (limbic and cortex), and speech and language problems (cortex). Perry's conclusion is that her problems were related to "one key set of neural systems, the ones involved in helping humans cope with stress and threat (p. 22)."

This and other cases led to Perry's development of a neurosequential approach (Perry & Szalavits, 2006) (Figure 3.1, in previous chapter) to trauma recovery. It is based on the fact that the brain develops sequentially and its plasticity allows it to learn and develop in relationship to what and whom it is exposed to in its environment. When normal growth is developmentally delayed by traumatic exposures, different symptoms appear at different times in that developmental period. For example, toddlers may develop aversion to touch and difficulty with relationships; middle school–age children may develop fears specific to elements of the event and engage in avoidant behaviors, and adolescents will experience an array of challenging emotions and behaviors.

Perry presents critical information that informs how to help children achieve self-regulation and underscores that sensory-based, somatic strategies are imperative and must match the areas of neurodevelopment that are impacted by traumatic events. Interventions are not based on age, but on the developmental needs of a child that were either delayed or affected by trauma. As previously mentioned, Melillo's approach of including developmentally appropriate activities to restore balance between the sides of the brain may have an older child crawling because when younger, crawling was limited to the point of not allowing the brain to take a normal developmental growth path. Melillo notes, "The brain is dependent on the body to provide the stimulation necessary for growth … the more activity it (the brain) gets (from the body), the more it grows in size and density … movement of all the muscles (the body) are directly correlated to the quality and quantity of functional capacity of the brain" (2009, p. 52). In sum, this means that the somatically based experience of physical movement helps to regulate functions of the brain including response to threatening, traumatic situations.

A School-Based Self-Regulation Study: Building Resilience

Lakes and Hoyt (2004) conducted a study to test the premise that "effective self-regulation not only increases a person's capacity for success (resilience) but also reduces self-destructive behavior" (p. 283). When thinking about self-regulation, it is important to consider regulation of thoughts, feelings, and body reactions. In the Lakes and Hoyt study, Tae Kwon Do was used with children from kindergarten through fifth grade over a three-month period. At the beginning of every session the children were asked to mindfully focus by asking themselves three questions: "Where am I? What am I doing? What should I be doing?" The outcome was then compared to the children who were not in this three-month Tae Kwon Do group. The study demonstrated that the Tae Kwon Do group had greater improvement in cognitive, affective, and physical (body) control. This translated into better classroom conduct, socialization, and performance on a mental math test.

Martial arts engage both left and right brain to build a balanced response to potentially dangerous situations; for children this means "This is a situation that is dangerous or stressful, but I now know I (my body) can manage. I can regulate my response." This study and others (Lakes & Hoyt, 2003) demonstrate that when children learn to control and self-regulate their bodies, they do better. From this perspective, teaching children to self-regulate can be preventative and lead to a more resilient response to fear and extreme stress.

The story of Sammy by Peter Levine and Maggie Kline in this chapter provides an example of how a trauma-informed play session months following a traumatic experience led to a reparative experience through self-regulation. Allowing Sammy to move back and forth from an unpleasant situation to a reassuring, protective one provided a renewed sense of resilience (regulation), confidence (empowerment), and joy (renewed sense of safety). In brief, this case demonstrates that a self-regulatory process can be learned.

THE STORY OF SAMMY

Peter Levine and Maggie Kline

Sammy is a little boy who is not yet 3 years old and is a good example of how setting up a trauma-informed play session months following a traumatic experience led to a reparative experience with a victorious outcome. It is also an example of what can happen when an ordinary fall that required a visit to the emergency room for stitches can go awry. Several months after the accident, Sammy's terrifying experience was transformed by using his body to complete an earlier thwarted attempt to escape from a terrifying experience. The play session allowed him to move back and forth from an unpleasant situation to a reassuring, protective one that provided a renewed sense of resilience (regulation), confidence (empowerment), and joy (renewed sense of safety).

Maggie Kline: Sammy has been spending the weekend with his grandparents, where I am their houseguest. He is being an impossible tyrant, aggressively and relentlessly trying to control his new environment. Nothing pleases him; he displays a foul temper every waking moment. When he is asleep, he tosses and turns as if wrestling with his bedclothes. This behavior is not entirely unexpected from a 2½-year-old whose parents have gone away for the weekend—children with separation anxiety often act it out. Sammy, however, has always enjoyed visiting his grandparents, and this behavior seemed extreme to them.

They confided to me that six months earlier, Sammy fell off his high chair and split his chin open. Bleeding heavily, he was taken to the local emergency room. When the nurse came to take his temperature and blood pressure, he was so frightened that she was unable to record his vital signs. This vulnerable little boy was then strapped down in a "pediatric papoose" (a board with flaps and Velcro straps). With his torso and legs immobilized, the only parts of his body he could move were his head and neck—which, naturally, he did, as energetically as he could. The doctors responded by tightening the restraint and immobilizing his head with their hands in order to suture his chin.

After this upsetting experience, Mom and Dad took Sammy out for a hamburger and then to the playground. His mother was very attentive and carefully validated his experience of being scared and hurt. Soon, all seemed forgotten. However, the boy's overbearing attitude began shortly after this event. Could Sammy's tantrums and controlling behavior be related to his perceived helplessness from this trauma?

When his parents returned, we agreed to explore whether there might be a traumatic charge still associated with this recent experience. We all gathered in the cabin where I was staying. With parents, grandparents, and Sammy watching, I placed his stuffed Pooh Bear on the edge of a chair in such a way that it fell to the floor. Sammy shrieked, bolted for the door, and ran across a footbridge and down a narrow path to the creek. Our suspicions were confirmed. His most recent visit to the hospital was neither harmless nor forgotten. Sammy's behavior told us that this game was potentially overwhelming for him.

Sammy's parents brought him back from the creek. He clung dearly to his mother as we prepared for another game. We reassured him that we would all be there to help protect Pooh Bear. Again he ran—but this time only into the next room. We followed him in there and waited to see what would happen next. Sammy ran to the bed and hit it with both arms while looking at me expectantly.

"Mad, huh?" I said. He gave me a look that confirmed my question. Interpreting his expression as a go-ahead sign, I put Pooh Bear under a blanket and placed Sammy on the bed next to him.

"Sammy, let's all help Pooh Bear."

I held Pooh Bear under the blanket and asked everyone to help. Sammy watched with interest but soon got up and ran to his mother. With his arms held tightly around her legs, he said, "Mommy, I'm scared." Note: This trust of safety would not happen without a solid attachment. Where healthy bonding is not the case, or where there is abuse, therapy is, of course, much more complex and also generally involves therapy for the parents or caregivers.

Without pressuring him, we waited until Sammy was ready and willing to play the game again. The next time, Grandma and Pooh Bear were held down together, and Sammy actively participated in their rescue. When Pooh Bear was freed, Sammy ran to his mother, clinging even more tightly than before. He began to tremble and shake in fear, and then, dramatically, his chest expanded in a growing sense of excitement and pride.

Here we see the transition between traumatic reenactment and healing play. The next time he held on to his mommy, there was less clinging and more excited jumping. We waited until Sammy was ready to play again. Everyone except Sammy took a turn being rescued with Pooh Bear. Each time, Sammy became more vigorous as he pulled off the blanket and escaped into the safety of his mother's arms.

When it was Sammy's turn to be held under the blanket with Pooh Bear, he became quite agitated and fearful. He ran back to his mother's arms several times before he was able to accept the ultimate challenge. Bravely, he climbed under the blankets with Pooh Bear while I held the blanket gently down. I watched his eyes grow wide with fear, but only for a moment. Then he grabbed Pooh Bear, shoved the blanket away, and flung himself into his mother's arms. Sobbing and trembling, he screamed, "Mommy, get me out of here! Mommy, get this off of me!" His startled father told me that these were the same words Sammy screamed while imprisoned in the papoose at the hospital. He remembered this clearly because he had been quite surprised by his son's ability to make such a direct, well-spoken demand at just over 2½ years of age.

We went through the escape several more times. Each time, Sammy exhibited more power and more triumph. Instead of running fearfully to his mother, he jumped excitedly up and down. With every successful escape, we all clapped and danced together, cheering, "Yeah for Sammy, yeah! Yeah, Sammy saved Pooh Bear!" Sammy had achieved mastery over the experience that had shattered him a few months earlier. The trauma-driven aggressive, foul-tempered behavior used in an attempt to control his environment disappeared, while his "hyperactivity" and avoidance (which occurred during the reworking of his medical trauma) was transformed into triumphant play.

Safety

The case (see "The Story of Sammy" text box) presented by Levine and Kline demonstrates that by being allowed to repeatedly move back and forth between unpleasant and pleasant (safe) behaviors, Sammy experienced different body sensations that allowed him to discover that he could regulate his fear response. One key word here is *repeatedly*. Too often, children are not allowed the time needed to repeat/practice those behaviors that are comforting, empowering, and safe. It is now commonly accepted that children with histories of multiple traumas need the opportunity to repeatedly engage in self-regulating behaviors (Perry, 2006; Stien & Kendall, 2004). Sammy's story demonstrates the need for, and the power of, the body to release the past traumatic sensations and to replace these experiences with safe, self-empowering sensations that help regulate reactions to frightening situations. However, this example also raises additional questions about safety.

Sammy knew Miss Kline; he had a relationship with her, making her a safe person. This intervention took place in Sammy's home, also a safe place. The questions we have to then ask about safety include

1. How do we determine who the child believes is a safe person?
2. How do we as practitioners, yet strangers to that child, present ourselves as safe?
3. What defines a safe intervention?
4. How do we create an emotionally safe environment for traumatized children?

How Do We Determine Who Is Safe?

Within a trauma-informed context, safety is not about reason and logic but about how that child experiences us as helping professionals no matter our skill level or years of experience. Trauma is not experienced in the cortical region where reason and logic prevail, but implicitly in the midbrain and brain stem where there is no language; in these regions, sensations, feelings, and instinctive survival responses can be triggered by any element in one's environment that is a reminder of traumatic experience. This includes the way we present ourselves to the child, our mannerisms, physical features, body language, and vocal tones.

We may be the most skillful trauma practitioners in our community but our features or mannerisms remind that child (activate an aroused response) of that bad person who did that bad thing to him. If this is the case, we simply may not be a safe person for that child. This means we may need to help that child find someone who provides a less activating response. Dr. Steele, founder of The National Institute for Trauma and Loss in Children (TLC), states repeatedly to practitioners, "There is no such thing as resistance in trauma. Either that child feels safe or he does not. The child ultimately determines who is a safe person."

How Do We Present Ourselves as Safe?

Even if our mannerisms do not trigger implicit memories, children will be wary of our efforts to help. So how can we help them feel safe with us? Obviously, meeting them with a supportive parent, caretaker, or other familiar face can help. What we say may also be helpful. Perry (Perry & Szalavitz, 2006) explains how he introduces himself to Amber, a teenager, in the following way, "Listen, you don't know me, you don't know anything about me, and you shouldn't trust me until you get to know me. So I'm going to say a few things. After I leave, you will have a chance to think about whether or not you want to spend any time talking with me. Whatever you decide is final. It's your choice. You are in control" (p. 184).

This approach first recognizes what most children and even adults are thinking and then introduces the terms *choice* and *control*. In trauma-informed care, children must always have the choice to say "no" to any intervention we propose or "stop" to any intervention in progress that is activating. For safety to exist, children must experience some level of control.

WORKING WITH CHILD SURVIVORS OF DOMESTIC VIOLENCE

Cathy Malchiodi

My earliest work involved developing therapeutic programs for children in shelters for domestic violence. What I learned immediately from this work was that children from violent homes did not want to talk about "what happened." While I believed at the time that I understood why they did not want to talk, I did not fully comprehend their responses until I later learned how traumatic events affects the body's reactions to seemingly unrelated situations involving professionals like myself who were trying to help.

I use expressive arts therapies and particularly art therapy in my work with traumatized children, including those who have witnessed violence and/or been physically or sexually abused. These interventions often serve as a catalyst for children to explore thoughts, feelings, and memories through a variety of senses including tactile, sound, smell, and taste. In many cases, these experiences facilitate self-regulation; in contrast, they can also become experiences that may trigger reactions related to past traumatic events. For example, some children respond with upset to a specific smell from a particular paint, felt marking pen, or adhesive that incites a sensory olfactory reminder of an uncomfortable memory. Some children who have been sexually abused may become hyperaroused when handling modeling clay; the tactile nature of the clay may bring on traumatic reactions related to past abuse or other distressful situations. Many children who have experienced physical punishment may simply be too afraid to play with materials for fear of reprisal in case they spill a paint jar or get chalk on their clothing.

In all cases, these children do not know why they are distressed. Additionally, these children may not know why they suddenly feel anxious or even fearful of the helping professional who has presented an activity that, under most circumstances, is perceived as fun and pleasurable. Remember, you may momentarily be an element of the sensory responses of traumatized children; when the paint is spilled, you may be expected to be the adult who punishes mistakes with physical abuse, the individual who reacts violently, or simply as an unpleasant reminder of an uncomfortable event. The important thing is that you begin to learn what tactile, sounds, or smells upset your young clients and begin the process of helping them to feel better through self-soothing experiences and activities.

Sammy's case underscores what can happen when a child loses control, but also what can happen when he experiences control.

Asking close-ended questions is another common mistake practitioners make that can inadvertently increase arousal and avoidance reactions in traumatized individuals. In contrast, it is important to be a witness and respond with curiosity rather than analysis. The way helping professionals seek information from traumatized children can either support safety or threaten children who will then, out of fear, say what they think adults want to hear or simply refuse to respond. In either case, the relationship is no longer a safe one. Olfason and Kenniston (2008) explain that in creating optional information gathering conditions (safety) for forensic interviewing, "open-ended questions are the most productive; even reluctant or non-disclosing children respond most fully to open questions" (p. 77). Although it is necessary to ask "yes" and "no" questions to understand all that happened or what the experience was like, the authors advise following a "yes-or-no" question with an open-ended question rather than asking multiple "yes" and "no" questions.

In other words, the more curious we are through the types of questions we ask, the easier it is for the children to bring us into their world. Open-ended questions should engage children in telling us about how they experienced what happened or is currently happening to them. From a safety, self-regulation standpoint, providing children with consistent and frequent opportunities to describe the range of reactions, sensations, feelings, and thoughts they are having about what they are doing, what we are doing, or what we might be talking about, gives them a voice. It is a way to allow them to stay safe by letting us know when it's time to stop a particular activity, continue it, or repeat it because it is helping or not helping.

For some children, any type of questions may be perceived as disruptive and uncomfortable, especially in early stages of intervention. In their research on Structured Sensory Interventions for Traumatized Children, Adolescents and Parents (SITCAP™), Steele and Raider (2001) emphasize implicit, sensory, expressive activities rather than language because it allows the child to direct the intervention (control) using activities they deem safe.

And, even though direct questions are generally avoided, the children present a very clear view as to how they now see themselves, others, and the world around them as a result of their traumatic experiences.

Finally, what further strengthens the sense of safety is an explanation of the intervention process; in other words, what the child will be asked to do and how it has helped others (psychoeducation). When intervention is structured, the process detailed for the child and the many physical, emotional, and cognitive reactions that the traumatized child can experience are normalized, and we make ourselves a bit safer because, to the child, we seem to know what it is like to be that child.

What Defines a Safe Intervention?

To select an intervention that may best meet that child's needs, a trauma-informed comprehensive assessment is necessary to identify the strengths and challenges the child presents, the time of earliest trauma, neurodevelopmental impact, how the child processes information (written, visual, and/or verbal), and what activities, environmental factors, and/or people are calming or activating to the child. As described in the two previous chapters on trauma-informed assessment, it is important to gather as much information about the child from developmental, cognitive, psychosocial, and sensory-based perspectives before designing specific interventions or strategies.

While many evidence-based interventions exist, it does not necessarily follow that they are universally safe for all children. There is simply no one intervention that fits every child and all practitioners must be flexible in their approach and proficient in several trauma-informed techniques, must consult others who can provide alternate approaches, or must obtain supervision or consultation if warranted. As previously mentioned, not all children will want to talk about what happened or have the memory or language to do so. Not every child will want to draw; others may not want to use props, toys, or sand trays to express themselves because sensory qualities of certain art mediums may actually activate some children. Our task is to keep the child safe by engaging those interventions that children identify to us as safe through words, behavior, or somatic responses. The challenge is always to find the intervention that fits that child.

Additionally, what makes an intervention safe is the process in which it is presented and applied. Both Perry and Levine emphasize the importance of moving at the child's pace. Olfason and Kenniston (2008) actually found that "the average child aged 5 to 7 takes about twice as long as adults to process a question and that Americans become restless and impatient after less than three seconds of silence" (p. 79). Not giving children the time they need to process a question or engage in repetitive reenactment no longer makes us safe as helping professionals because it takes control away from children. *Titration* is a somatically based term that refers to pacing—providing interventions in small doses and a little at a time. During this form of pacing, it is important to carefully listen to and watch for cues of hyperarousal and avoidance in children in order to adjust the pace of intervention. In Sammy's case, the authors wrote, "Without pressuring him we waited until Sammy was ready and willing to play the game again." This respected his safety needs because the practitioner followed Sammy's pace by *titrating* his experience. They added, "If the child's response appears to be moving in the direction of construction of compulsive repetition instead of expansion and variety ... slow down ... by breaking the play (intervention) into smaller increments."

Finally, any intervention session needs to begin in a safe place and end in a safe place with trauma-focused work accomplished in the middle. That is why a structured process is perceived as safe, especially for traumatized children. Activities that allow children to return to their "fun place, comfortable place, safe place" before they leave helps to identify helping professionals as "safe people " and the intervention process as safe. They give children repeated opportunities to experience their abilities, to move from the unpleasant to the pleasant, and to learn to self-regulate. Knowing what the child enjoys can be used to begin and end intervention. At a sensory level, relaxation activities, guided imagery, play, and music are helpful. The point is for them to be enjoyable and so it is important to check with children to be sure they are absolutely enjoyable rather than anxiety inducing. What might be enjoyable for some may be stressful for others, so any activity must be sanctioned or driven by the child.

Van der Kolk (2005) notes, "safety, predictability and fun is essential for the establishment of the capacity to observe what is going on, put it into a larger context and initiate physiological and motoric self-regulation" (p. 47). Only after children master the ability to engage in pleasurable activities without becoming hyperaroused or distressed do they have a chance to develop the capacity to play with other children, interact with adults, participate in simple group activities, and address more complex, cognitively based issues. He adds that we do not want to remind children of their trauma until they can consistently experience pleasure and mastery over their body sensations and emotions. In essence, helping traumatized individuals self-regulate their bodies becomes the resilient factor in the healing process.

Key Elements of Safe Interventions

The four areas of safety and self-regulation presented in this chapter can be operationalized as follows:

1. Introduce choice and control.
2. Use a structured approach.
3. Be a witness rather than an analyst.
4. Use open-ended questions and be curious.
5. Teach children to be mindful of the sensations associated with interventions.
6. Instruct children to stop at anytime interventions become too activating.
7. Instruct children to stop us when what we are asking is too activating.
8. Follow the child's pace and practice titration.
9. Begin the session in a safe place and end in a safe place.
10. Help children recognize the pleasant and unpleasant sensations in their bodies always resourcing those pleasant sensations when children are experiencing unpleasant, activating sensations.
11. Incorporate appropriate strategies according to principles of neurodevelopment.
12. Repeat interventions used to regulate or deactivate the child frequently in order to build new sensory memories.
13. Identify and involve at least one adult familiar to the child when possible to reinforce what is learned.
14. Keep in mind that the child always remains the best expert as to what is helping and what is hurting.

In addition, Table 4.1 focuses on children's reactions and needs and summarizes many of the basic principles presented in this list.

Conclusion

Safety and self-regulation are experiences that support an internal sense of control and self-efficacy; they are affected by environments including

Table 4.1   Children's Reactions and Children's Needs

Reactions	Needs
Anxiety	Security
Guilt	Reassurance
Terror/Fearfulness	Adult protection, acknowledgment, patience, simplification of tasks
Constantly worried that something else will happen (hypervigilance)	Structure, consistency, facts, information, simplification of tasks
Helplessness	Physical nurturing, simplification of tasks and expectations
Chaotic or out-of-control feelings and emotions	Calm, peaceful environment
Fatigue	Sleep, predictability, calmness
Repetitive telling of the story or reenactment in play of incident	Someone to listen
Fear of being alone (difficulty leaving parent or letting parent leave)	Safety and conviction that self and others will be safe
Confusion, forgetfulness, inability to concentrate	Simplification of tasks, repetition, structure, patience. Teachers and counselors may need to be made aware of this inability to concentrate.
Worry about something else happening to him/herself	Reassurance, sense of safety

Source: Copyright TLC 2011, http://www.starrtraining.org/tlc. Used with permission.

physical aspects, systemic aspects, and organizational structure. The next chapter outlines specific elements beyond safety that define a trauma-informed environment as well as the processes needed to sustain its viability and integrity. In reality, assessment, environments, relationships, resilience, and trauma integration are interconnected because emotional safety is at the core of all components of trauma-informed practice. It will also address environment as a central factor in trauma-informed practice and how organizations themselves can enhance a sense of safety and set the stage for self-regulation through establishing values and beliefs that support growth and recovery in children and adolescents.

Chapter 5

Creating and Sustaining Trauma-Informed Environments

This chapter explores the role of the environment in trauma-informed intervention with children and adolescents. Trauma-informed practice suggests that trauma recovery involves not only focused intervention, but also the interrelationship of the individual with others within a community, whether that is residential care, a shelter setting, hospital, school, organization, or family. These environments may either help or impede a child or adolescent's progress toward trauma integration.

Successful trauma-informed environments include psychosocial, physical, and sensory aspects. For example, values and beliefs are central to an organization or agency; in order to reach a consensus on appropriate trauma-informed values and beliefs, education of all stakeholders in that organization or agency is necessary. To maintain a successful environment with trauma-informed values and beliefs, accountability is also essential. Finally, strategies and adaptations that help create an emotionally safe environment that respects the individual's values, beliefs, and cultural preferences are fundamental to trauma-informed practice. In brief, all aspects of an environment must be trauma-informed, attending to the developmental and psychosocial needs and cultural values and beliefs of traumatized individuals.

To help readers understand the complexities and interrelationships inherent in environmental influences, this chapter begins with the story of T (Brendtro, Mitchell, & McCall, 2001), a young person who faced numerous challenges and traumatic events during his childhood and adolescence.

A Fire Burns Within

On December 1, 1958, at Our Lady of Angels elementary school in Chicago, 92 students and 3 teachers died in a fire set by a student at the school (Brendtro, Ness, & Mitchell, 2001). T (whose name has been protected) was born in a home for unwed mothers after his mother was allegedly raped by her own stepfather. When she was 15 years old, T's mother planned to put her son up for adoption, but couldn't let her child go. Troubles at home were compounded by problems experienced in school. He was mercilessly ridiculed and bullied by peers. His mother was aware of the problems and did all she could to protect him. She and her child moved to Chicago where the young man's childhood was filled with chaos and uncertainty. He began setting fires at the age of 5.

It would take years for the truth to come to light and for authorities to connect the young man to the fire. Area fire investigators kept a roster of students enrolled in the school at the time of the fire. In any other case when arson was suspected, the police cross-checked the names of juvenile suspects against the roster. Police were unaware that shortly after the Angels fire, T, who attended the school and was in fifth grade at the time, moved from the parish to a suburb of a large urban area. His single mother had married and T now had a stepfather. He also gained a new name, but retained his old ways. For three years, authorities were unable to connect this boy to the fire that killed 92 students and 3 teachers.

T loathed school as he proved with poor attendance and grades. According to neighbors, T's stepfather was abusive. He reportedly beat T with rabbit punches and held his hand over the gas burner. T was terrified of the man who told him, "The next time you set anything on fire and if you kill anybody, and if the police don't get you and give you the electric chair, I'll come after you myself and kill you."

The fire occurred on the first of December, a date that T didn't forget. In the weeks around the third anniversary of the tragedy, T was implicated in a string of suspicious fires. He seemed to want to be caught. On the other hand, he was terrified of what his stepfather might do. When interrogated by police, T was usually accompanied by his mother and he denied any wrongdoing.

T's past caught up with him early in December 1961. He admitted to police that he set some fires. The motive seems to have been retribution: "I wanted to get even with the kid who lives there. He pushes me around a lot and I don't like him." He later retracted this statement. As investigators zeroed in on T, his parents hired an attorney. His mother vigorously protested that her boy was being harassed and pestered by authorities. She charged that they were interrogating him at school whenever there was a fire and interfering with his education. She had kept a list of 11 such fires. She conceded he might have started one or two of them, but certainly he had not started them all.

At the suggestion of their attorney, the parents agreed to a polygraph test. They hoped to clear the boy of some allegations. Their attorney retained a prominent polygraph expert, lawyer, and former police officer. In January 1962, a newspaper reported that a 13-year-old boy had confessed to setting the fire at the school that took the lives of 92 children and 3 nuns. This was the last the public would hear about the matter for a generation.

The judge sealed all records and ordered that T be locked in a juvenile home. He was held in complete isolation from other youth. Even police and investigators were not allowed to interview him. The court psychologist found that T scored in the bright-normal range on the Wechsler Intelligence Scale. A panel of psychiatrists determined that T was not psychotic and was competent to stand trial.

Closed juvenile court hearings began shortly after. On advice of his attorney, T pled not guilty to all charges. He claimed he gave a confession because he was frightened and tired. Under Illinois law at that time, a 10-year-old could not be held criminally liable. The boy obviously needed mental health treatment. It was uncertain whether he had intended to harm anyone.

At the completion of the trial phase, the judge found T guilty of certain fires. He threw out the Angels charge, citing inconsistencies in the boy's story. In reality, nothing would have been served by reopening this tragedy. The judge had few options. He might have sentenced the boy to the children's ward of a state hospital, a century-old snake pit that was infamous for abuses. Alternatively, if he placed T in the juvenile corrections system, he was likely to be abused by other delinquents. The state training school was the spawning ground for delinquent youth gangs that existed for many years. In fact, placement anywhere in Illinois increased the risk that someone might tie the boy to the school fire. He would likely be murdered if his identity were widely known. This suggested that placement outside the state of Illinois might be in the best interest of the child.

The court was now to be legally responsible for raising this boy. This was a highly troubled youngster who was a threat to his community. The court kept T locked in solitary confinement from January through March. While isolation was for his own protection, T felt bitterly abandoned. The detention facility became his private Alcatraz. T needed to be removed and placed in an environment that placed him and others at risk and placed in an environment where children could flourish. He wanted out of that facility but to be sent away from his family was to lose everything. He had never left his mother since she had refused to give him up at birth. But on a mid-April morning, T took his scant possessions with him to another environment, a residential treatment facility. (T's story adapted from *No Disposable Kids*, Brendtro, Ness, & Mitchell, 2001.)

Being trauma-informed means we believe that the environment shapes the child. Therefore, we have to ask what kind of environment would change T's life? This question can be answered by discussing environmental changes and what constitutes a trauma-informed environment. At the end of this chapter, T's story will demonstrate how trauma-informed environments can help in reparation and recovery.

Changing the Environment

What are the processes and criteria needed to successfully change and sustain integrity and viability of a trauma-informed environment? Environments are not just physical places, but also situations that are defined by the actions, interactions, and reactions of their members. These actions, interactions, and reactions are driven by the core values and beliefs held by the members within that environment. External environmental factors also challenge these behaviors over time and can severely strain otherwise stable, viable environments, put its members in crisis, alter their behaviors, and induce trauma in any one member or the entire environment. The list can be quite extensive: war, terrorism, community, family and school violence, racism, poverty, economic disasters, environmental disasters like hurricanes, floods and fires, chronic illness, loss of a member, introduction of a new or unwanted member, or corrupt, coercive, inadequate leadership.

Fortunately, there is a growing amount of literature detailing the principles of trauma-specific practices and trauma-informed care. However, practitioners and caregivers have varying degrees of success initiating, implementing, and sustaining change while attempting to achieve goals. This raises several critical questions that are generally not addressed in the literature. What are the core factors that contribute to trauma-informed environments? What allows some environments to not only successfully make the changes needed to become trauma-informed, but more important to consistently sustain viability and integrity? How can environments overcome the factors that challenge and traumatize families, schools, residential and community-based programs, mental health, juvenile justice, and other service delivery agencies?

Neuroplasticity of Environments

Gluckman and Hanson (2006) note that it is easier to change the environment than to change the human brain. Given the neuroplasticity of the brain and its ability to adjust, compensate, and redesign itself (Grafton, 2007) in response to biopsychosocial changes in the environment, it makes sense that efforts focus on creating and sustaining trauma-informed environments to help ameliorate the deleterious effects of trauma and promote resilience. Today the evidence is very strong that "trauma-informed environments, where healing and growth can take place, are a necessary precursor to any formal therapy that might be offered to any child" (Bath, 2008, p. 17). Children are exposed to a far greater number of traumatic events in their young lives than seen in previous generations (Burnham, 2009). This dictates why creating trauma-informed environments must be designed not only to help traumatized children, but also to prepare and ready all children to thrive despite the subsequent traumatic events they may face.

For a number of years, Malinowski (1960) and others have substantiated that when the environment fits biopsychosocial needs, children and youth flourish (Bronfenbrenner, 2005; Yehuda, 2004; Bloom & Farragher, 2010; Brendtro, Mitchell, & McCall, 2009). The emergence of *epigenetics* reveals that experiences within the environment actually change the genetic expression within families and transgenerationally influence changes in offspring (Cloud, 2010; Sweatt, 2009). Practitioners have also known for years that the one constant environmental characteristic associated with resilient children is connection to caring, protective, and compassionate adults; this is what allows some children to do better than others when faced with the same terrifying, traumatic situation (Werner & Smith, 1992; Bowlby & Winton, 1998).

Criteria for Trauma-Informed Environments

For the purpose of this chapter, trauma-informed environments are defined as those situations in which at least one or more adults are interacting with one or more children. For example, a single parent raising a single child can

THE EPIGENETICS OF CHILD ABUSE

Cathy Malchiodi

Recent studies offer intriguing research data on how early negative experiences cause developmental changes in the brain, biochemistry, and psychosocial responses. Many researchers in the area of child abuse and early intervention note that there is wide agreement that providing nurturance, positive interactions, and experiences of safety have a long-lasting impact on children's brain development.

When abuse goes undetected or is allowed to continue to impact children's development, abused individuals may be diagnosed with a major psychiatric disorder by adolescence. Additionally, brain scans of individuals who have experienced abuse during childhood show abnormalities in areas of cognition and emotion. But something even more intriguing is also detectable in the brain function of children who are abused and maltreated. Changes in neurodevelopmental areas go even deeper than just brain function; abuse literally can change one's genes.

Simply put, the influence by environmental and social factors on our genes is a field of study known as *epigenetics*. In brief, when an epigenetic change occurs, the biochemistry of how the gene is expressed is altered. In the case of child abuse, how gene expression is changed by abuse may tell us why many of the effects of child abuse do not appear until adolescence and why many maltreated individuals eventually become abusers themselves. A study of the brains of individuals who committed suicide may underscore the profound influence of abuse and just how it may alter genetic expression (McGowan et al., 2009). Of the individuals who committed suicide and who were the subjects of this particular study, some had been abused early in life and others had not. The brains of those who were abused showed significant genetic changes in the hippocampus function that could predispose them to lifelong stress responses; those who were not abused, but had died from suicide, did not show similar changes. Individuals who died of natural causes also did not show changes to the hippocampus.

This finding may imply that abuse causes severe alterations in the hippocampus in those who have experienced abuse in childhood; these alterations are not found in others, even those individuals who may have conditions such as depression or anxiety that predispose them to suicide. And while these changes occur early in life, their presence may not be observed behaviorally until later in life, making early detection and intervention for abuse all that much more critical. Because of the nature of epigenetic changes, some speculate that these alterations may be present for at least two generations, a possible partial explanation for the intergenerational cycle of abuse that trauma specialists see in their work with abuse and domestic violence.

Despite the profound impact of child abuse, we know that we can counter the effects through early intervention and identification of maltreatment and provision of care giving and environments that provide positive social interaction and stimulation. As trauma specialists, it is undeniable that we face difficult challenges in our work with abused children and the impact of maltreatment over the lifespan. Fortunately, emerging research continues to inform us on how to better meet these challenges on behalf of children and how to improve our efforts as trauma-informed practitioners.

constitute a trauma-informed environment. A therapist and client, a teacher and a classroom, community-based programs, organizations that deliver services to children and families, juvenile justice settings, protective services, mental health, and pediatric hospital units can all be defined as environments that can benefit from being trauma-informed.

Trauma-informed environments apply specific processes and criteria to create and/or change an environment so that its members can engage the kind of relationships, practices, and processes that do not inadvertently traumatize children and or retraumatize previously exposed children. This applies regardless of whether these environments are residential settings, schools, community-based programs, childcare, or homes. In brief, there are five criteria to consider when creating a trauma-informed environment:

1. Establish a core set of values that addresses the developmental needs of traumatized children while defining for all members of that environment "who they are, what they stand for, and what they live by."
2. Establish sustainable trauma-informed beliefs that align with the core values and drive the behaviors and practices of the members in that environment.

3. Educate organizations to provide the appropriate training so each individual can engage the necessary trauma-focused interactions within their specific roles and area of responsibility.
4. Establish measures of accountability that help sustain a trauma-informed environment.
5. Initiate a specific process for identifying and initiating trauma-informed values and beliefs and sustaining trauma-informed integrity in the environment.

Core Values: Respect, Cooperation, and Kindness

In most literature on trauma-informed care one rarely finds mention of the important role that value formation and belief systems play in creating healing, trauma-informed environments. This is puzzling because from a developmental perspective, values and beliefs emerge naturally in early childhood and are reinforced or reshaped by the attachment experiences of children's environments (Tancredi, 2005). According to Thames (2008), "values are a reflection of our culture, who we are and … [they] enable and empower us to establish priorities and make decisions we can live with and by." When the attachment process is a traumatic one, values and beliefs are shaped or selected because they serve one purpose—survival (Donovan & McIntyre, 1990; Brendtro, Ness, & Mitchell, 2001). "The fact is one cannot create positive ecologies for children and youth without a unifying theme of shared beliefs and values" (Wolin & Wolin, 2000, p. 52). Therefore, it makes sense that trauma-informed environments provide traumatized children with experiences that support trauma-informed values associated with resilient, thriving children.

Healthy environments include deep moral values of respect, cooperation, and generosity. Tancredi (2005) notes that by elementary school, children have an inner moral voice rooted deeply in cooperation, generosity, and respect for others. When environments are traumatizing or when children are victimized by those they respect, these moral values are reshaped and become ways to control and manipulate the environment for the sole purpose of surviving in a culture of disrespect. Kindness turns to aggression, respect and cooperation to manipulation, and people are no longer to be valued but feared. The values and beliefs of traumatized children are not characteristic of resilient children but those of terrified children seeking power and control for survival's sake.

Respect

Using the value of *respect* and applying it to interaction between teachers and students, helping professionals could prevent undue trauma to already at-risk students. Irwin Hyman, former head of the School Psychology Division of the American Psychological Association, has documented how experiences in schools can create enduring trauma in many students (Hyman & Snook, 1999). Hyman found that 60% of the most traumatic events reported by students were related to peer ridicule and mistreatment. But he was astounded to find that 40% of these destructive encounters were with school staff. For example, a student reported: "One day in Spanish class, I told the teacher I was lost and didn't know what was going on; in reply he said, 'There is a place for people like you to go and it's called the lost and found.' The whole class laughed but to me it wasn't funny and I was embarrassed" (Brendtro, Mitchell, & McCall, 2009, p. 83). Practicing the value of respect can prevent further wounding of already traumatized children as well as help children develop an appreciation of others as helpful and supportive rather than hurtful and dangerous.

Developing Respect

Key processes for developing respect in children are modeling, reinforcing, correcting, and expecting the behaviors that are associated with respect that we want children to develop. We obviously want to model the behavior we are trying to teach children. We want to reinforce respectful behavior with praise and by talking about how it feels to respect others and for others to respect them. It is important to correct disrespectful behavior immediately by talking about what may have been happening that caused the child to be disrespectful, how that may cause others to react, and then providing ways to respond differently in the future. Children will work hard to live up to expectations, so it is important to expect that they will be respectful at all times. There are many excellent Web sites that provide numerous ways for parents to teach respect. The chapter on trauma-informed relationships (Chapter 6) discusses developing relationships that allow traumatized children to eventually respect our efforts to be helpful to them.

Cooperation

Through valuing cooperation, children learn naturally that they can often achieve more together than alone (Laughlin, Hatch et al., 2006). Unfortunately, traumatized children can become less than cooperative because their "private logic"—their experiences—tell them no one is to be trusted, and that "when I cooperate I get hurt." Cooperation is developmentally essential to satisfying the universal need to belong, to be connected to others, and subsequently to become a contributing member in the varied environments children must navigate.

Developing Cooperation

We teach children cooperation by also modeling, reinforcing, correcting, and expecting behaviors such as the following:

- Listening when others are talking
- Taking turns when others want to do the same thing or nobody wants to do what is asked
- Experiencing the value of doing things together
- Learning that there are many different ways to accomplish something
- Learning to respect the value others provide in the way of ideas
- Learning that others have experience and unique skills
- Realizing what others can contribute to benefit everyone's needs or efforts

Support groups are a wonderful example of the value of working together for the betterment of every member in the group.

Generosity

The value of *generosity* or "the quality of being kind" (*Merriam-Webster Learner's Dictionary*, 2010) actually has biological and psychological reparative value that benefits traumatized children. Zak, Stanton, and Ahmadi (2007) present a neuroscience perspective that the experience of generosity releases the hormone oxytocin. One group of individuals was given an oxytocin nasal spray while the other group was given a saltwater spray. Each group played a game that required them to decide whether or not to give away money. The presence of oxytocin increased generosity by 80%. Oxytocin actually calms the brain and creates trust, which facilitates bonding with others (Carter, 2007; Ratey, 2002); in traumatized children, trust is frequently absent as a result of broken attachments. A trauma-informed environment will promote the value of generosity and provide the opportunities for traumatized children to learn and feel the benefits of becoming generous; these include social bonding, trusting attachments, being valued by others, experiencing the self as having value, and the reduction of hyperarousal as a result of the more frequent production of oxytocin.

Developing Generosity

Supporting respect and cooperation encourages the development of generosity. However, generosity is a value that is not necessarily a focus for many families, especially traumatized families. Generosity is seldom a focus of treatment plans, which is also unfortunate. Essentially, generosity is doing good things for others without expecting anything in return. Empathy is essential to generosity, and therefore we must teach children the importance of thinking about others, what is helpful versus what is hurtful.

For generosity to be valued and practiced, its benefits must be experienced. Again, children will take their lead from us. Modeling, reinforcing, correcting, and expecting children to be generous is how they learn. Encouraging children to offer to help, to think about others, to be kind, and to engage them in volunteering, may seem to be an oversimplification, and yet this is how children develop the spirit of generosity.

Revisiting T

In reexamining T's story, these three values did not develop as a result of the trauma experienced at school. T was frequently ridiculed and bullied. His teachers failed to provide him with the safety, care, and respect he needed. Denied opportunities for safety and respect precluded acts of generosity on his part. At some point, T's recovery would depend upon being in an environment that would give him the opportunity to revisit and complete these developmental periods.

These three values—respect, cooperation, and generosity—are important because of their emergence in early childhood, their association with resilience, and their role in meeting the biopsychosocial needs of all children, but especially traumatized children whose attachment, attunement to others, and empowerment has been disrupted. Other values such as honesty, compassion, fairness, and responsibility can be added to this list, but in fact, all other values derive from experiences of respect, cooperation, and generosity.

Core Beliefs

When discussing values, it is also necessary to consider what members of an environment believe. Beliefs and values in some ways are mutually inclusive. We value what we believe; we believe what we value. The difference between the two is that a value represents who we are (I am respectful); a belief represents the actions we engage in that we believe makes us respectful (I am courteous). Because what we believe drives our behavior, it is important to determine whether our beliefs align with our values.

Children initially become traumatized in environments that fail to keep them physically and emotionally safe and do not allow them physical and/or emotional escape from the sources inducing trauma. As a result of experiences with the people in their environment, they develop a *private logic*, which is a set of beliefs to help them survive (Adler, 1930). For example, traumatized individuals come to believe any or all of the following:

■ The world is threatening and bewildering.
■ People are unpredictable and not to be trusted.
■ I must do whatever I need to do to control you because if I let you control me, I am vulnerable to your abandonment and abuse (physical, verbal, emotional) again and again.
■ The world is punitive, judgmental, humiliating, and blaming.

These variations of private logic then ultimately drive traumatized individuals' behavior. Their behaviors (beliefs) make sense to them and reflect their efforts to survive even though they can be self-defeating and destructive. This process is no different in organizations and families. Beliefs, old and new, can either support a cultural change or prevent it. In brief, for any environment to be trauma-informed, members must embrace those beliefs that drive trauma-informed care (Connors & Smith, 2009).

There are no assessment tools to identify our private logic. It is revealed in our responses to our experiences and the experiences themselves. When we take the time to listen to children's stories, the experiences they have enjoyed and those they have survived, their private logic emerges (private logic will be discussed in detail in Chapter 6 covering trauma-informed relationships). Private logic changes as children are exposed to new experiences. Experiences that are trauma-informed will promote a strength-based, resilience-focused logic. Within this context, the beliefs in the context of that environment are critical to shaping trauma-informed experiences.

According to Yehuda (2002), "The normal path [of trauma survivors] is recovery, which is facilitated by supportive environments" (p. 35). From this perspective it makes sense that a supportive, trauma-informed environment is shaped and governed by a core set of beliefs. These beliefs allow the environment to be one that is experienced as physically and emotionally safe, as predictable and that affords new experiences and learning opportunities that are empowering, that provides the opportunity to experience others as respectful, fair, honest, and compassionate rather than punitive, judgmental, humiliating, and blaming.

Practices Driven by Beliefs

Starr Commonwealth is a nonprofit program that has been creating environments where children flourish for nearly a century. Established in 1913, the core belief penned by Floyd Starr, its founder, was "There is no such thing as a bad boy," later changed to "There is no such thing as a bad child," to reflect the care of girls as well as boys. This one belief dismissed the idea that troubled children were pathological, but instead simply not afforded the kind of environment needed for their strengths to emerge. Today we would refer to this belief as trauma-informed and resilience focused. Over time, Starr has added the following trauma-informed supported beliefs (not inclusive) (http://www.starr.org/mission):

■ **We believe** everyone has the responsibility to help and no one has the right to hurt, physically or verbally. (This single belief guides their approach to creating an environment that is both physically safe and emotionally safe. It supports the National Center for Trauma-Informed Care's [NCTIC, 2005] primary essential focus on safety as the framework for delivering trauma-informed care.)

- **We believe** people can change and problems are solvable opportunities that facilitate growth and development (resilience focused).
- **We believe** in recognizing and developing the strengths of all children and families (strength based).
- **We believe** all people are spiritual beings and must be given opportunities for spiritual growth. (*Spiritual* refers to doing what has personal meaning, brings about a sense of making a difference, and an opportunity to be of service).
- **We believe** in the oneness of humankind and will embrace all people as social equals, valuing their diversity. (This belief supports sensitivity to the factors that influence the *efficacy of interventions in that child's cultural context*. Cultural and community values, for example, exert profound influence over a victim's willingness to disclose [or not] a particular incident of violation or abuse, making it essential that trauma-informed environments provide multiple healing processes and programs [Harvey, 2007].)

Families, schools, or larger communities could easily adopt these beliefs. These beliefs shape the expectations of community members, the youths served by them, the varied programs they may provide, and the practices in which they engage. However, for any set of beliefs to be effective they must be clearly identified, consistently communicated, practiced, and within a trauma-informed context, align with what neuroscience supports about the developmental needs of traumatized children. They also need to become part of the evaluation criteria (Peterson, 2006) used to consistently monitor and insure that the policies, procedures, behaviors, and interactions of everyone in that environment align with its core beliefs (and values) so the environment meets the biopsychosocial and developmental needs of every child.

One Unifying Belief

Trauma-informed environments are best guided by a unifying belief of what constitutes trauma-informed care. The following section provides two examples of programs that capitalize on a unifying belief to support a trauma-informed environment: the Sanctuary Model and the Circle of Courage.

It is impossible to present the many excellent models available in this chapter. In summary, the three absolutely essential elements for creating and sustaining a viable, trauma-informed environment or care delivery system

THE SANCTUARY MODEL AND ITS UNIFYING BELIEF

Sandra Bloom

The Sanctuary Model (Bloom & Farragher, 2010) represents an evidence-supported, attachment-based, trauma-informed model for upgrading human service delivery organizations. It is based on the following belief: "We believe that the core issue for traumatized children who present with complex problems is disrupted attachment and that one single therapeutic approach is unlikely to be a sufficient remedy for all that is disrupted in the child's basic operating system because of the intertwined complexity of the developmental impacts." In essence, although it presents multiple strategies for supporting the efficacy of the model, it is unified, grounded, focused, and driven by the one belief that disrupted attachment is the core issue, and if resolved, can change the lives of traumatized children.

The model focuses on the seven key domains of attachment. These domains are then used to evaluate the operating systems of the organization. For example, the first attachment domain is *safety and security*. A crisis-driven environment is created when members do not experience safety and security in their environment. It becomes anxiety ridden, resistant to and fearful of change, vulnerable to major staffing issues, which increases performance and efficiency deficiencies. The same practices used to restore safety and security for the traumatized child are then used in the Sanctuary Model to redesign operating systems that have been traumatized.

are: (1) establishment of and a shared commitment to core values; (2) shared commitment to a trauma-informed belief or set of beliefs that drives every practice, program, procedure, and organizational policy; and (3) the clear communication of these values and beliefs in actions and words.

Values and Beliefs Matter: The Rest of T's Story

[T's story adapted from Brendtro, Ness, & Mitchell, 2001.] (Values and beliefs are in *italics*.) When T arrived at the Starr Commonwealth campus he probably felt disoriented; many helping professionals who work in clinics or

CIRCLE OF COURAGE AND ITS UNIFYING BELIEF

Larry Brendtro

Circle of Courage is an example of another model that has a unifying belief (Brendtro, Brokenleg, & Van Bockern, 2002). It is an international youth developmental model that integrates brain science, resilience science, practice wisdom, and tribal knowledge. The curriculum used to put the Circle of Courage into practice was initiated in South Africa when President Nelson Mandela created a national commission to transform programs for children and youth and is now present in over a dozen countries (Brendtro & du Toit, 2005). Its unifying belief is that children in all cultures have four universal growth needs: belonging, mastery, independence, and generosity. Its entire model is guided by strength-based, resilience-focused practices that align with the development and the presentation of experiences that allow youth to fulfill these four universal needs. In residential settings it provides an alternative to coercive methods of restraint, seclusion, and exclusion, and as such meets the National Center for Trauma Care (NCTIC, 2005) trauma-informed guidelines.

hospitals might be, too. Could this possibly be a school for troubled students? The 350-acre campus has a pristine lake and is surrounded by pine forests and farms. The campus rivaled any private boarding school in the nation. Its founder, Floyd Starr, *believed that beauty is a silent teacher.* Many boys came from lives of deprivation and ugliness. He would say, "I wanted to send them a clear message. This beautiful place is for you because you are of value." Like all new boys, T was assigned to a residence on the main campus. He was welcomed by the other youth, but living in a home with a dozen other boys was scary for a lad who had spent most of his life without siblings or friends. Huge Tudor-style houses built between the world wars made the campus look like a fashionable suburb.

It was awkward for T to hear the other boys call the house parents "Mom" and "Pop." They weren't his parents. They were strict, but the other boys didn't seem afraid of them. The boys were *responsible* for keeping the cottages spotlessly clean. T's name was added to the chart on the wall for chores. Setting tables, serving, washing dishes, carrying garbage, mopping bathrooms—all of these chores were part of a system that seemed strange to T. A favorite job was being a buffer boy. With polishing pads under their feet, boys skated around polishing hardwood floors to a high shine. The boys had to keep their lockers and beds in perfect condition. T was given the small handbook with tips on cleanliness and good manners. The most important rule was that *selfishness was off limits*. As Floyd Starr would say, *"Commonwealth means we all share in common every good thing that happens."*

All the boys knew the Creed because *it was posted and proclaimed everywhere*. It began with the declaration *(belief)* that every boy will be good if given an environment of love and activity. The activity part was easy in this beehive of work, study, and play. But boys like T import painful experiences and private logic that convince them they are unworthy of love. "Why should I trust these people?" T was starving for love, but kept to himself.

Heading the counseling staff was Al Lily, a former teacher who went on to earn a graduate degree in social work. The founder was leery of therapists who thought kids could be changed by "the 50-minute hour," but he trusted Al Lily, who shared his philosophy of *environmental intervention* and loved kids. Lily explained, "Many students entered with very little self-control. When at first adults had to exercise external control, they talked with the student about self-control and *also involved the more seasoned students in those talks*. Students started out in highly structured cottages. When they learned to be responsible, they earned their way to more relaxed, ranch-style residences. By *making good decisions*, they *were preparing to return to the community*. They also gained insight into how their own families had broken down, and they learned a new style of family living." Lily saw the big picture: He was training troubled youth for their future role as positive parents. Said Lily, "The cycle of abuse has to be broken. It begins here *with all of us believing we can bring out the good in every child.*"

T needed to learn to bond to adults, respect authority, get along with peers, be a friend, succeed in school, plan for a vocation, and find a purpose in life. In today's terms, these were strength-based interventions. Mr. Lily chose Jerry to be T's counselor. Jerry was a zestful young man who in later years became a decorated sea captain. He was a pied piper for hard-to-reach kids. T had been caged like an animal for three months and was very guarded. Jerry had little to go on, as the case files had been "sanitized." *The expert on T would have to be T himself,* who had never trusted adults.

Counselors consulted with one another on difficult problems. Jerry was still in his 20s and realized he was more of a big brother than a father figure or therapist. He believed that T would benefit from a more mature and seasoned counselor. So Jerry and Mr. Lily decided to invite Max to join T's treatment team.

Max was a former Ohio state police officer who was also much admired by the students. Six-foot-four and middle-aged, Max was a gentle, fatherly role model. Now T had two strong male models who believed in him. "Our goal," said Jerry, "was to *immerse students in* experiences that helped them *make sense out of their lives.* We tried to *provide as many normal growth opportunities* as possible. As they surmounted challenges, they built confidence in themselves."

For more than three years T was reparented and reeducated. An alienated boy learned to belong, a failing student found success, an out-of-control adolescent learned responsibility, and a self-absorbed youth became a friend to others. Grade 11 was the upper limit of the school's curriculum at the time. Most students returned home to finish high school. Military recruiters were hunting for young men who would respect authority, *work as a team member, and get along with diverse groups of people.* T qualified on all counts. He decided on his future, and with the court's approval, he enlisted in the Marines.

T's time in this environment came to a close. From being a boy who was a risk to the community, he was now a strong young man set out to risk his own life in the service of his country. After completing his tour of duty, T returned to civilian life where he continued to do his part to support his community while his identity remained protected (adapted from Brendtro, Ness, & Mitchell, *No Disposable Kids*, 2001).

This story demonstrates that respect, cooperation, and generosity were not only held to be of the utmost value, but also practiced and clearly communicated throughout the campus. T's story illustrates that when the values and beliefs of an environment are clearly defined and shared by the members of that environment, traumatized children can flourish. When that environment also provides the strength-based, developmentally appropriate opportunities that children were previously denied because of their traumatic environment, progress can be made and the resilience associated with the successful completion of these normal developmental tasks can now help children and adolescents thrive.

Family Environments

"Families are bounded by its values and beliefs. Family beliefs are the basis for the formal and informal rules [practices and interactions] that guide its members in the ways they behave toward each other, other people and the groups that comprise the other systems in their environment" (Steele &

Raider, 1991, p. 21). When helping professionals approach the family as a system, they can begin to appreciate that when one member is traumatized, the entire family is impacted. Berg (1994) observes what most practitioners believe, noting that "the best way to provide services to a child [who is traumatized] is through strengthening and empowering the family as a unit" (p. 1).

To function effectively, the family itself must feel safe as a unit and empowered in its various functions as a unit as well as members within that environment. From this perspective, all that is introduced in this work applies to families. Although we do not focus on families, we do understand that efforts to heal a hurt child, a traumatized child outside the context of his family environment, simply will not yield the same lasting outcomes seen when the entire family is trauma-informed. Therefore, our intent is that the core elements and specific strategies identified as being trauma-informed apply to the family as well as the classroom, community-based programs, and services caring for the well-being of children.

Organizational Environments

For environments to succeed, core values must be accepted by all members of a group and commitment to these values must be shared through mutually agreed upon beliefs and practice. Therefore, it is first important to address core organizational values and the role they play in creating and sustaining a trauma-informed environment.

The importance of values related to successful, sustainable relationships within organizations constitutes a text of its own. However, it is foolish to believe that service delivery systems, for example, can actually sustain, manage, or achieve mandates regarding the objectives of trauma-informed care without first reframing and defining the values that address organizational integrity (Connors & Smith, 2009). They also must address the developmental needs of traumatized children, adolescents, their families, and their environments (van der Kolk & Pynoos et al., 2009) and the criteria for evaluating the achievement of the goals of that environment (Peterson, 2006).

The formation of the National Center for Trauma-Informed Care (NCTIC) in 2005 acknowledged at a federal level that organizations, especially childcare delivery systems, should become trauma-informed. However, even prior to this time, efforts were under way to educate outdated delivery systems and processes (Donnovan & McIntyre, 1990; Bloom, 1997; Harris & Fallot,

2001). As of 2010, the National Child Traumatic Stress Network (NCTSN) developed and made available a number of resources for law enforcement agencies, child welfare, education, healthcare, juvenile justice, and other service delivery systems to assist in creating trauma-informed environments.

In order to be trauma-informed, organizational systems and individuals within them must make significant changes in the way they think, what they believe and what they value, and in the practices in which they engage, and then have in place a process that sustains these changes consistently over time. By taking the time to define desired core values, outcomes can be achieved more efficiently and with much less conflict and disruption (Collins, 2009; Connors & Smith, 2009).

Actually, from the time system theory was introduced, it became quite clear that a change in one member's behavior altered or influenced the behaviors of the other members in that environment. It was also realized that for any change to be supported and embraced, its value needed to be clearly understood, doable, and most importantly, believed to be in the best interests of everyone in that system and the system's position and relationship in its ecology (Kantor & Neal, 1985; Bowen, 1990; Fallot & Harris, 2006). In the classic book *Good to Great*, Collins's (2009) research of what allowed organizations to successfully move from good to great and then endure, were their core values. The many suggestions and recommendations today regarding goals, objectives, and strategies for creating trauma-informed environments are well thought out and certainly trauma based. However, without clearly defined core values and beliefs that are embraced by all members in that environment, change will present significant challenges.

Organizational values drive the overall policies, procedures, administration, and management of the organization and its staff. Fallot and Harris (2009) identify five organizational values that support a trauma-informed culture: safety, trustworthiness, choice, collaboration, and empowerment. As with individuals, these core values define the culture of the organization— "what it considers important, how it understands the people it serves and how it puts these understandings into daily practices" (p. 3).

Connors and Smith (2009) identify three core values found in the most successful organizations that sustain organizational integrity—"follow through, get real and speak up" (p. 224). These three values speak to what allows organizations to sustain their culture as well as help it and its members flourish. "Follow through" (do what you say you are going to do) reflects the value of respect in which we come to trust that people mean what they say they mean. "Get real" speaks to the value of honesty between individuals or within organizations. "Speak up" is a value that cannot exist if the first two values are not practiced. It takes courage to speak up, and it is easier to do so when in a culture of respect and honesty (transparency). If the environment is a punitive or retaliatory one, or if a family system is a closed, authoritarian one, members will be very cautious. When members are fearful of speaking up, then respect, cooperation, and generosity are difficult to practice. Without these values, environments simply do not flourish, nor do their members, and the quality of care they provide suffers.

In essence, the values attributed to the success and integrity of trauma-informed organizations are the same values we would hope to instill in families, teachers, and practitioners. If values do in fact define who we are and what we do, developing a trauma-informed environment begins with establishing, clearly communicating, and reaching full consensus as to its core values.

Value-Driven Education and Training

What is needed to be trauma-informed and to practice trauma-informed care is also presented and referenced throughout the text. The purpose here is to address the process for considering how to initiate and sustain education and training efforts within a trauma-informed environment. Although the information presented here is directed at professionals, it can also be applied to the education and training of families. Even training needs to be value driven if it is to be effective in bringing about long-term change. The International Society for Traumatic Stress Studies (ISTSS) sponsored an extensive two-year study resulting in the article "Guidelines for International Training in Mental Health and Psychological Interventions for Trauma Exposed Populations in Clinical and Community Settings" (Weine et al., 2002). They concluded that training "ought to be based on a central set of values and this set of values ought to be made explicit" (p. 159). They stressed that "values tied professionals to humanity and to professions and … guide professionals in addressing the dilemmas that arise from compelling or conflicting obligations" (p. 159). Respect, cooperation, and generosity are listed as essential values related to attending to the uniqueness of individuals, families, communities, and engaging multiple resources to develop content because there are multiple perspectives and strategies that support trauma recovery. Honesty and transparency are also important because these values help to acknowledge what we know or do not know.

They also impart confidence to consumers of trauma-informed services; additionally, consumers' honesty and transparency helps practitioners and trauma-informed environments arrive at strategies that are feasible, practical, and respect diversity and cultural preferences. They help practitioners determine which evidence-based or other approaches to meet the needs of children, adolescents, and families are respectful and include clients' input.

Training and Accountability

The purpose of education and training is to increase awareness, influence practice, interactions, and relationships, develop specialized skills, and ultimately bring best practices to the members in that environment. Therefore, training is a process and one that ought to be supported by accountability outcomes. As new information about trauma presents itself, content should be adjusted to include this information so others can consider its relevance to their practice and their environment and members in their environment.

Evaluating outcomes following the use of these new skills, strategies, and interventions also needs to be a constant objective of training, especially when that training is introducing new practices. It is particularly important when training families because it is so easy for them to fall back upon past practices when their anxiety increases or the results of their initial efforts are less than anticipated. Determining how participants actually use their new practice knowledge, how long they actually continue to use it, and evaluating the benefit it has brought to those receiving help, is accountability. This is by no means easy to achieve, yet it supports the ethical responsibility to do no harm, the moral responsibility to provide best practices, the social responsibility to provide what is actually adaptable and helpful, and the professional responsibility to remain accountable for what is presented to others.

Establishing Sustainable Trauma-Informed Practices and Processes

This chapter opened with T's story to illustrate how environments can traumatize children and to pose the question of what constitutes a trauma-informed environment. It explored the importance of core values to define who we are, what we live for, and what we stand by. It examined the importance of core beliefs because they drive behavior and support the practices we engage in to support the values we strive to maintain. The rest of T's story illustrated how powerfully influential values and beliefs are in creating an environment where T and youth like him can flourish, especially when those values and beliefs are shared by all its members. Most importantly, T was introduced to new experiences that helped him complete past developmental tasks necessary for the *good in him* to flourish, a part of his personality that was obstructed by his traumatic childhood and trauma-inducing environment.

In summary, one unifying belief can be the cornerstone for a comprehensive trauma-informed, resilience-focused model of care. Attention to accountability underscores the importance of consistently holding all members accountable for their practices. Integrity, the ability of an environment to sustain its value and viability, are dependent upon three values—honesty, respect, and the courage to speak up, which cannot happen in environments of disrespect, or environments ruled by fear, coercion, and power. Finally, efforts to educate and train parents, teachers, practitioners, and organizations themselves to be trauma-informed require that education and training also must be value driven to be successful.

Ultimately, helping professionals can be trauma-informed and organizations can have policies, procedures, and mission statements written in trauma-informed terms. However, for any environment to be a place where the Ts of this world not only can flourish, but also can stop the transmission of trauma to their own future generations, all the members of that environment must consistently demonstrate a shared commitment to engage in those practices that support and align with clearly defined, trauma-informed, strength-based core values and beliefs. The following are recommendations for initiating and sustaining a trauma-informed environment.

10-Point Process: Identifying and Sustaining Trauma-Informed Values, Beliefs, and Environmental Integrity

1. List, present, and discuss your values and beliefs with each other.
2. Identify what each value and belief means to you.
3. Provide the opportunity for members to discuss their values and beliefs with each other.

4. Document how these values and beliefs support what you know about trauma and the needs of traumatized children using available knowledge of group members, research literature, best practices, and cultural preferences. Come to a consensus on no more than five values and five beliefs for your primary focus. Identify the values and beliefs all members can agree to share.

5. Define what behaviors and practices (policies, procedures, and programs) support the shared values and beliefs.

6. Evaluate the developmental appropriateness of the defined behaviors and practices (policies, procedures, and programs). Remember that the expectations regarding behaviors must be developmentally appropriate rather than age appropriate. This is best determined, if needed, by trauma-informed assessments. (For example, a traumatized 16-year-old may be developmentally functioning as a 10-year-old. Therefore, programs and practices must reflect developmental expertise.)

7. Get to work, but establish a *practice period*, a time limit at the conclusion of which outcomes need to be evaluated. During the practice period, monitor interactions to determine whether people do what they say they value or believe. If the behavior is contradictory to what was decided, it must be discussed and reevaluated from the perspective that (a) changes in the environment may preclude or dictate different behaviors; (b) the experiences of those involved have since changed what is now valued and/or what is believed; or (c) there is a need for additional support, guidance, information, and skill building to support the behaviors.

8. At the end of the agreed-upon practice period, evaluate all members' commitment to and experiences with the declared values and beliefs.

9. Restate shared commitments to the established values and beliefs and their alignment with expected behaviors.

10. Set regular periods to evaluate the ongoing status of efforts.

Managing Change

Following this 10-point plan is not a difficult process, but one that must be ongoing because environments change along with what the field of trauma-informed practice continues to learn or discover about trauma changes. Anticipate that practices change because environments change, members change, what they know changes, and what they learn changes. While

ORGANIZATIONAL ACCOUNTABILITY

William Steele

Obviously every organization's level of implementation of the trauma-informed components discussed is going to vary. There are excellent tools to assist in evaluating implementation levels. Hummer & Dollard (2010), through the Department of Behavioral and Community Sciences, University of Florida, developed "Creating Trauma Informed Care Environments: An Organizational Self-Assessment." This tool can be used by those just beginning or by those already practicing trauma-informed principles. Significant aspects of the assessment are based on two other instruments: "Trauma-Informed Services: A Self-Assessment and Planning Protocol, Version 1.4" (Fallot & Harris, 2006) and "Trauma Informed Care in Youth Serving Settings: Organizational Self-Assessment" (Traumatic Stress Institute of Klingberg Family Centers, 2008).

These are excellent tools, but they do not address the process for bringing all members of that environment to a shared commitment to invest in the stated trauma-informed values and practices that align with those values. The importance of core beliefs, as they support values and direct practices, also are not examined. This ought to be a major concern because all too often programs "adapt the language" but fail to understand the role that process plays in helping staff with major paradigm shifts in practices that being trauma informed dictates. In reality, given the abundant resource of information available on trauma, identification of trauma-informed values, beliefs, and practices is not all that difficult or time consuming. At the same time, all helping professionals should be concerned with successfully implementing and sustaining these recommended practices.

values may not change, when this occurs, it becomes important to evaluate the current appropriateness of the core beliefs; for example, an organization or its members may need to change the core belief that talk therapy is the intervention of choice. Neuroscience now underscores that sensory-based intervention is also critical and even mandatory for healing to take place. Therefore, a previously accepted belief may need to be expanded or a new belief added to ensure that attention is given to best practices. When change is necessary, this will happen more rapidly than when following a systematic process like the one previously described.

No process or change is useful in the long term without accountability. All members must be committed and agree to be accountable in this process. Appropriate measures must be used frequently and consistently to help (not force) members to continually work toward aligning their practices, policies, and procedures with their values and beliefs. The two points that individuals and organizations often dismiss or forget are (1) monitoring that they are doing what they say they will do as directed by their core beliefs and values (point 7) and (2) consistent accounting of their efforts and outcomes (point 10). Ignoring these two actions can do more to weaken trauma-informed environmental sustainability than any other.

Trauma-Informed Practices for Creating Safe Environments

In this section, practices that support an emotionally safe trauma-informed environment are described and recommendations for various environments are offered. In general, many of the practices presented can be applied to most settings. For additional information, see the previous chapter on safety and self-regulation and subsequent chapters on relationships, resilience, and posttraumatic growth and trauma integration.

Key Principles

In addition to an overall trauma-informed environment, the following basic principles are recommended:

1. Children are given the opportunity to express what does or does not feel safe in or about the environment, and helping professionals remain open and curious to recognizing what helps children feel safe.
2. Children are allowed to bring to the environment those items or engage in those activities and relationships that are calming and soothing.
3. The environment always offers several options, resources, and activities to help children self-regulate so if one or the other is not helping, additional choices remain available to children.
4. Routines, schedules, structure, and rules remain predictable.

5. Whenever possible, the beginning and end of children's time in that environment is experienced as pleasant.

As a result of these practices, ultimately the environment supports and enhances children's abilities to self-regulate and feel safe.

Recommended Practices

Practice One: All practices must be engaged within the framework of safety. The child must know: (1) my body is safe; (2) my feelings are safe; (3) my thoughts, ideas, and words are safe; and (4) my work—the things I make, the materials I use—are safe (Levine, 2008). These practices should be applied at home as well as in the treatment setting and classroom, and are the responsibility of significant adults in the child's life—parents, teachers, counselors, coaches, and trauma-informed practitioners. When safety rules are broken, whether by verbal disrespect, ridicule, shame, or failure to listen, adults must reiterate the rules of the environment that support the environment as safe. For example, "We do not interrupt while another is ..." or "We do not make fun of what someone ..." or "We do not touch other's materials without permission."

Practice Two: All interactions must begin in a safe, pleasant manner and end in a safe, pleasant, simple manner, and this must be consistently predictable. Consider the most critical transition periods in a child's daily life. They include:

■ Rising in the morning
■ Leaving for school and entering their classroom
■ The last class or school activity of the day
■ Arriving home
■ Going to bed

As simplistic as these may seem, they represent opportunities to support consistent self-regulation throughout the day. Many traumatized children are living in violent homes and communities. They bring to school their survival responses reinforced by what happened the night before, before they left home for school, or what happened on the way to school. How they are greeted in their first class can activate or calm. From a trauma-informed perspective, when that teacher and classroom is safe

(Practice One) that child will find it much easier to self-regulate. When that class always begins with safe, enjoyable, nonthreatening interaction before beginning the process of learning, the traumatized child's limbic system is given the time needed to regulate.

Practice Two must be consistently applied to the major transition periods from the first interaction in the morning and the last interaction at night. Young children love for their parent to read a short book to them before turning off the lights, if in fact the parent appreciates how critical this transition period is to regulation. Equally important is waking to calm, predictable, supportive interaction in the morning. Transition periods that are not marked by consistent predictable interactions that are not safe and pleasant are simply more prone to inducing anxiety, worry, and resulting in unpredictable responses from children in their environment.

Practice Three: Reduce stimuli in the environment. Traumatized children are constantly navigating their environments at a sensory brain stem, midbrain, or limbic level. What they see, hear, and sensations of touch and smell can become very activating. This does create a challenge, especially for the learning environment where multiple stimulations are part of the learning process. However, it is important to appreciate that the brains of traumatized children do not do well with multiple stimuli as it causes them to feel a loss of control. The same children will manage stress levels differently on any given day depending upon what preceded that moment in time. From this perspective, helping professionals must be able to recognize that if traumatized children are acting out, they are likely in need of being in an environment with limited stimuli until they can self-regulate. In clinical settings like play rooms, only set out those items needed for that play session. Traumatized children tend not to do well with too many choices.

Practice Four: When activated, traumatized children need to be reassured that they are safe emotionally and physically. To help children move from lower parts of the brain to more cognitive areas, verbalize what you see them doing: "I notice you are looking down"; I notice you are tapping your foot," and so on. Ask them to change what they are doing: "Let's get up and walk for a minute" or "Let's sit down." Focusing on their bodies and what they are doing or changing what they are doing helps to regulate their response to whatever may have activated them. Once they begin to calm down, continue to verbalize that they are safe, and ask what they need or need to do to feel safe.

Practice Five: Determine several activities, actions, or resources that children enjoy to help them regain a sense of safety and to feel better when they are stressed. Provide them with the opportunity to initiate those actions until they once again feel some sense of control or safety. In this regard, keep in mind that what worked the previous day may not work the next day; therefore, have multiple options available.

Practice Six: Find and repeat engagement in areas of competency. Traumatized children need repetitive experiences of mastery. Non-traumatized children will generally experience mastery with fewer repetitions, whereas traumatized children will need multiple repetitions over time. During stressful moments, what might appear to be regressive behavior may be a traumatized child's return to an activity he or she has mastered as a way to feel safe and to regulate trauma reactions. The more opportunities practitioners can offer traumatized children to discover areas of competency, the more resources are available to help young clients regulate their reactions and behaviors.

Children as Experts

The following list provides sample questions that can help identify ways to make the environment an emotionally safe one for children. Keep in mind that these questions are being asked within a trauma-informed environment and as an integrated part of safe practices.

- I am really curious as to what you like best about this room when you look around?
- I have a number of chairs. Why don't you try out all the chairs and tell me which one you like the best. That can be your chair if you like, or you can sit on the floor.
- Where would you like me to sit?
- What would make the room more comfortable for you?
- When something or someone really upsets you, what or who calms you the most?

In a school setting:

- I'm curious. Where in this room/building do you feel the most comfortable, the safest?

TRAUMA-INFORMED ENVIRONMENT FOR INFANTS AND TODDLERS

Caelan Kuban

When creating a trauma-informed environment for infants and toddlers, we must remember to see, smell, listen, feel, and taste the world from the perspective of a young child. The younger the age at which a child is removed from adversity and placed into a nurturing, safe, and stimulating environment, the greater the expectable improvement. The environment includes everything that surrounds a child, namely the people and places the child encounters every day. A trauma-informed environment is one that is consistent and predictable. Caregivers and activities should be reliable and routine consistent so that a child can learn who and what to expect at various times of the day. This dependable schedule will provide infants and toddlers with a sense of safety and security.

A nurturing and consistent caregiver provides attachment. The maturation of the brain is heavily mediated by interactions between the infant and its primary caregiver. Attachment experiences directly influence optimal brain development including maturation of the right brain and the development of coping responses. Growth-facilitating environments, those rich with secure attachments, create strong neuronal connections, integrate brain systems, and strengthen the capacity to cope with stress. All are essential for optimal cognitive, emotional, and behavioral development in children.

A trauma-informed environment would include both calming and stimulating things to see, hear, touch, and explore. For example, colorful patterns and smiling nursery characters will arouse a child during playtime, while blankets with soft textures and classical music will help to soothe a child when it is time for rest or sleep. During an infant's first year, the focus should be on helping the caregiver read, interpret, and respond to infant cues. Attunement between caregiver and infant improves a caregiver's sense of efficacy and increases the number of positive interactions that the caregiver and infant experience. It is through the repeated process of caregivers helping their children self-regulate that children learn how to manage their feelings by themselves and with the help of others, as well as develop an understanding of the role emotions play in relationships.

Promoting playfulness and exploration as well as the importance of allowing a child to take the lead is important during the second year. At this age, crawling, pulling things out of cupboards or baskets, and other developmentally appropriate toys for play will provide many opportunities for the use of emerging communication, motor, and emotional skills.

The third year of life requires continued promotion of playfulness and help with resolutions if traumatic play is constant. Again, interventions should be consistent and predictable, repeated, nurturing, and provide the child with some control. Play should follow the normal process of development and allow children to look, touch, explore, and learn. Play provides the use of toys/props as words so that children can play out behaviors and concerns. This ultimately facilitates communication, releases feelings, and renews and allows for problem solving. Introducing books with themes that the child can relate to is often helpful following trauma. Dress-up clothes, mirrors, building blocks, puppets, musical instruments, texture boxes, doll houses, sand and water tables, and craft supplies are just a few of the items that help create a trauma-informed environment for infants and toddlers.

- With whom do you feel the safest?
- Of all your classes, in what class do you feel the safest?
- Of all the activities you take part in during the week, what is your favorite?
- When something or someone really upsets you, what or who calms you the most?

At home:

- I'm curious. What part of the day do you like more—the morning or evening?
- What is it that you like about that time?
- Where is your favorite place here (at home)? (Do not assume the bedroom. We say home because the safest place may not be in the house.)
- What is your favorite thing to do at home?
- What is your favorite possession, toy, and so on?
- When something or someone really upsets you, what do your parents do that helps you feel better (or worse)?

These few questions can reveal a good deal about what helps children feel safe. Additional questions could be added, but the point is to give children the opportunity to reveal what can make *our place* emotionally safe for them. Children must be given the opportunity to control some aspect of their environment, to have their *safe place* and *safe behavior.*

Cultural Competence and Trauma-Informed Environments

Cultural competence refers to the capacity and abilities of programs and practitioners to treat diverse traumatized populations in ways that are acceptable and effective. However, what currently constitutes culturally competent trauma-informed care varies widely, largely because there are multiple complexities and challenges unique to each culture. Some individuals and families also frequently face the stress and even secondary trauma of acculturation.

Children who come from diverse backgrounds must often navigate dual cultures—their family culture and their peer culture (in school). They are often used as interpreters for their parents, which places them in conflicting roles when communicating for parents at school conferences. Traumatized children frequently do not do well academically because of trauma's effect on cognitive processes; add to this the stress of having to deal with the discrimination and language limitations in school settings. Children in refugee or displaced populations must also deal with the stress of resettlement in communities where diverse cultures may themselves be in conflict or at least in competition for mental health resources. These and other challenges underscore the obvious need for cultural competency in all trauma-informed organizations and environments. In addition, there are a limited number of trauma-trained professionals available to provide services in the native language of those seeking help.

In 2005, the National Child Traumatic Stress Network (NCTSN) Refugee Trauma Task Force, in collaboration with International Faces Heartland Health Outreach, completed *Mental Health Interventions for Refugee Children in Resettlement White Paper II* (NCTSN, 2005). In essence, they found that trauma intervention with children was helpful in mitigating trauma symptoms, but not school functioning, largely because intervention did not address the resettlement and acculturation issues. On the other hand, psychoeducational parenting programs that involve only mothers appear to be helpful in multiple areas of functioning.

There are no studies that show that being trained to be culturally competent actually improves outcomes for culturally diverse groups. However, the one common factor related to efficacy found across the literature is that when ethnically matched professionals are available, retention and intervention benefits improve over those who receive services from nonethnically matched professionals (Snowden, Hu, & Jerell, 1995). When such a match is not possible, using supervising paraprofessionals to provide intervention can be beneficial within an environment or organization. Obviously, a trauma-informed environment would match professional staff to the diverse populations seeking help.

An organization's responses to culturally diverse clients are a unique part of the overall environment's values and beliefs. Here are some recommendations on how to value diversity and respect the belief systems of all individuals (children, adolescents, and adults) who are encountered in trauma-informed environments:

1. Always request permission to do things or discuss issues before actually beginning any assessment, intervention, or activity.
2. Explain the purpose of assessment and intervention, but especially the need and reason for asking questions.
3. Be curious about the individual's culture and give permission to adult, child, or adolescent to inform you of what is and is not acceptable.
4. Acknowledge your limitations in the way of language, speaking, and understanding, and knowledge about customs and norms.
5. Apologize when you do or say something that is not acceptable.
6. Know the "dress code" for that culture.
7. Always be courteous and attempt to greet and part with hello and goodbye using the native language.
8. Know what is appropriate from a spiritual perspective, as many cultures have a strong spiritual belief system.

From a systems perspective, culture-specific centers and clinics provide an environment in which clients are likely to stay longer in treatment versus those in nonmatching environments (Snowden, Hu & Jerrell, 1995). In fact, limited research shows that the gains seen in culturally specific environments are greater than those seen in environments that are not culture specific, even when working with a culturally matched professional. Given the earlier discussion about the influential power of environments, this makes sense. Most agree that a great deal more outcome research is needed

CULTURAL COMPETENCE IN SHELTER SETTINGS
Cathy Malchiodi

Having worked for many years in domestic violence and homeless shelters, I am acutely aware that experiences of trauma leave many individuals feeling helpless and powerless when they arrive at the facility. Of course, traumatic events happen to people from all ethnic backgrounds that have a variety of worldviews. Despite the fact that the brain's response to traumatic events is similar in most people, culture has an important role in how trauma is defined and managed by various survivors. It also dictates what supports and trauma-informed interventions may be most useful and effective.

Domestic violence has different meanings in various cultures; it has different meanings within cultures, too. Religious beliefs in particular impact how interpersonal violence is perceived, including any solutions or recommendations to survivors whose beliefs may prevent them from leaving even the most dangerous situations on occasion. In all cases, eventual recovery is affected by these beliefs and their meanings and trauma integration takes place within that meaning-making process. Practitioners must be aware of their own responses to interpersonal violence because the families and children they serve may have very different beliefs and attitudes; accepting those beliefs and attitudes is the first step to helping these individuals reexamine any behaviors that endanger themselves and their children.

Engaging people through their cultural beliefs or worldviews is actually relatively easy in most cases. Offering opportunities to participate in cultural rituals and traditions, religious practices, and even cooking specific foods in residential settings goes a long way to establish connection and trust. These gestures indicate a culturally respectful environment that honors individuals' identities and preferences; it builds a sense of self and connection to the staff and practitioners. In establishing a culturally sensitive art and play therapy room, I try to display colorful and culturally diverse artwork that is child-appropriate; include "live things" such as fish tanks and plants; and have comfortable seating with options for pillows; rocking chairs; and calming music (at a resting heart rate). If possible, I always try to enlist children and residents in adding to the space or decorating it with items that provide a sense of their culture and preferences, too.

Above all, it is important to make sure that everyone understands any rules, expectations, and routines to enhance a sense of safety and control; this practice crosses cultural boundaries because all individuals want to feel safe and empowered. Everyone should be introduced to staff that will be involved in their care, including who will check on them during evenings and how and when this will happen and why. In particular, everyone should know how a shelter or other program responds to violent behavior or suicidal statements. If possible, psycho-educational information should be posted where everyone can access and read it. Translations are also helpful if available so that individuals can read the materials in their own languages when they are ready and able, knowing that most survivors are overwhelmed and initially may not be able to take in too much information.

regarding culturally sensitive trauma intervention. Based on what is known about the need for safety in trauma-informed environments, seeking help from trained professionals that match clients' cultures within a culture-specific environment (clinic or center) is more likely to support this essential component of trauma-informed care.

Conclusion

Environments are complex and include multiple systems; they include individual clients, family and/or caregivers, practitioners, support staff, and organizational values and beliefs that govern day-to-day operations and interventions. Overall, young clients and their families need to trust these environments and the helping professionals within those environments. The next chapter will address trauma-informed relationships that enhance individuals' success with achieving a sense of safety and challenges of self-regulation, and enhance the success of any environment or organization in helping traumatized children and adolescents.

Chapter 6

Trauma-Informed Relationships

Arina is a 5-year-old girl from Russia who was abandoned at birth and sent to an orphanage to live until an American couple recently adopted her. Little is known about Arina except that the orphanage she lived at was an over-crowded facility where childcare workers had little time to spend with each child. While Arina knows and understands some English, she prefers to communicate through playing with her favorite toys, a baby doll and a stroller. On some days she puts the doll in the stroller, rocking it forcefully until it falls out of the stroller; in response, Arina becomes withdrawn and often walks away from the doll, leaving it on the floor while she finds a self-soothing toy to cuddle or blows bubbles. On other occasions, Arina behaves like a baby herself and crawls on her hands and knees or demands to be held and rocked until she feels content. Her new adoptive parents are worried that she may not bond to them and that she may not be able to start school like other children in her age range.

Marla is a 10-year-old girl who experienced repeated physical and sexual abuse since approximately the age of 3 years. In early childhood, she was assaulted physically and sexually by a stepfather and was put into foster care until her mother received treatment for drug abuse. When Marla was returned to her mother's custody, the mother became physically and verbally abusive to Marla; protective services made several attempts to again remove the child from her mother's custody, but all attempts failed. More recently, Marla was repeatedly sexually assaulted by a group of boys at her school. Because she feared that she would be separated from her mother again, Marla kept the incidents a secret until a teacher at her school witnessed one of the assaults near the school grounds. The child is now in a residential treatment center where therapists report that she is regularly wetting her bed, is socially withdrawn, has poor personal hygiene, and in general, behaves more like a 3-year-old child. In fact, Marla actually prefers to play with the younger children at the facility and to engage in the activities that preschoolers enjoy rather than those of children her own age; even her human figure drawings are more like those of a preschooler (Figure 6.1).

Jacob is a 15-year-old adolescent who has recently been in a juvenile detention facility because of various crimes including assault of another teen and robbery. His parents divorced when Jacob was 3 years old, and since that time he has had several stepfathers. When interviewed by a psychologist who was treating Jacob at the detention facility, the mother reported that at least one of his stepfathers was physically violent and physically assaulted Jacob on many occasions. At 7 years old, Jacob's older brother died in a homicide at school; this was a complicated grief because Jacob witnessed some of the events associated with the homicide firsthand. Jacob's older sister also struggled with her grief about her brother's death and is currently in drug rehabilitation for addiction to opiates and pain medications; Jacob is preoccupied with worry about her hospitalization and thinks she "will probably die of an overdose." Jacob's most critical problem involves anger management and he believes that he may "always be angry."

Figure 6.1   Marla's human figure drawing. (Reproduced with permission of C. Malchiodi.)

These three brief case examples underscore the importance of relationships and how, when primary relationships are disrupted by traumatic events, children and adolescents are put at risk for a variety of symptoms, behaviors, and responses. For Arina, Marla, and Jacob, experiences of neglect and abuse heighten the importance of safe and appropriate relationships with trusted and caring adults. In their cases, the establishment of trauma-informed relationships is the cornerstone of recovery and resilience. Regardless of the environments children must navigate daily, those memories that help traumatized children thrive when facing multiple exposures are those related to what others did with them, to them, and for them throughout their lives (Steele, 2009; OACAS, 2006; Tweedle, 2007: Brendtro & Long, 2002). Gharabaghi (2008) stresses that the limited focus on evidence-based practices "ignores broader qualitative studies showing that the interpersonal relationships yield more impact than technique" (p. 30).

This chapter addresses the importance of relationships in trauma-informed practice. The impact of trauma on early attachment and how trauma-informed relationships can reestablish secure attachment are discussed with an emphasis on safety, trust, and respect in interventions; understanding individuals' private logic; applying sensory experiences as relational mediators; the importance of modeling and empathy building; and establishment of trauma-informed relationships with parents and caregivers.

The Power of Caring Relationships

Gharabaghi (2008) says, "Relationships are the interventions" (p. 31). What parents, practitioners, or educators say, do, and provide children in the way of experiences are all equally important. When asked, "What is your favorite thing to do at home?" the child who says, "Play with my mom" will do better than the child who replies "Sleep." When asked, "What kinds of things does your parent say to you that makes you feel special?" the child who cites three or four very specific statements will do better than the child who can only cite one statement. Unfortunately, the power of relationship is often overlooked in favor of more "profound" treatment strategies. Larson (2008), citing the work of the Commission on Children at Risk (doctors, research scientists, mental health and youth service professionals), notes that the principal reason that growing numbers of American children are failing to flourish is a lack of positive connectedness—close connections to other people and deep connections to moral and spiritual meaning.

DeBoer and Coady (2007) conducted research comparing outcomes between the quality of good helping relationships in child welfare and poor relationships characterized by impatience, not listening, being judgmental, not taking the time to understand, and being too professional or too formal. Client outcomes were far more positive when workers related to clients "in a person-to-person, down to earth manner … including talking and dressing in a manner that decreased professional distance … using small talk to establish support … self disclosure, returning phone calls, being on time for appointments and completing tasks as promised as these actions conveyed respect and helped to building trust" (p. 38). A similar qualitative study (Shelden, Angel et al., 2010) found that "not only was trust associated with greater gains in student achievement, but also with lasting gains in achievement" (p. 159). In brief, those who took the time to listen and communicate an attitude of acceptance, warmth, accessibility, and knowledge engendered more trust. Finally, in a longitudinal study that tracked high-risk children over three decades, those who succeeded had at least one person in their lives who accepted them unconditionally (Werner & Smith, 1992).

In a qualitative study (Steele, Kuban, & Raider, 2009) involving children ages 6 through 12 years the question was asked, "What allowed some of these children to do better than others although all did well?" In the previous year, these children were screened for the presence of clinically significant trauma and other related mental health symptoms. They were then randomly placed in treatment groups and wait list groups. All children eventually received evidence-based intervention with three- and six-month follow-up measures, and all experienced a statistically significant reduction in symptoms. The qualitative study included focused interviews with these children, their parents, and school social workers. An analysis of these verbatim interviews indicated that the quality of the connection with a parent was correlated with those who saw the greatest positive gains. Their parents played with them more, spent more time with them, and provided their children more varied experiences and positive value statements than did the parents of those children who did not perform as well. These results support the widely accepted premise that self-regulation is the direct outcome of the quality of children's primary attachment relationships (Osofsky, 2004).

All of these studies underscore the importance of connection through quality relationships. As Bronfenbrenner (2005) implies, all children need at least one adult who is "irrationally crazy" about them, underscoring the significance of relationships as primary sources of positive outcome. Siegel (1999) emphasizes "interpersonal neurobiology" and how social relationships shape the brain and the ways that individuals of all ages adapt to emotional stress. Finally, Perry (2009) notes that relationships mediate the major developmental experiences during childhood as well as how traumatic experiences are processed. For example, children with few positive relationships during or after a trauma have a more difficult time reducing stress reactions and have more ongoing trauma symptoms over time. Overall, caring human relationships buffer the effects of stressful events and literally support the neural networks involved in bonding, attachment, attunement, social interactions, and affiliation. Thus, it is essential that helping professionals understand how to construct trauma-informed relationships to provide the necessary intervention to support and enhance children's ability to attach and attune to others.

Trauma's Impact on Children's Relationships and Attachment

The quality of early attachment experiences is widely accepted to be the most important influence on psychosocial development (Bowlby & Winton, 1998). *Attachment* is generally defined as the strong emotional bond with caregivers that is formed during infancy and early childhood and is a predictor of future developmental and psychosocial consequences. In the cases of Arina and Marla, multiple childhood traumas affected their subsequent relationships with adults because their relational environments were disrupted in some way. While having basic needs for food and shelter met, Arina may have experienced severe neglect and lack of consistent care giving during the first several years of her life. Marla was subjected to multiple abusive relationships, inconsistent relationships, abandonment, and other traumatic events. Because all individuals are born with an innate disposition to seek closeness from others, when this natural tendency is disrupted by trauma or other events, all later personality development may be impacted.

Attunement is another important aspect in every caring relationship and is central to attachment. In the caretaker–infant relationship, it is the caretaker's sensitive responses to the infant's cues; these responses either enhance or disrupt the quality of an infant's attachment. In a series of now classic studies on attachment, Ainsworth (1967) found that when parents or caretakers promptly and successfully responded to infants' cries, the infants cried less by the end of their first year than babies who did not receive similar caring responses. In brief, most infants quickly learn that the adults who expediently respond are reliable and that that attention to needs is recognized and provided.

Ainsworth also distinguished two different types of attachment: secure and avoidant. Secure infants may reach out to adults in a number of ways to seek physical contact through vocalizations, smiles, cries, or other obvious behaviors with a goal of renewing engagement with caregivers. Those who experience avoidant attachment may avoid parents or caregivers or fail to find comfort in social interactions in these relationships; some may even appear nondistressed, but are also disengaged and display avoidant behaviors as their dominant response.

These early relationships lay the foundation for emotional regulation, but more importantly, the formation of relationships between the self and others. It is not difficult to understand some of Arina's inability to respond to her caring, adoptive parents because Arina may have experienced a lack of caring relationships during her first years of life in a crowded Russian orphanage. Marla's young life began with abuse and possible neglect from infancy onward. In Marla's case, she may have been vulnerable to abuse by peers because disrupted attachments may cause children to become victimized by others since they may not be perceived as socially competent or likeable. For both Arina and Marla, their attachment problems may also cause adults, including helping professionals, teachers, and caregivers, to unconsciously repeat negative relationship patterns with them or have unrealistic social expectations for them.

Arina's disrupted attachment is evident in her play activity; she may lovingly take care of her baby doll and then suddenly absentmindedly drop the doll on the floor, neglecting it as she was once neglected early in life. When there has been inconsistent, frightening, or abusive caregiver behavior, children's relationships remain in conflict, leaving them both wanting to be close to a caring adult but at the same time, wanting to flee or dissociate from others. Helping professionals and caregivers may even be perceived as sources of fear and worry when traumatized children's brains react with survival responses. In brief, initial experiences that involve relationships early in life are not erased over time, but are retained and subsequently impact all future development, particularly in the area of relationships. These disrupted attachment experiences are believed to predict dissociative problems throughout adolescence and young adulthood (Gil, 2003a).

ATTACHMENT

Sandra Bloom

Early childhood attachment determines whether a child's brain, body, sense of self, capacity for relationships, and conscience all develop properly. In the Sanctuary Model we focus on seven key domains of attachment: (1) safety and security, (2) emotional management, (3) learning, (4) communication, (5) participation in relationship, (6) reciprocity and justice, and (7) coping with loss and change. The grandfather of attachment studies, Sir John Bowlby, referred to attachment as creating for the child an "internal working model" that determined the child's view of self and others across the lifespan. We have updated this notion with the idea of an "operating system," with the child's brain and body representing in this metaphor the "hardware," and all that the child learns over time, the "software." We believe that the core issue for traumatized children who present with complex problems is disrupted attachment and that one single therapeutic approach is unlikely to be a sufficient remedy for all that is disrupted in the child's basic operating system because of the intertwined complexity of the developmental impacts. Let's look for a moment at what disrupted attachment frequently does to a child.

When the child has a less than optimal attachment experience as a result of exposure to conditions of toxic stress, the damage to the normal developmental integration of body, brain, mind, and soul can be extensive, but is likely to appear differently in every child. In the Sanctuary Model we group these complex problems in parallel with the main attachment domains: (1) lack of basic safety, security, and trust; (2) lack of emotional management and chronic hyperarousal; (3) learning problems ranging from mild to severe, impaired decision making, problem solving, judgment; (4) poor communication skills; (5) problems with authority ranging from passivity to defiance to bullying; (6) inadequate moral development, impaired sense of reciprocal relationships; and (7) reenactment behaviors, inability to grieve, and inability to imagine future outcomes, including consequences of actions.

Finally, disruption of attachment during infancy and early childhood is not an ending to the development of secure attachment later in life; even adults who have had abusive or difficult childhoods have the opportunity to revise their responses to create more secure and positive relationships to others. Trauma experts like Perry (2009) advocate for early intervention because a younger brain is more malleable than a more mature brain; infancy provides the organizing framework for future stress responses. However, others like Siegel (1999, 2003) propose that all individuals can find the emotional security missed, even if they experienced neglectful or violence-ridden childhoods, if intervention focuses on the relational aspects that involve on attachment and attunement. Both stances provide a basis for trauma-informed relationships. One values the importance of early intervention with traumatized individuals and supporting secure attachment when possible; the other emphasizes that the brain can remodel itself through experiences provided by helping professionals and caregivers that replace previously insecure or avoidant relationships.

Helping Children Through Trauma-Informed Relationships

While safety, self-regulation, and environment are essential to trauma-informed practice, relationships are the foundation for facilitating trauma integration and resiliency responses. Without successful relationships, traumatized individuals will not have the necessary relational skills to support safety and healthy self-regulation that lead to resolution of trauma reactions. As underscored in the introduction to this chapter, the ability to establish connection to others is key to the experience of secure attachment. Because practitioners eventually encourage traumatized children and adolescents to acknowledge their worries, fears, and distressing experiences, developing safe, trustworthy, and respectful relationships with practitioners is essential.

While many components go into successful trauma-informed relationships, two overarching concepts are particularly important: (1) right brain and relational (limbic) interaction between clients and helping professionals are often more important than strictly cognitive or behavioral interventions; and (2) reparative and repetitive experiential activities that enhance the experience of secure attachment between practitioner and client are important ,and particularly those activities that meet the individual needs of children and adolescents in development of interpersonal skills (Steele & Malchiodi, 2008; Malchiodi, 2008). Therefore, the next section covers the

PROVIDING BONDING, PASSION AND JOY

John Micsak

Behavioral models of child rearing are historically the greatest limitation to healthy relationships with children and are the models that most of us still utilize. This bias has seriously limited our ability to reach and provide healing for children with neurodiversity issues. Older behavioral models may have worked somewhat with some behaviors, but are terribly insufficient in reaching the sequential bottom-to-top wiring, brain chemistry, and brain architectural issues evident in various degrees with traumatized children. The key is to create relationally based blueprints that enhance and prioritize regulation from a hierarchal standpoint. Focus must start with the biology of arousal patterns (hypo or hyper arousal) followed closely by emotional or affect regulation, and then cognitive, social, and moral regulation. It is crucial that we focus on building or reorganizing the foundation of children who have neurobiological risk factors. Relational-based approaches are more effective than traditional cognitive or behavioral approaches that merely try to correct or modify external behaviors.

Bonding is the behavior an adult provides for a child; *attachment* is the neurobiological response of a child to bonding opportunities. Without bonding opportunities, children cannot attach. It is important to provide hundreds and perhaps thousands of bonding experiences focusing on attention, affection, and attunement. *Attention* is spending time with the child, displaying age-appropriate interaction including eye contact, singing songs, laughter, fun, and play, and talking in a soothing and reciprocal voice. It is recognizing the child as a valued human being and providing encouragement and support. *Affection* is providing loving physical contact and gestures, unconditionally caring about a child, and providing sensory soothing, deep warmth, and congruency through actions. *Attunement* is being aware and responsive to the cues of a child or the process of getting "online" with the child. It includes empathy, understanding, and intuition to tune in to what the child needs and providing the appropriate response. Attunement involves rhythm, synchronicity, and triception (understanding the body, mind, and relational triad) orchestrated by a loving adult presence. It is crucial to provide these bonding experiences, particularly during transitional periods such as morning, after school, and bedtime.

Unfortunately, some adults who work with challenging children spend most of their relational time on managing disruptive behaviors or modulating negative affect. In contrast, they do not provide experiences that foster positive emotions such as joy, passion, fun, love, and support—emotions that are often absent in traumatized children. Passion and joy allow a child to divert from pervasive fear, uncertainty, and vulnerability. On a biological level, joy and passion create more oxytocin, which we know is the bonding/trust hormone in the body.

following aspects of trauma-informed relationships to support these concepts: establishing safety, trust, and respect; identifying and understanding private logic; sensory experiences as relational mediators; modeling and mirror neurons; relationships with parents and caregivers; and the impact of trauma-informed relationships on practitioners.

Safety, Trust, and Respect

Children and adolescents like Arina, Marla, and Jacob all have had life experiences that leave them feeling vulnerable and often fearful or anxious. In Jacob's case, his primary response is anger while Marla has become a silent victim of abuse. In all three cases, these individuals have learned that their worlds are not safe and each has developed adaptive coping skills to meet challenges through avoidance, hyperarousal, anger, dissociation. and other responses.

Chapters 4 and 5 addressed in detail the importance of safety in trauma-informed practice. However, because it is central to trauma-informed relationships, the basic principles are also summarized here. In order to accept helping professionals' offers of help, children and adolescents must first experience them as "safe people." Although individuals ultimately determine who is safe, practitioners can present themselves as safe by verbally acknowledging and normalizing the concerns (fears, worry, suspicion) that many traumatized children generalize about all adults. Young clients should always be presented with the power to choose how much time they spend with practitioners to the extent possible. Once the relationship begins, they should also be able to choose what activities they find helpful or not and, of course, should be protected from endangering themselves and others.

Practitioners also can project an atmosphere of safety in the questions that they ask, including open-ended questions and being present to both verbal and nonverbal responses (play, body language, breathing, and other cues). As described in Chapter 4, children should be helped to identify resources and activities that help them feel safe, stable, and calm when trauma reactions emerge. In particular, in order to create a safe relationship, children and adolescents should have a voice in what is needed in their environment to help them relate to helping professionals with trust and comfort. Additionally, beginning and ending all interactions with safety and positive outcomes in all situations is basic to trauma-informed relationships.

Finally, trust and respect are central to any therapeutic relationship, including trauma-informed relationships. Trust and respect are earned in part from creating a sense of safety between the client and the practitioner; these values can also be conveyed in other ways. For example, practitioners convey respect when allowing children to make decisions about participation in an activity or even responding to questions. Providing adequate information about sessions and activities in developmentally appropriate ways is also helpful because it suggests what will happen and what to expect. Being trauma-informed means that a sense of shared power and responsibility in the relationship is communicated, with the goal of empowering individuals to move from being victims to survivors to eventual thrivers. The long-term goal is to help children and adolescents become individuals who can trust not only the helping professional, but also find the experience of secure attachment in others. Here are some statements reflecting the shared relationship:

- In this room (playroom, office, recreation room), we will be working together.
- When we are together, we can do many things you like to do. Sometimes you will be the boss and decide what we will do. Sometimes I will decide what we will do. We will take turns being the boss.
- Sometimes when we work together, you will be able to play or draw pictures on your own. Sometimes we will play or draw together or just talk. We will decide together if we will play, draw, or talk each time we meet.
- If we play this game (do this activity, play with these puppets), you can be the one to tell me what to do.

In order to create a sense of safety, trust, and respect, a few ground rules are also necessary to establish an effective trauma-informed relationship between the helping professional and the child or adolescent. For example, a practitioner might say the following:

■ In order to help you and other children feel safe in this room, there are a few rules. There is no hitting or breaking toys or games. No hitting or hurting yourself or me.

■ Sometimes children wonder if I will tell your parent (foster parent, care-taker, teacher) what you say while you are here. I promise not to tell anyone what you tell me unless you are hurting someone else or your-self, or somebody is hurting or might hurt you. If you might be hurt or hurt someone else, I will need to tell someone (case worker, social worker, etc.) about it because I want to make sure you are safe and OK. Before I tell someone else, I will always tell you first.

These statements do not have to be made at the start of the session; they are actually more effective if helping professionals weave them into conversa-tion during the initial and subsequent meetings. Because many children may not immediately understand these rules, it is important to repeat them over several sessions. In conveying any rules for safety and respect, remember to consider cultural preferences for eye contact, proximity to the helping profes-sional, and talking. In addition to culture, children who have experienced neglect, abuse, or chronic trauma have developed an idiosyncratic worldview (private logic; for more information, see next section) because of their experi-ences. For example, Arina is used to inattention and can remain still for long periods of time or play by herself without interacting with adults. In her case, it may be helpful to sit by her side rather than confronting her face-to-face and making gentle, nonjudgmental comments about what she is doing or creating. The goal is to lay the groundwork for security and establish that there will be consistency and reliability in the relationship as much as possible.

Finally, as narrative therapists say, "the person is not the problem, the problem is the problem." Many children and adolescents have come to believe that they are "defective" and they are problems that others respond to with frustration, hopelessness, or confusion. When working from a trauma-informed perspective, it is important to communicate to young cli-ents that they are more than the sum of what has brought them to therapy, counseling, or treatment. Reinforcing a sense that problems are separate from the person is central to developing an atmosphere of respect for the individual as unique and capable of change. It also conveys and facilitates a trust in the process of working together to solve problems without blame or shame, two emotional beliefs that many traumatized individuals internalize.

Relating to Traumatized Children's Private Logic

Being trauma-informed dictates that helping professionals accept that they cannot know what that trauma experience is really like for any individual; in other words, practitioners cannot completely relate to what a child or adolescent has endured or survived. This is why it is so important to be a witness rather than a clinician within a trauma-informed relationship and to take a stance of being curious (relational) rather than analytical (cognitive). If asked "What are we likely to witness," Steele (Steele & Raider, 2001) would reply "terror, feeling totally unsafe and powerless, hurt, anger, revenge, and layers of accountability" (p. 2), of all of which are manifested in various body sensations, implicit memories, images and feelings. These adjectives define the pain that traumatized children and adolescents live with every day. As mentioned previously in Chapter 2, individuals create what Adler referred to as a *private logic* (Griffith & Powers, 1984); it is a way of thinking that then shapes the often misunderstood and misdiagnosed, primal survivor behaviors. Traumatized individuals' behaviors will always be consistent with their private logic. In brief, the private logic of traumatized children and adolescents is rooted in terror and in the anticipation of pain.

These behaviors, as illogical as they may seem, are an attempt to regain power over, avoid, or escape the "whom" or "what" in the environment that triggers those deep-brain traumatic memories. When developed as a result of multiple traumatic experiences, this survivor response becomes the automatic, implicit, nonthinking response to a perceived threat. A child who lives in a violent home discovers that when she runs she can avoid being hurt and exposed to acts of violence. She runs. She is not harmed, so the next time danger approaches she runs again and again. She quickly picks up the cues and signals that the people in her environment give just prior to violent things happening— the things being said, the tone of voice, the sounds, certain behaviors, mannerisms, and facial features. These become synaptic memories in the brain.

Unknowingly, helpers, teachers, and others in her life may display similar mannerisms that activate and arouse this youngster. Unable to distinguish (reason) between the *then* and the *now,* she runs even when those in her environment and the environment itself is safe. She experiences her running as an attempt to stay safe—to get away from what her trauma memory knows to be the precursor of violence. However, others who have not seen the way she experiences life, who are not trauma-informed, will see her as oppositional, defiant, impulsive, immature, and manipulative, and the labeling goes on as do the less than helpful interactions and increasing frustration of those trying to help this child.

A trauma-informed approach acknowledges that something she is relating to in the environment—a person, interaction, or sensory element—is activating her survival response and her inherent need at that time to be safe. Understanding this makes it acceptable for her to run, but also includes a way to structure the behavior so that she runs to a safe place and to selected others she feels can keep her safe. In other words, helping professionals, shelter staff, or childcare workers would help her identify and repeatedly rehearse where to run to, such as predesignated places and people identified as safe. By having her use her body as the source of information, practitioners can clearly communicate to her that they want her to be safe and can help her be safe. This in turn begins to allow this youngster to experience her environment and those in it as safe. In the process, stronger connections and relationships are being established. The more she can feel safe (the more her arousal is self-regulated), the less she needs to run.

The problem many traumatized children face is that they are forced to fit into the environment rather than the environment finding ways to fit itself to the child. When their behaviors do not make sense, remember that the experience of trauma is one of terror and pain that activates the deep midbrain survival response and their private logic. From a *nontrauma* perspective, children's behaviors may look like self-defeating behaviors; from a *trauma* perspective, these behaviors allow individuals to momentarily feel safe and in control. In their world, these behaviors allow them to survive. The private logic says, "I must do something to let you know I'm terrified. I will do whatever I need to do to control you and control your responses in order to survive. If I let you see how sad I really am, you will take advantage of me. I will fight any experience, any activity, any person that I see as a threat to me—any person who tries to "control" me because if I let you control me I am vulnerable to your abuse and abandonment, again and again." By understanding the source of private logic, practitioners can appreciate that efforts to control or change the resulting behavior rather than alter experiences will only be met with primitive survival responses: fight (aggression, assault), flight (physical, cognitive, and emotional avoidance), or freeze (immobilization in thought, movement, or emotion).

BE CURIOUS, NOT ANALYTICAL

William Steele

In the discussion on safety and self-regulation, the Structured Sensory Interventions for Traumatized Children, Adolescents, and Parents (SITCAP™) model is mentioned as a structured sensory approach for accessing children's implicit memories and their iconic view of self and others. The two examples that follow illustrate how being curious rather and analytical helps us meet the child where he is living, and provides the child the opportunity to help us see what he sees and often the private logic that exists.

Elizabeth was 5 years old when her 15-year-old stepsister was brutally raped and murdered. One year later, her mother reported that Elizabeth was constantly fighting with her 4-year-old sister and had become extremely oppositional. In Mom's words, "She has gotten a really bad mouth on her." After spending some time letting her know that we would be doing some drawing and asking her questions, either of which she could decide not to do and that would be OK, we began by simply asking her to draw us a picture about which she could tell us a story. She was told she could draw anything she wanted to draw.

This structured sensory process always begins and ends in a safe place, all the while taking its lead from the child. Elizabeth had fun drawing and telling us about her drawings. The drawing that taught us the most was a picture of her family doing something. She included her pet, older brother, sister, and mother. Mom was a single parent following divorce. The father was never seen in this intervention. Elizabeth described what the family was doing, but did not include herself in the family activity nor in the drawing (Figure 6.2).

When Elizabeth was asked, "Where are you?" she placed her finger on the drawing of her mother and said "I am here." In this curious process, we simply followed her story and replied, "Where is here?" She responded "I'm in Mommy's tummy." The analytical response would be "How did you get there?" or "Why are you there?" The curious response, which would allow us to be present with the child in Mommy's tummy, is "What is it like in Mommy's tummy?" or "What are you doing in Mommy's tummy?" In response to "What is it like?" her eyes got really big, her face

Figure 6.2 Elizabeth's drawing of her family "doing something." (Copyright TLC 2011, http://www.starrtraining.org/tlc. Used with permission.)

broke out in a smile, and she replied "I am the only one there, no one else is there, wherever Mommy goes, I go."

This was a brutal killing with a great deal of media coverage. Mother did a remarkable job trying to alleviate the impact this had on her four children as well as herself. Understandably, her own pain and grief, the new worries this created about the safety of her children, and the emerging problems developing in her 11- and 15-year-old son and daughter all took her attention away from Elizabeth. Elizabeth could never find the words to explain why she was always fighting with her youngest sibling and sassing her mother. However, this one drawing and our being curious as to her story, not about the details of what happened but about how she was experiencing everything since, allowed her to let us know (her private logic) that Mommy needed to go back to the ways she was interacting with her before this traumatic loss occurred. She did, and Elizabeth's posttrauma behavior ceased. Although there were significant crises facing this family, there was just this one major traumatic event.

The next story is related to repeated exposures prior to the most recent traumatic incident that led to removal from the parents. R was 16. Her parents were drug addicts. Life at home was chaotic, always unpredictable, and terrifying. Juvenile justice removed R from home after the following horrific experience. Her parents took her to a crack house where she was trapped for several weeks and repeatedly raped. Her pretest scores on the Briere Trauma Symptom Checklist (Briere, 1996) and the Youth Self-Report (Achenbach & Rescorla, 2001) were all in the clinically significant range.

PTSD, depression, aggressive rule-breaking behavior, internalizing, externalizing, and dissociation were understandably severe. Following the use of the SITCAP model, there were statistically significant reductions across all subcategories within the two assessment tools (Raider, Steele et al. 2008, pp. 167–185). R chose not to talk about the details of what happened but responded fairly well to using the structured drawing activities related to her worry, hurt, anger, and other themes related to the experiences of trauma that SITCAP addresses.

When asked to draw a picture of herself (Figure 6.3), she did so and then finished by writing down some of the feelings she was having but also hung a sign around her neck (in the drawing) and wrote "The Used." In essence she externalized into a visual format what she sees when she now looks at herself, a view that had not been previously verbalized. It is quite easy to hear the private logic that emerged from this iconic identity of self. Figure 6.4 depicts the extent of her anger. Her drawing allowed her to bring us into her world in ways talk could never accomplish. It was empowering for her as well as for us.

The SITCAP process is based on the belief that eventually trauma victims need to be able to cognitively reframe their traumatic experiences and their trauma-driven private logic in ways they can manage. However, that reframing begins by first presenting them with the opportunities to experience helping professionals and themselves differently, by bringing practitioners into their implicit world to see what they see when they look at themselves, to hear what they think but cannot speak (private logic), and to see how they view those around them and the environments they must still navigate. It is this view that helps determine the kinds of experiences that may be helpful in replacing the sense of being a helpless victim with a strong, resourceful, resilient individual.

This is a picture of _____ Me _____ when it happened:

Figure 6.3   R's drawing of herself. (Copyright TLC 2011, http://www.starrtraining.org/tlc. Used with permission.)

Sensory Experiences as Relational Mediators

For many traumatized children and adolescents, reason and executive functions are not readily available. In general, trauma memories are understood implicitly as sensory-based experiences that are kinesthetic, auditory, olfactory, visual, and/or affective in nature. Therefore, sensory-based experiences govern relationships because individuals respond from lower brain and limbic systems rather than strictly cortical areas (executive functions) of the brain. According to some theories, trauma is essentially the inability to transform sensory memories of distressing events into explicit (cognitive) memory, where these memories could be reframed and managed and where what is happening now (no danger or threat) is distinguished from what happened then (traumatic event).

Figure 6.4   R's image of her anger. (Copyright TLC 2011, http://www.starrtraining. org/tlc. Used with permission.)

Practitioners working with traumatized individuals cannot depend on specific cognitive approaches or children's ability or willingness to use words to describe their experiences. A broad range of methods and activity-based experiences are often necessary in addition to strictly verbal interviewing techniques. Trauma-informed relationships, therefore, should initially involve sensory activities that allow children and adolescents to express these implicit memories (Gil, 2006; Malchiodi, 2008; Steele & Raider, 2001). Expressive therapies (art, music, movement, play and props, sand tray, and bibliotherapy) are particularly useful and tap both hands-on and creative capacities of children and adolescents to express events and memories, to reduce distress, and to develop a relationship with a caring adult who provides these opportunities to create and communicate (Malchiodi, 2008). A brief list of the most prominent methods is included here, but practitioners are encouraged to explore these methods via coursework if unfamiliar with these approaches:

PRIVATE LOGIC

John Seita

When I was 5 years old, I watched my father relentlessly beat my mother. During a short argument at dinner, he exploded at my mother and nearly jumped over the kitchen table, the one that we'd gotten at a garage sale, pulled her forcefully from her chair, grabbed her by the hair, and threw her against the wall. He banged her head repeatedly against the kitchen wall. The crack, crack, crack of her head bouncing off of the wall sometimes even now makes an impression in my mind; I can still hear it. After only a few seconds of this beating, I saw blood gushing from her skull and then splatter on the wall. She screamed that she was "seeing stars." I remember her pleading that he "may as well go ahead and kill her." Then he abruptly stopped beating her, loaded us into an old blue Pontiac, and drove my battered mother to the hospital emergency room. Shortly thereafter, they were divorced and my life soon took a turn for the worse, if you can imagine that.

Without a doubt, that event was memorable, traumatic, and damaging. But I soon experienced new and other kinds of traumatic experiences that were equally memorable and damaging, and in their own way just as acute. On the worst day of my young life, I was 7. My mother brought us three kids with her in a dirty cab to the court building in downtown Cleveland. She said she had to talk to a judge and told me I was the oldest and should watch over Jimmy and Maria. Some people whom I had never seen before took us from my mother to sit on a wooden bench outside of the courtroom. In a few minutes I heard my mother screaming; I ran to the room and looked inside to see who was hurting her. I saw her lying on the floor rolling around, crying, "I love my babies. Please don't take my babies away!" I tried to rush to her aid, but the workers restrained me. I never lived with my family again.

I then unwillingly started on an odyssey that did not end until I was well into adulthood. I was moved and lived in roughly 15 different foster homes in an 11-year span. For years I never dared to trust others again; I could not risk additional pain, suffering, and rejection. My own sense of betrayal by adults, including my parents, emerged and evolved out of the kind of traumatic and toxic events described earlier.

Well-meaning adults who tried to reclaim me and to connect with me were rebuffed, rejected, and were often spectacularly unsuccessful.

To them I must have seemed antisocial and almost intimidating. I was once described in one social work report as nearly autistic; I now know that my behavior, my private logic, made perfect sense at the time under those conditions. Through the lens of time and maturity, I now understand that my defiant behavior could better be described not in negative terms or in terms of weakness or deficits, but rather as strength and as adaptive behavior in a maladaptive environment. I was simply seeking ways to cope, to understand, and to survive in what seemed to be a hostile, uncertain, and abnormal life. It turns out that I did not fail 15 different foster homes; I succeeded at getting kicked out of 15 different foster homes.

Nearly all of my obnoxious and relationship-distancing behavior as a kid in care could be attributed to the toxicity of abuse, neglect, and the constant movement from placement to placement to placement. It is clear to me by way of time and the wisdom of personal and professional hindsight that only when I found myself in a safe, structured, and caring environment where others took the time to connect with me by being consistently patient but also curious as to what I thought, what I believed, how I looked at myself, as well as what I saw in those trying to help, did my mistrust fade, my trauma ebb away, and my healing begin.

Since we now know more about the science of youth development, resilience, and of trauma than we did when I was in care, our opportunity and our obligation is to apply what we know in a way that is intentional, strategic, and purposeful. No longer can we expect children to steer without a rudder, navigate without a map, or seek without a friend.

■ *Art therapy* is the purposeful use of drawing and other art materials and media in trauma intervention and other forms of psychotherapy and rehabilitation; it is used with individuals of all ages, families, and groups.

■ *Play therapy* is the purposeful use of toys, props, games, and other media in trauma intervention and other forms of psychotherapy; most often used with individual children, it also is used with families and adults.

■ *Sand play or sand tray therapy* is the specific application of toy miniatures and a sand tray to assist the individual (child or adult) in self-expression.

■ *Expressive therapy* is a general term used in reference to a variety of creative methods and approaches including, but not limited to, art therapy, music therapy, dance movement therapy, drama therapy, poetry therapy and creative writing, and play therapy.

Art, play, sand play, and other expressive methods can provide remarkable access to those implicit memories of traumatic events that may not be apparent through other forms of evaluation or strictly verbal interaction. However, the process of developing a relationship with a caring adult through expressive methods is possibly the most important relational reason for using creative interventions with traumatized children and adolescents. Unlike strictly verbal counseling, bringing creative expression into a relationship between client and helping professional sets up a unique dynamic that has the potential to enhance attachment and attunement on a sensory level. For example, the practitioner has the opportunity to become the "third hand" (Kramer, 1998; Malchiodi, 2010) in the relationship, providing materials and props to support and encourage the individual's abilities to create and express independently. Additionally, being an attuned and focused witness to a child's efforts to complete a hands-on task and assisting those efforts when appropriate mimics the neurobiological relationship between a caring adult and child. For some children, repetitive experiential, self-rewarding experiences that include a positive and attuned witness are central to repairing disrupted attachment and developing a sense of security and confidence (Perry, 2009).

In inviting children and adolescents to create and draw, using one's curiosity rather than interpretation is important for two reasons. First, being curious and inquisitive about creative expressions maintains an open mind to multiple meanings as well as the private logic that each traumatized individual has. Also, curiosity communicates that you are genuinely interested in the child or adolescent rather than passing judgment or analysis of their circumstances, personality, or challenges. A list of basic questions is presented in Table 3.4 in Chapter 3 (sensory-based, trauma-informed assessments).

While Greenwald (2005) notes that it is possibly unethical to use art, play, or other expressive methods within an unstructured approach, these approaches by their very nature demand that the trauma-informed practitioner remain open-minded to possible modifications and adaptations of activities within sessions. When using creative interventions that tap implicit memories, it is less possible to control outcome or expectations according protocol. The structure, however, comes from applying trauma-informed

THE IMPORTANCE OF DRAWING AS A SENSORY INTERVENTION

Cathy Malchiodi

The idea that trauma is encoded in a sensory fashion by mind and body is now widely accepted by professionals who work with individuals with stress reactions, including posttraumatic stress disorder in children and adults. Well-known traumatologist Bessel van der Kolk observes that when terrifying events such as trauma are experienced, but do not fit into a contextual memory, new memories or dissociations inevitably are established. In other words, when a traumatic memory cannot be articulated with words, it remains at a symbolic level. So to retrieve it, it must be externalized in symbolic forms such as images. This iconic symbolization gives experiences a visual identity because the images created contain all the elements of that experience—in other words, what happened, our emotional reactions to what happened, and the horror and terror of the actual event.

What Bill Steele and I concluded more than a decade ago is that one of the best ways to begin to address the needs of children in trauma is to begin with drawing as a form of intervention. What we began to slowly find out over the next 10 years was exactly why having children engage in drawing and similar creative activities made a difference. Here's a brief summary:

1. *Drawing taps implicit memory.* Trauma and drawing are largely sensory experiences; drawing pictures about aspects of "what happened" prompts sensory memories of traumatic events.
2. *Drawing actively engages children in the process of repair and recovery.* It provides the possibility to move from a passive to an active role in the treatment process.
3. *Drawing provides a symbolic representation of the trauma experience in a concrete, external format.*
4. *Drawing makes us a witness to children's trauma experiences.*
5. *Drawing increases children's verbal reports about emotionally laden events.* Research supports that drawing encourages children to provide more details and to organize their narratives in a more

> manageable way than children who are asked only to talk about traumatic experiences.
>
> 6. *Drawing assists in reduction of reactivity (anxiety) to trauma memories* through repeated visual re-exposure in a medium that is perceived and felt by the client to be safe.
>
> This list is a very simplistic overview of why drawing helps children in trauma. Fortunately, we now have a growing body of research to support the reduction of posttraumatic stress in children and adolescents who participate in structured intervention using drawing as a core activity. As a researcher and helping professional, I continue to be intrigued by just how drawing helps bring about recovery, whether through decrease of worry or fear or reduction of more complex acute trauma and posttraumatic stress reactions. But of equal importance, giving traumatized children the opportunity to express through images what is often impossible to say with words underscores my responsibility to bear witness to their very human suffering, honoring those voices that might otherwise have remained silenced.

principles of safety, self-regulation, and relationship in place to ensure that use of sensory methods have meaning and purpose.

Modeling and Mirror Neurons

Being trauma-informed requires that we meet the children in their worlds, which is often where sensations, images, and feelings rule without apparent reason. "The power of synchrony can be exploited for good purposes. On one occasion in the Netherlands, a herd of some 120 horses got trapped on a patch of dry pasture in the middle of a flooded area. With 20 horses already drowned, people were attempting to save the others. One of the more radical proposals was for the army to erect a pontoon bridge, but the local riding club came up with a simpler solution. Four brave women on horseback mixed in with the stranded herd, then splashed through a shallow area and, like pied pipers, drew the rest with them in single file. The horses had to swim a few stretches, but all made it safely to terra firma. Movement coordination both reflects and strengthens bonds" (deWaal, 2005, p. 5).

The same synchronization takes place with humans. Yawning in a crowd will generally cause others to yawn. We actually have *mirror neurons* that play a critical role in our being empathetic, feeling what others feel at the time. Mirror neurons are believed to be one of the major neuroscience discoveries of recent years and refer to brain cells that fire both when a person is in action, and when he or she observes someone else engaged in the same action. Neuroscientists like Ramachandran (2011) believe that these neurons are connected to imitation and perhaps language acquisition. While the processes behind these neurons are not completely understood, it appears that they have implications for modeling behaviors to others, including empathy.

The way we begin to "sync" with traumatized children and adolescents is to first meet them in their world. Practitioners must be present as witnesses, seeing and accepting what children and adolescents see when they look at themselves and everyone around them. Siegel (2003) calls this process *mindsight*, the capacity for insight (knowing what one feels) and empathy (knowing what others feel); Perry (2009) refers to this as *attunement*, the ability to be able to read the nonverbal communication and rhythms of others. In other words, it involves perceiving not only what children and adolescents say, but also attending to eye signals, facial gestures, tone of voice, and even breathing rate. In brief, the deceptively simple practices of "being present" and mindful are at the core of being "in sync" with traumatized individuals.

In establishing trauma-informed relationships, helping professionals have the opportunity to use nonverbal cues and actions to make connection with their young clients. Verbal communication can accomplish this to some extent, but actions may be more effective with children whose neuro-developmental needs are lodged in lower brain and limbic functions rather than cortical areas involving cognition. For example, Arina may respond to exposure to activities that include repetition, positive and appropriate touch, rocking, and soothing rhythmic activities. Even Jacob's anger management challenges can improve to some extent with active modeling of ways to handle impulsivity and arousal reactions via the practitioner enacting less volatile resolutions to upsetting situations; in Jacob's case, no amount of cognitive intervention alone will change his fight responses to distress and recurrent reminders of threats in his world.

Rituals are particularly important because they not only model appropriate responses, they also provide consistency in relationships and trauma-informed intervention. Rituals soothe the lower parts of the brain, reduce stress responses, and induce calmness; they also actively communicate ways that things are stable and constant in the child-helping professional relationship. Some common rituals include: (1) greeting rituals (handshakes, high-fives, or other interactions agreed upon by participants), (2) appreciation rituals (congratulations for a "good job" or celebration of completion of a task or project), (3) life-event rituals (birthdays or other special days), and (4) closure rituals (ending of therapy and good-byes in general). All of these experiences can serve to actively model relational skills, particularly if complemented by sensory experiences such as specific songs, storytelling, play activities, or movement exercises.

In brief, while there are many specific modeling strategies that can be used in individual situations, there are several areas that are helpful to focus on in trauma-informed relationships with children and adolescents, including: (1) reinforcing through actions and sensory experiences that they are capable individuals who can achieve self-efficacy and competence over time, (2) conveying that they are valuable and courageous individuals whose lives and contributions make a difference, and (3) establishing through activities and relationships that they do belong to a community despite any neglect or disruptive attachment experiences earlier in life.

This view supports the previous discussion of the importance of movement and balance in restoring safety and self-regulation. The following strategies are useful for developing the capacity to be present and to engage opportunities that balance the relationship.

Building Relationships With Parents and Caregivers

Being trauma-informed not only involves building relationships with children and adolescents, but also with their parents or caregivers. In some cases of abuse and neglect, parents may not be available and caregivers such as foster parents may be temporary or unavailable. Nevertheless, extending any trauma-informed intervention to adults in children's lives is important, no matter what extenuating circumstances exist. In many cases, parents and caregivers can be capable and effective allies who can assist the progress of children in the short and long term.

A discussion of trauma-informed relationships with parents or caregivers could easily be an entire chapter in and of itself. Therefore, this section provides a brief overview of this topic with an emphasis on enhancing relationships between parents and children during intervention and treatment through the following practices:

BEING PRESENT
Kiaras Gharabaghi

Being present includes being with children within the therapeutic relationship, but also outside of the relationship. Practitioners should seek to engage the young person in a relationship by first and foremost avoiding the pressure points of a young person's pain. Relationships in their early stages are neither directive nor corrective, and the goal is not to "change" the young person or his or her conduct, but rather to allow the young person to stabilize the sense of self, security, and trust under the gentle and always patient guidance of the practitioner. When possible, the practitioner seeks out engagement opportunities that balance interpersonal engagement (between practitioner and young person) with third-party (implicit) engagement such as recreational activities, music, art, and the like. Such balance allows the young person to move in and out of the relationship based on his own assessment of pain responses; when things get too painful, he can focus on the basketball game, but when pain subsides, he can focus on the presence of the practitioner. Relationships in this way are wavelike, much like the ocean's relationship with the shore; the ocean can shift effortlessly from calm periods of coexistence to exciting periods of engagement and interaction. And no matter how calm or exciting things get, one can always count on the patterns of mutual engagement to continue; the capacity to be present for both the ocean and the shore is endless.

AVOID IMPOSITION, INTERVENTION, AND EXPECTATIONS, AND FOCUS INSTEAD ON BEING PRESENT

Relationships cannot be based entirely or even predominantly on the need to come together with the young person *in order to* achieve a particular objective. Relationships must acknowledge the value of being together and of being connected *as an end in itself.* Being present in a relationship therefore means that our focus is on acts of kindness (or caring) such as offering hot chocolate on a cold winter day, cleaning up the young person's bedroom when we know he is emotionally stressed, and spending time sitting with the young person in silence or silently listening to his stories. A key component of being present is to find a place within the young person's life space that is safe, nurturing, and ultimately not one characterized by performance expectations.

HAVE CONFIDENCE THAT SCIENCE SUPPORTS THE CENTRALITY OF RELATIONSHIP IN THE HEALING PROCESS, BUT NEVER ACT SCIENTIFICALLY—RELATIONSHIPS ARE HUMANISTIC ENDEAVORS

Practitioners bring to their work with young people the knowledge, skills, and a rich repertoire of evidence-based practices that draw on scientific discovery and research. Relationships are not just a good idea, but in fact, their usefulness in the therapeutic process has been scientifically demonstrated in brain research. While this is a positive development, it is crucial to remember that the everyday interactions with young persons are fundamental human processes. Particularly from the perspective of the young person, the presence of the practitioner is what restores his sense of belonging, trust, comfort, security, and value. These, in turn, are humanistic concepts that must be reinforced every day through acts of caring and nurture, guidance and direction, discipline and expectations. All of the routine tasks of the practitioner, therefore, must be rooted in humanity rather than science; whether we are setting boundaries for our work with young persons or enacting treatment plans, ultimately the interaction itself must be one that confirms our interest in the young person and our desire to be there with him.

Safety, trust, and respect. The same principles of trauma-informed relationships with children and adolescents apply to relationships with parents and caregivers. In order for intervention to proceed and be effective, parents must feel safe with helping professionals who work with their children. First, it is always important that they know that the goal of intervention is not to take over their role as parents and that they play a central role in assisting their child's or adolescent's recovery process. Not all parents will be able to undertake this role because of their own challenges (see the following text for more information). Nevertheless, practitioners should communicate that they are willing to help parents and caretakers learn ways to support their children's progress.

As in any therapeutic relationship, it is important that parents and caregivers be informed of the purpose of interventions and activities. Because children and adolescents may be encouraged to engage in sensory-based interventions that involve play, drawing, and other activities, it is important that all adults involved in their care understand the purpose of these interventions. For example, it might be helpful to tell parents and caregivers that children, even those who are not traumatized, do not have the verbal language to express themselves; even a teenager like Jacob may find it more comfortable to express his anger on paper through a drawing or with a set of drums rather than talking about his feelings. Cultural background influences how adults see play, drawing, and other creative expression, and even that it is acceptable for children to be engaging in these activities rather than work or goal-oriented tasks (Gil & Drewes, 2006; Malchiodi, 2005). Respect for preferences and questions about methods will earn practitioners respect and trust from parents and help to establish trauma-informed relationships among caregivers, children, and practitioners.

Reinforce connection. As discussed in Chapter 7 (resilience), the supportiveness of parents and caregivers is one of the major predictors of resilience in children. For example, practitioners can encourage parents and caregivers to help in evaluating changes in their children between visits or sessions if possible; we can also impart skills to help parents relate appropriately to their children's behaviors and reactions. Finally, it is important to repeatedly reinforce connection through statements such as, "If at any time you have additional questions or concerns, I hope you will call me (the facility, school, or agency)."

Give parents and caregivers support. Parents and caregivers are also often survivors of trauma, especially if distressful events over time have impacted the entire family system. Foster parents and other caregivers are subject to stress in similar ways and from the experience of care giving with children and adolescents who have histories of chronic trauma. Therefore, it is safe to assume that many have unresolved trauma reactions from their own series of distressing events and struggle with guilt, shame, anxiety, hopelessness, and sadness. Just like helping professionals, they can develop secondary traumatization, have intrusive thoughts, or be hypervigilant.

If feasible and with modifications, practitioners can use the same sensory-based activities that they use with children and adolescents to help parents self-regulate and mediate reactions. The self-regulation activities described in Chapter 5 (safety and self-regulation) can be adapted and applied to a trauma-informed relationship with parents and caregivers. Adults who learn these skills firsthand will be able to more effectively relate to their own children's use and progress with these activities.

Finally, practitioners can offer support and information to parents and caregivers on how to relate and respond to children and adolescents in appropriate ways. For example, here is a brief list of responses to children in treatment that parents can practice with the helping professional (adapted from Steele & Raider, 2001).:

- I didn't know you thought about these things. Thank you for helping me to understand.
- I am really glad you can tell me about this and about how you feel.
- Now I understand how scary (sad, upsetting) that must have been. I get scared (sad, upset), too. It's OK to be scared (sad, upset).
- It's doesn't matter what you draw (create, toys you like). I like watching you draw (create, play) and listening to your stories.
- I will be talking with (helping professional's name) so I can keep on helping you feel better.

The Impact of Trauma-Informed Relationships on Helping Professionals

Helping young clients feel safe and learn self-regulation skills is challenging work, and developing and sustaining relationships is hard work requiring focus, energy, dedication, and patience. Being trauma-informed requires that helping professionals regularly reexamine how their relationships with young clients are affecting them emotionally and interpersonally. Working with traumatized individuals may take a greater toll on the practitioner than working with other types of clients. How we respond to the inherent stress of this work eventually impacts the quality of intervention we provide to children and adolescents.

Many terms have been used to describe the impact of traumatized clients on practitioners including compassion fatigue (Figley, 1995), vicarious traumatization (McCann & Pearlman, 1990), and simply burnout (Freudenberger, 1974). In all cases, helping professionals, caregivers, and family of traumatized individuals are most at risk for compassion fatigue or secondary trauma reactions. Ironically, the empathy—the capacity to feel others' feelings—that enhances trauma-informed relationships also makes practitioners more vulnerable to distress as a result. In order to monitor the impact of work with traumatized clients, Rothschild (2011) advises thinking of one's empathy as being controlled by a dial; it is important to mentally turn that dial down when it is necessary to gain distance from trauma work (for example, when a practitioner starts to have the same fears or nightmares that a traumatized child is having). Conversely, helping professionals can train themselves to move the dial up when they need to call on their empathy to help them understand their young clients.

Finally, being trauma-informed also underscores that practitioners can benefit from the same self-regulatory techniques they use with children and adolescents. Taking time to explore the size of a worry through a simple drawing or where a client's traumatic memories are perceived in our own bodies through a body scan activity can be helpful to the practitioner just as much as for the traumatized individual. The same trauma-informed advice given throughout the previous chapters applies to all professionals; the more we are able to take care of ourselves, the better we will be able to engage in meaningful and effective trauma-informed relationships with others.

DEVELOPING A RELATIONSHIP THROUGH PLAY WITH TRAUMATIZED CHILDREN AFTER A DISASTER

Eric J. Green

Having been a part of a few natural disaster mental health relief teams over the last several years, I'd like to summarize a couple of common themes discovered in my clinical work and research when working with traumatized children. Children who endure a situational crisis, such as a hurricane or earthquake, may face a variety of deprivations to their psychological and physical safety including familial discord, exposure to mass hysteria, loss of valuable or irreplaceable personal items, separation from family members, and death. During a natural disaster, typical patterns of posttraumatic responses in children can be codified into the following three distinct phases: (a) emergency (or acute), (b) inhibition or avoidance, and (c) adaptation. It is typically during the *adaptation* phase that we augment the strategies from psychological first aid, which is typically administered during the acute phase.

When a family's social support system becomes overwhelmed during or immediately following a natural disaster, mental health concerns may materialize. This effectively renders children psychologically defenseless in the wake of simultaneous attacks on their tenuous residual resources as their primary caregivers are coping with their own emotional vulnerability. A disaster and the possibility of subsequent interpersonal separation affect not only the familial system as a whole, children are especially vulnerable and can display reactive behaviors along with pronounced psychological deterioration when caregivers or previously stabilizing adult figures in their lives are rendered inadequate. Symbolic communication, which may be temporarily severed during extreme trauma, guides a child toward healing and fulfillment by connecting the unconscious to the ego. Children who are separated from or lose family members to death during a natural disaster may suffer a *disconnect* (rupture) in their ego's stability in managing the external world. Specifically, children affected by disasters often display an extremely poor connection with their unconscious because of the erosion of the "transitional space" between their outer and inner worlds due to the destabilization of their "good enough" parental introjects (images and the feelings associated with those images of the good mother or good father archetypes that provide safety). For the child's ego to mitigate the devastating effects of trauma, a meaningful integration must occur. One such integrative component is the salubrious nature of the play therapy relationship, where a child is not judged, is allowed to make decisions in a play space, and is supported by a competent, caring adult. The play therapy relationship often results in strengthening the child's ego and its capacity to explore polarities that are both excruciating and comforting following a natural disaster.

The helping professional must accept three principles when counseling traumatized children: (a) each child can and will reveal him or herself symbolically through spontaneous drawings, play, or dream content; (b) though play, drawings, and dreams are not direct forms of communication with a child, they are valid and have meaning; and (c) the mind and the body are linked together, thereby allowing continuous communication between the two spheres, so that if something is troubling a child psychically, the body will communicate this and vice versa.

My best advice to therapists wanting to form helpful relationships with children following a traumatic event is to provide them with the therapeutic space to play and reconnect with their inner healing capacities. One of the things we should advocate for in shelters after natural disasters is a space (usually separated by a boundary of tape or blankets), that is labeled "the children's corner." Once you are seen regularly as a positive, empathic, nonanxious presence, children will seek you out and want to play games and draw with you. And remember—we cannot give to children what we have not given ourselves. During a time of crisis, don't neglect self-care. Reignite the archetypal imagination within your psyche (find a coloring book, watch cartoons, meditate/pray, spend time outside the therapeutic setting, and venture into nature if possible). I also encourage you to move your play sessions to the outdoors, with the caretaker's permission, to permit children the chance to be outside and in nature, which is inherently healing. In the end, children do not remember what elegant interventions we prescribe after a natural disaster, but they do remember the kindness and compassion we show them.

Conclusion

Of all trauma-informed practices, developing and maintain trauma-informed relationships are among the most important. When they are applied effectively, they enhance attachment experiences by reinforcing primary connection between children and caring adults and developing a sense of safety, trust, and respect in young clients. When relational work is extended to parents and caregivers, traumatized individuals inevitably will benefit from additional trauma-informed relationships outside the treatment or intervention setting. Finally, relational work is key to supporting and increasing resilience and the potential for trauma integration, the subjects of the final two chapters in this book.

Chapter 7

Supporting Resilience and Posttraumatic Growth

Anna—A Picnic Gone Wrong

Peter Levine and Maggie Kline

Eight-year-old Anna has enormous brown eyes. She could have been a model for one of the popular Keane paintings of almond-eyed children. The school nurse has just brought her in to see us. Pale, head hanging, and barely breathing, she is like a fawn frozen by the bright lights of an oncoming car. Her frail face is expression-less, and her right arm hangs limply, as if it were on the verge of detaching itself from her shoulder.

Two days earlier, Anna went on a school outing to the beach. She and a dozen of her classmates were frolicking in the water when a sudden riptide swept them swiftly out to sea. Anna was rescued, but Mary (one of the mothers who volunteered for the outing) drowned after courageously saving several of the children. Mary had been a surrogate mom to many of the neighborhood kids, including Anna, and the entire community was in shock from her tragic death. I had asked the school nurse to be on the lookout for children who displayed a sudden onset of symptoms (e.g., pain, head and tummy aches, and colds). Anna had already been to see the nurse three times that morning, reporting severe pain in her right arm and shoulder.

One of the mistakes often made by trauma responders is to try to get children to talk about their feelings immediately following an event. Although it is rarely healthy to suppress feelings, this practice can be traumatizing. In these vulnerable moments, children (and adults as well) can easily be overwhelmed. Previous traumas can resurface in the aftermath of an overwhelming event, creating a complex situation that may involve deep secrets, untold shame, guilt feelings, and rage. For this reason, my team sought out, and learned, some of Anna's history from several helpful elementary school teachers (and the nurse) prior to seeing the child. In this way, we could have information that either was consciously unknown to the child or might be dangerous to uncover given her fragile state. We learned that at age 2, Anna was present when her father shot her mother in the shoulder and then took his own life. An additional detail that compounded Anna's symptoms was provoked by an experience she had prior to the picnic. She had been infuriated when Mary's 16-year-old son Robert bullied her 12-year-old brother. There was a strong possibility that Anna had been harboring ill will toward Robert before the drowning, and was seeking retribution at that time. This raised the likelihood that Anna might feel profound guilt about Mary's death—perhaps even believing (through magical thinking) that she was responsible for it.

I asked the female nurse to gently cradle and support Anna's injured arm. This could help Anna contain the frozen "shock energy" locked in her arm, as well as heighten the child's inner awareness. With this support, Anna would be able to slowly (i.e., gradually) thaw and access the feelings and responses that could help her come back to life.

"How does it feel to be inside of your arm, Anna?" I ask her softly.

"It hurts so much," she answers faintly.

Her eyes are downcast, and I say, "It hurts bad, huh?"

"Yeah."

"Where does it hurt? Can you show me with your finger?" She points to a place on her upper arm and says, "Everywhere, too." There's a little shudder in her right shoulder followed by a slight sigh of breath. Momentarily, her drawn face takes on a rosier hue.

"That's good, sweetheart. Does that feel a little better?" She nods, and then takes another breath. After this slight relaxation, she

immediately stiffens, pulling her arm protectively toward her body. I seize the moment.

"Where did your mommy get hurt?" She points to the same place on her arm and begins to tremble. I say nothing. The trembling intensifies, then moves down her arm and up into her neck. "Yes, Anna, just let that shaking happen, just like a bowl of Jell-O—would it be red, or green, or even bright yellow? Can you let it shake? Can you feel it tremble?"

"It's yellow," she says, "like the sun in the sky." She takes a full breath, and then looks at me for the first time. I smile and nod. Her eyes grasp mine for a moment, and then turn away.

"How does your arm feel now?"

"The pain is moving down to my fingers." Her fingers are trembling gently. I speak to her quietly, softly, rhythmically.

"You know, Anna, sweetheart ... I don't think there is anybody in this whole town that doesn't feel that, in some way, it was their fault that Mary died." She briefly glances at me. I continue, "Now, of course that's not true ... but that's how everybody feels ... and that's because they all love her so much." She turns now and looks at me. There is a sense of self-recognition in her demeanor. With her eyes now glued on me, I continue, "Sometimes, the more we love someone, the more we think it was our fault." Two tears spill from the outside corners of each eye before she slowly turns her head away from me.

"And sometimes if we're really angry at someone, then when something bad happens to them, we also think that it happened because we wanted it to happen." Anna looks me straight in the eye. I continue, "And you know, when a bad thing happens to someone we love or hate, it doesn't happen because of our feelings. Sometimes bad things just happen ... and feelings, no matter how big they are, are only feelings." Anna's gaze is penetrating and grateful. I feel myself welling with tears. I ask her if she wants to go back to her class now. She nods, looks once more at the three of us, and then walks out the door, her arms swinging freely—in rhythm with her stride.

In order to sustain and maintain positive developmental outcomes as a result of trauma-informed intervention, enhancing young clients' capacity to overcome future challenges is essential. The fact that children and adolescents can overcome disastrous life experiences or deplorable living circumstances indicates that they can emerge from these events with encouraging outcomes. For example, numerous studies have demonstrated that many children living in war zones where there is violence, poverty, or high terrorist activity can constructively adapt to these conditions (Betancourt & Kahn, 2008). Other studies of children's adjustment after they have witnessed life-threatening natural disasters provide additional understanding of how some individuals actually can do well despite massive disruption. In brief, many children and adolescents who have experienced tragedy do emerge with optimism, continue to form fulfilling relationships, have success at school, and develop abilities to effectively deal with future misfortunes.

But what about children and adolescents who do not recover so quickly? Helping professionals and caregivers often wonder if it is really possible to help these individuals overcome past challenges and make the adaptations necessary for a healthy and productive life. This chapter addresses two core principles that can help sustain and maintain positive developmental gains in traumatized individuals—resilience and post-traumatic growth (PTG). In addition to operational definitions and salient research, the relationship between these concepts and trauma is discussed along with strategies for instilling, enhancing, and supporting resilience and PTG in children and adolescents.

Resilience

In 1991, Garmezy identified resilience as demonstrations of ability and competence in children despite exposure to stressful events. Masten (1994) defined resilience simply as successful adaptation in the face of risk and adversity, despite developmental status or chronic challenges. Ginsburg and Jablow (2006) write, "Resilience is a trait that parents hope to develop in children so they will be equipped to navigate a stressful, complicated world while relishing its abundant pleasures" (p. 4). He suggests that one of the major processes found in resilient children is that they push themselves and learn from their mistakes. Brendtro and Longhurst (2005) observe that resilience is a term that was derived from physics to describe the resilience of objects to withstand extreme stress (cold, heat, pressure, winds) by being flexible without breaking. Wolin and Wolin (2000) describe resilient youth as those who come back from stressful situations even stronger "with an inner strength that has been called 'survivor pride'" (p. 52). Resilience has also been described as the ability to recover or return to a level of functioning present before adversity occurred with only minimal reactions following that exposure (Bonanno, Papa, & O'Neill, 2001).

In general, resilience is defined as the ability to thrive and grow during adverse and/or chronically disruptive experiences (physical, social, or environmental). In essence, resilience is an individual's capacity to "bounce back." Individuals' resilience begins to develop at the very first moment their parents hold their newborn child. The consistent comfort, soothing, and joy children receive from their parents during infancy and early childhood is critical to developing resilient minds and bodies. The ability to bounce back is, in part, the result of parental modeling; later in life, it is what children learn from their extended family, peers, teachers, and other adults in their lives. Resilient children are thought to be far less vulnerable to posttraumatic stress disorder (PTSD) and trauma reactions in general. They have learned to regulate their responses to stress and have experienced sufficient mastery to be confident that challenging situations are only temporary and that things will eventually become better.

Given the exposure children have today to worldwide media coverage of terrifying situations on a daily basis, building resilience has become much more challenging. Burnham (2009) reports that being raped, experiencing terrorism, hurricanes and tornadoes, or war, being poor, witnessing shootings, and being kidnapped made up most of the major fears of children from 2nd through 12th grade. Ample research clearly documents that children's exposure to terrifying situations increases their anxiety and repeated exposure leads to a view of the world as not safe, not friendly (Pfefferbaum, Nixon et al., 1999; Duggal, Berezkin et al., 2002; Burnham, 2009). Progressively over the past several decades, numerous studies have shown that children's repeated exposure to varied forms of media increases their risk factors for anxiety and similar responses. Ginsburg and Jablow (2006) state, "[I]n 21st century America stress seems to be chronic—24/7—permeating everyone's lives" (p. 11). Today there are also challenges such as cyber bullying and Internet predators; children's involvement with texting, poking, and surfing is believed to be "hardwiring" their brains in ways that prevent processing information and the ability to focus (Conley, 2011), which may be compromising resilience and adaptability.

Resilience Characteristics

What allows some children to do better than others when exposed to similar situations? Researchers identify numerous conditions, events, and experiences that are associated with overall resilience in children and adolescents (Cloitre, Martin et al., 2004). Charney (2004, p. 7) provides one of the most comprehensive lists of protective factors related to resilience:

1. **Optimism.** Individuals who are very optimistic often show greater resilience, demonstrating that those who have a positive view can more readily bounce back.
2. **Altruism.** Individuals who are resilient are often those who find that helping others is good way to handle stress and enjoy "giving back" in exchange for the satisfaction of what they receive for it in return.
3. **Having a moral compass.** Having a set of morals or strong beliefs.
4. **Faith and spirituality.** Prayer, religion, spirituality, or belief in a higher power is often found in resilient individuals.
5. **Humor.** Like optimism, the ability to be able to laugh and see the lighter side of things is often associated with resilience.
6. **Having a role model.** Resilient individuals often draw strength from role models; helping people use or discover a role model has been found to be helpful in the development of resilience.
7. **Social supports.** Individuals who have connections with trusted and significant others and with whom one can share problems or difficult experiences is key to resilience.
8. **Facing fear.** Leaving one's "comfort zone" (but not necessarily engaging in dangerous activities) develops resilience through self-efficacy and development of self-worth. Individuals who are more resilient also seek novel experiences over repetitive ones.
9. **Having a mission.** Individuals who have a mission or meaning in life have a reason to live and tend to be more resilient.
10. **Training.** Most importantly, people can learn to become more resilient through educational experiences and intervention; in particular, resilience training has implications for young people who can learn how to overcome challenges at an early age and take this skill into adulthood.

Others echo and expand Charney's list of resilience factors. Cheever and Hardin (1999) found, for example, that connections or connectedness, a sense of control and coherence, and the ability to make sense of their trauma experiences or find positive meaning in these experiences are directly related to resilience. In general, the most frequently researched resilience factors are social support and personal control, particularly in the prevention of PTSD (Berkman & Glass, 2000; Zautra, Hall, & Muray, 2010). Cheever and Hardin (1999) found that those individuals who have a connection to a significant other did better than those who did not when exposed to traumatic situations. Harvey (2007) notes that those who have a high *self-potency* score (empowered with choice) also did better when exposed to the same traumatic experiences than those who do not feel empowered.

Resilience in Children Following Acute Trauma

In recent years in the United States, people have learned that they are not protected from the effects of mass violence and even terrorism as a result of the events of September 11, 2001. In fact, in the months following that tragedy everyone learned to be afraid of airplanes, tall buildings, and even mail delivery. Because the events impacted almost everyone through television and the Internet, children who either directly or indirectly witnessed the attacks became preoccupied with the possibility of more "hurt" happening. Depending on their previous experiences with traumatic experiences and social support, among other factors, some children developed heightened anxiety, fears of being alone or being subjected to danger, avoidance reactions, and/or physical symptoms.

Following exposure to disaster or other traumatic events, even resilient children may experience transient reactions, but not the clinically significant symptoms of PTSD (Bonanno, Pap & O'Neil, 2001). In other words, it is not correct to assume that an experience is traumatic or that it calls for formal trauma-specific intervention or a prescriptive intervention like debriefing. Trauma-focused interventions are for the more severe reactions individuals may experience. For example, debriefing has become a standard prescriptive form of intervention following traumatic interventions, yet research is revealing that debriefing can be ineffective and actually impede recovery when used as a first response on large groups who are not truly participating voluntarily and who directly or indirectly are told that this intervention is necessary for healing (Bisson, Jenkins et al., 1997; Mayou, Ehlers, & Hobbs, 2000).

Resilient children can benefit from the initial support of others, but are not at risk for PTSD. Therefore trauma-focused interventions may hinder and even weaken their resilience. To assume everyone needs the same prescriptive intervention because they have been exposed to trauma simply does not take into account that resilient children will bounce back with limited support. This limited support is generally in the form of crisis intervention, which is a much less intrusive process than debriefing and other trauma-focused interventions. Following a traumatic event, the least intrusive form of intervention should be applied while giving children time to process their experience and demonstrate, by their behaviors and symptom formation, that more trauma-focused intervention may be needed. This initial form of intervention is crisis intervention—normalizing reactions, attending to basic needs, offering support, providing safety, shelter, food, connection to caring adults and peers, the opportunity to self-express, time to self-regulate and return to previous routines and relationships (Echterling, Presbury, & McKee, 2005). This basic approach essentially allows children within the context of support to call upon their resilient characteristics to bounce back. The research shows that the majority will bounce back and adapt (Wilkenson, 2003).

To help children and adolescents become more resilient when faced with traumatic events, here are some recommendations that reflect trauma-informed practice:

Establish and maintain close relationships with trusted adults. Even under the most adverse circumstances, most children and adolescents can cope as long as they have connections to adults, including helping professionals and caregivers. Young people who have someone they know is concerned about their well-being; provides them with guidance, structure, and information; and spends frequent time with them do better than those who do not have such relationships. While parents are usually the source of support, others (counselors, teachers, childcare staff) can also supply a sense of meaningful connection.

Ensure a sense of safety. All children need to feel safe, but particularly those under stress. In acute trauma situations like disasters, sharing knowledge of what is being done to help everyone feel safe and secure is important. Many individuals have a tendency to worry more than usual after a catastrophe or negative event; for example, some children believed that airplanes could hit their homes after the events of September 11, 2001. Helping professionals and caregivers can assist them by providing age-appropriate and realistic information to reduce undue fright, anxiety, or obsessive thinking. Monitoring children's exposure to violent images or reports of death or disaster will also reduce feelings of vulnerability and the sense that "it is happening again" when, in fact, there may no longer be a threat. Finally, children and teens also need to know that their immediate environment and relationships are safe and stable; strategies discussed in Chapter 4 that address safety can be adapted for use in short-term intervention.

Practice self-regulation techniques. Knowing a method or two to relieve emotional and physical tension can enhance and build resilience over time. Play is a natural form of self-regulation if it calms and relieves the individual. Talking, drawing, making music, or physical activities or sports can help, too. For children and adolescents who are anxious or showing signs of hyperarousal, many of the self-regulation activities and strategies (breathing, mindfulness, and muscle relaxation) described in Chapter 4 are useful; mastery of a resilience-building skill is a positive resilience factor, in and of itself.

Encourage optimism. Traumatic events like disasters make it difficult to feel positive about the world; even children and adolescents who have a natural tendency to see a positive future can be emotionally shaken by certain events. Those individuals who believe that these events are temporary will do better than those who obsessively believe that things will not change for the better. It is extremely important that helping professionals and parents help children and adolescents develop a sense that they can effectively deal with stress.

Identify values and beliefs. Charney's list of resilience factors includes several concepts that underscore the importance of values and beliefs in trauma-informed practice. Individuals who are altruistic, for example, and seek to help others in need build personal resilience and reduce depression and anxiety in the process. Values that involve connection to others are particularly important because they reinforce connection to a larger group and emphasize the welfare of others. After a traumatic event, beliefs about religion or spirituality are also a source of resilience for some individuals; trauma-informed practitioners can help identify these beliefs within a framework of cultural sensitivity for individuals' and families' preferences for sharing information on religious or other practices.

Practice all of the above. This list of recommendations began with the importance of relationships in resilience building after a traumatic event, underscoring that one of the most significant factors in resilience and trauma recovery is a meaningful relationship with either a parent or a helping professional. In order to make that possible, parents and professionals must be able to be available and supportive. Practitioners must make sure that they are feeling safe, calm, well rested, and in good emotional health in order to implement the resilience-building strategies in this list. Practitioners can also help parents and caregivers understand and practice these same principles so that they can be available and supportive to their children.

Finally, it is important to look for any trauma reactions even months after exposure to an acute event; it is common for individuals of any age to begin experiencing symptoms two to three months after the occurrence. Anxiety, depression, avoidance of certain situations, problems with cognition and concentration, and irritability can signal that some resilience enhancement is in order. If reactions persist, professional assessment may be appropriate to make sure children and adolescents retain the ability to function at home, school, and with peer groups.

Developmental Guidelines for Promoting Resilience

Many of the strategies used to enhance and promote resilience are the same ones used to encourage a resilient response to trauma. In working with children and adolescents, practitioners must always be aware of developmental factors, remembering that chronological age is not always the same as developmental level. The following recommendations are presented within a developmental context and can be applied immediately and throughout the six-week period following exposure to a traumatic event:

Ages 0 to 3

- Avoid any prolonged time away from the child.
- Increase touching, holding, comforting, play (friendly baby talk).
- Avoid talking about what happened in the child's presence because the emotional brain (limbic system) will pick up the tension and stress you have about what happened.
- Maintain sleeping and eating routines.

Ages 3 to 6

- Follow the same guidelines for ages 0 to 3.
- Think in terms of the importance of finding pleasant, fun things to do in the midst of what is happening.
- Listen patiently to their story of what happened as often as they wish to tell it.

- If the child's behaviors regress, allow this to happen. It is his way of reclaiming some sense of safety.
- Make nighttime a comforting time; give physical comfort and read a favorite book.
- Delay introducing anything new into the child's routine.
- Answer questions as simply as possible.
- Anticipate calmly some different reactions like nightmares or new fears. Assure the child you are not afraid and know these will change.
- Begin the child's day with something pleasant and fun and end the day in the same way.
- Give the child opportunities to draw what happened. Be positive in your verbal communications that this is only temporary, that you are confident everyone will bounce back.
- Check on how the child is doing at school or at home if signs of stress are observed by teachers.

Ages 6 to 12

- Follow the guidelines for ages 3 to 6.
- Look for new ways to experience some sense of calmness and regulation—music, play, and games. Provide the child with choices to talk about what happened or not talk, to do more of what they do well as a way to feel better or avoid thinking about what happened.
- Help the child think about ways he may help others if others were involved.

Ages 12 to 18

Adolescents benefit from play, staying active, comforting, connecting with peers, basic routine, and support, but will also benefit from the following:

- Have conversations about why they think this happened and what it means to the way they think about life and their future.
- Encourage activities directed at helping others who may have been victims.
- Provide sensory activities that help express their feelings—compiling a CD of songs that reflect their thoughts and feelings, creating a collage, or writing in a journal.

Resilience and Chronically Traumatized Children and Adolescents

Some individuals experience repeated trauma including physical and sexual abuse during many years of their lives; other children have been exposed to environments where chronic domestic violence or, in some parts of the world, war and terrorism are daily events. In all these cases, primary relationships are disrupted and in some cases, there is a fundamental breach of trust between a child and significant adults who would have served as reliable social supports and a source for resilience. However, even with this breach, there are many children and adolescents who display their own unique form of resilience under these circumstances.

Resiliency for children and adolescents who have been abused is somewhat different than for children who have experienced an acute, nonviolent trauma. They often use a number of adaptive coping skills (Malchiodi, 1997, 2008; see the "Adaptive Coping and Resilience in Domestic Violence" text box) to manage relationships and the environment. For example, despite intense physical abuse, some children and adolescents defend their parents' behavior, feeling that their parents still love them; they manage to continue to love their parents despite physical violence. Even when angry or disappointed with parents, they can remember the "good things" their caregivers have done for them, like a birthday cake or a new bicycle. Some children and adolescents reframe the parents' actions as "having a bad day" or "he was drinking too much and that made him angry." In brief, they are able to use their adaptive coping skills to compartmentalize parents' abusive actions from those moments when parents provide positive support or rewards.

During teenage years and young adulthood, individuals also explain that they believed what was happening in terms of childhood abuse was normal because it was happening on a regular basis and they simply had no knowledge that it did not happen to others, too. Some state that these beliefs helped them to feel less trapped and also enhanced their abilities to adapt and plan ways to escape situations that could become violent. Others work hard to feel safe by "flying under the radar" and reducing their chances of encounter with an abusive parent; staying in one's room, out of the home for long periods of time, or simply keeping one's distance or remaining quiet are all strategies children and adolescents use to avoid initiating an abusive event and to stay safe. Many also mention activities that help them escape including playing with favorite toys, drawing, engaging in make-believe, writing in a journal or diary, or sports. Dissociation, which is frequently categorized as an emotional disorder, is another way distress is avoided; in terms of adaptive coping, this response is also one of few ways that some children and adolescents can take themselves away from situations involving violation (Malchiodi, 1997, 2008).

There are two other resilience factors that many chronically traumatized children and adolescents display. Despite recurrent abuse, including physical, sexual, or verbal, many survivors state that they were able to maintain their own self-worth. Some of this is derived from beliefs and values, including faith-based concepts like "God always will love and protect me;" in other cases, innate resilience is present and helps individuals overcome negative thinking and self-deprecation. Other children have been fortunate to encounter one or more positive adult role models outside the abusive home, and as a result, have internalized that someone does care about them.

Finally, many individuals have a sense of a more positive future even in the midst of serious or life-threatening challenges. In other words, they have hope, maintain a dream or vision for better days, and look forward to independence from current circumstances. Some focus on "the day I will graduate high school and get a job" or similar goals that they believe will eventually lead to positive changes for themselves. Underlying these beliefs is one of the core resilience factors previously mentioned—optimism and a sense that things will not always stay the same and that the future has possibilities for improvement. This type of adaptive coping is a resilience skill that mediates the impact of adverse events to some extent and makes it possible for many individuals to not only survive, but also survive with expectations for change and opportunity.

Of course, not all children and adolescents will have this form of adaptive coping; temperament, genes, relationships, and environment have an impact on each individual. It is not reasonable to expect that all individuals can easily develop these adaptations for that reason, just as it is not reasonable to expect that anyone should have to find ways to mediate and survive abusive or violent environments. However, knowing that resilience may take on a slightly different appearance in chronically traumatized individuals in contrast to those who have experienced acute or nonviolent trauma is important to trauma-informed practice. Cultural sensitivity is a key factor in trauma-informed care; in the same sense, understanding the culture that abuse or violence creates for children and adolescents helps to inform practitioners about why their adaptations constitute a form of resilient behavior within exceptionally difficult life situations.

ADAPTIVE COPING AND RESILIENCE
IN DOMESTIC VIOLENCE

Cathy Malchiodi

Despite exposure to domestic violence, some children are remarkably resilient and display few trauma reactions as a result of their experiences. There is limited information on why some seem to bounce back quickly from exposure to violence; of course, a stable environment like a trauma-informed shelter or residence with appropriate intervention and resources is helpful. There are also various mediating factors such as level of exposure to violence, personality traits and adult support, particularly from a parent or relative.

In working with domestic violence survivors for many years, I quickly came to realize that children often had a well-developed set of adaptive coping skills. They knew much better than I did how to handle dangerous situations and had well-developed routines for addressing threats in the environment. Others knew how to remain "invisible" to others through specific behaviors.

For example, Elena, a 9-year-old who was brought with her 6-year-old brother to a domestic violence shelter by her mother, used a variety of adaptive coping skills to survive her circumstances. In particular, she became the parent in her family (a role her mother gladly relinquished due to her own depression), which gave her a sense of control. Elena was also able to distract herself through engaging in parent-like activities including house cleaning, caring for her younger brother, and meal preparation. She spoke of physical abuse to her mother and herself through narratives that disclosed her father's violent behavior as well as his kindness in giving toys to her and her brother and taking them to the amusement park on weekends. In fact, after years of witnessing and being the target of extremely violent actions by her father, she consistently expressed her love for him and that, one day when she was grown up, the hurting would never happen again. Of course, shelter staff and I worked to protect Elena and her family from future violence; in their case, they were eventually able to separate themselves from violence and moved to another state with relatives where Elena's mother received treatment for her depression. Most importantly, Elena, despite challenging circumstances, developed ways to cope and a future sense of better days ahead even while in the midst of distressful and abusive family dynamics.

Trauma-Informed Interventions Supporting Resilience

First, it is important to remember that in some cases, like acute trauma, the passage of time will help resilience emerge and only the basic trauma-informed interventions (attention to safety and social support) may be necessary. Children who have risk factors such as abuse, neglect, exposure to multiple traumatic events, or lack of social support may be in need of specific interventions to support and develop resilience. Malchiodi, Steele, and Kuban (2008, pp. 287–288) provide a helpful list of questions to help practitioners get a sense of coping skills in children and adolescents:

- With all that has happened, what makes you smile, even just a little?
- Despite all that has happened, have you been able to laugh a little when things strike you funny?
- On a scale of 1 to 10, with 10 being the most positive, how positive do you feel after this difficult crisis? (With younger children, it is more helpful to use pictures, engage them in drawing, or provide an image of a feelings thermometer to communicate the idea of scaling.)
- On a scale of 1 to 10, with 10 being the most stressful, where would you rate the stress (hurt, worry, fear) you are experiencing?
- Do you believe you will bounce back from this? Have you already begun to do so?
- Have your plans for the future changed as a result of what happened?
- Do you find you push most of what happened out of your mind?

Interventions to support and enhance resilience should focus on the following: (1) parent– or caregiver–child relationship; (2) children's feelings of safety, self-esteem, and capability, and (3) if children are interested, positive memories. In general, interventions with young children (3 to 6 years) should emphasize enjoying activities with a parent or adult to reinforce attachment; for older children (7 to 12 years), activities should include those that reinforce attachment and include specific themes related to resilience. For example, an adult and child might co-create a scene with miniature toys in a sand tray or make a puppet together to reinforce attachment through a sensory-based activity, and thereby capitalize on social support as a resilience factor over time. For older children, an adult and child can co-create a collage from magazine pictures or photographs that represent a positive memory or an image of "the Good Things About Me" to enhance the child's sense of self-efficacy and esteem. For more information on these types of creative, sensory-based activities for resilience building, please see Malchiodi, Steele, and Kuban (2008).

USING RITUALS TO SUPPORT RESILIENT FAMILIES

Cathy Malchiodi

Trauma specialists and helping professionals in general often ask, "How do I help enhance resilience in children?" Research tells us that resilience in children is often predicated on attachment and bonding with parents and other relatives and the degree to which social support is present in their lives.

Kuban and Steele (2009) have a practical suggestion for helping raise resilient children. They note that parents should brainstorm with their children about the rituals their family already has in place. For example, families can write words or draw pictures that represent the rituals and start practicing these rituals today. With children and families, I have adapted this activity using magazine pictures in addition to drawing. If you are a therapist or counselor working with a family, have a shoebox or small basket of precut pictures ready for everyone to choose from; home-oriented, sports, and outdoor magazines are a good source for images. I recommend cutting pictures from magazines in advance of your meeting with the family to prevent your participants from leafing through too many magazines and getting distracted from the task at hand. It also gives you a chance to create a set of images that represents not only common activities, but also to introduce other ideas to help the family imagine new rituals for the future. Be sure to include images that represent diversity (ethnicity, gender, and societal), too.

Once the pictures are selected, ask the family to work as a group to glue the images to a large piece of colored construction paper, cardboard, or poster board. After the family completes the task, I often ask each family member to talk about their creation and what rituals are most important to them in their picture. I also ask if there are any activities or rituals missing from the picture, if there are any they would now like to add as a family, and any family mottos or sayings that we can add to their collage. Finally, I recommend that the family hang their final creation in a prominent place at home to reinforce positive actions and rituals they can engage in as a family in the future.

Identifying rituals and activities as a family may seem like a simple intervention, but it is, in fact, an activity that has a potentially important impact on family cohesion, bonding among family members, and children's sense of safety and security. Family therapists Imber-Black and Roberts (1992) note that, "Rituals have existed throughout time—they seem to be a part of what it means to be human" (p. 10). For this and other reasons, family rituals ease difficult life transitions, commemorate personal history and relationships, and celebrate life in the most basic sense. The families we see in our work are yearning to recapture, reinvent, or rediscover meaning in their lives; they are also longing to reduce the alienation that trauma and loss often increase among family members. Fortunately, as trauma specialists, we can help them reconnect with each other and, in doing so, address the impact of crises on children and enhance their capacity for resilience in what is often a traumatic world.

Posttraumatic Growth

At age 9 years, Lisa was anxious and depressed for several months after her grandfather and younger brother were killed in a violent tornado that destroyed her grandparents' and parents' homes in a matter of minutes. Usually an independent child, she clung to her mother, often refused to eat, and slept in her bedroom closet when she could not get to sleep in her own bed due to worry. Two years later and with good intervention from counselors and support from her parents, Lisa still has worries, but she has also changed in many ways. Her parents report that they see many new behaviors in Lisa including a strong empathy for those who have survived disasters, more caring relationships with her family and friends, and even some unexpected creativity in the form of handmade crafts that she enjoys giving to others as gifts.

It is possible that Lisa is displaying *posttraumatic growth* or PTG. In 1996 a group of psychologists coined the term PTG in an attempt to define the positive personality traits and emotional growth that emerges after traumatic experiences. Tedeschi and Calhoun (1996) describe PTG as development beyond pretrauma exposure and functioning, resulting in beneficial changes in cognition and emotion. They state that PTG is "a changed sense in one's relationships, a changed sense of self, and a changed philosophy of life. Posttraumatic growth can involve an experience of deepening of relationships, increased compassion and sympathy for others, and greater ease at expressing emotions. The change in self-perception may include an increased sense of vulnerability, but an increased experience of oneself as capable and self-reliant. Finally, some individuals report a greater appreciation for life, a changed set of life priorities, and positive changes in religious, spiritual or existential matters" (Tedeschi & Calhoun, 2004, p. 16).

Turner and Cox (2004) indicate that PTG is manifested in several clearly defined behaviors and thought patterns not necessarily present prior to traumatic exposure such as, "If I survived this, I can survive anything." PTG has also been defined as "the experience of positive psychological change following highly challenging and traumatic life experiences" (Levine, Laufer et al., 2008, p. 42). In a study evaluating PTG following the diagnosis of cancer, Morris, Shakespeare-Finch, and Scott (2007) found four coping processes similar to those mentioned previously—"positive interpretation, social support, active coping and venting emotions" (p. 8).

Summarizing the work of Ungerleider (2003), Janoff-Bulman (2004), Tedeschi and Calhoun (2004), and Calhoun and Tedeschi (2006), PTG experiences of children and adolescents include

1. More compassion and empathy for others after personal trauma
2. Increased psychological and emotional maturity when compared to age-related peers
3. Increased resilience or the ability to bounce back
4. A greater appreciation for life when compared to age-related peers
5. A deeper understanding of one's personal values, purpose, and meaning in life
6. A greater value for interpersonal relationships
7. A deeper spiritual focus (value for self, others, and community)

In Lisa's case, she started to relate to the experiences of other individuals who survived disaster and endured the losses of significant others. Like other people who may have these types of growth experiences, she may now see the world in a different way, be able to problem solve more easily, feel more capable, and in general, feel closer to other individuals. In a sense, distress and challenges encountered by Lisa actually stimulated a growth process in her case, despite her initial worries, depression, and fears.

Coping strategies play a major role in PTG. For example, research demonstrates that children who use a repressive coping style (refusal to talk about what happened) tend to have fewer psychological and somatic symptoms, and fewer health problems than others who do not use repressive coping (Weinberger, Schwartz, & Davidson, 1979; Weinberger, 1990; Coifman, Bonanno et al., 2007, pp. 745–758). It also appears that the individuals who go on to experience PTSD have generally been unsuccessful in repressing their experiences, but can achieve PTG through developing a narrative and meaningful *reframing* of their experiences that supports PTG. Turner and Cox (2004) and Tedeschi, Park et al., (1998) have cited several additional coping strategies that may contribute to PTG:

1. Ability to express their reactions and create a meaningful narrative
2. Ability to positively reframe their experiences as a resource
3. Greater attention to the quality of life
4. Placing greater value on relationships

There is one major difference between resilience and PTG. The characteristics of resilience are viewed as being present at an early age and prior to traumatic exposure (Bonanno, Papo et al., 2001). Additionally, many of the factors for resilience described earlier in this chapter are believed to protect children exposed to traumatic situations from actually developing trauma reactions and PTSD. While resilient individuals may experience challenges in functioning capacity following a traumatic experience, overall they have the capacity for healthy functioning and adaptation including seeing the positive aspects derived from the experience (Morris, Shakespeare-Finch, & Scott, 2007). Resilient children may share similar characteristics with those who experience PTG, but their coping mechanisms may be different and suggest that these characteristics help facilitate PTG. This is of interest to trauma-informed practitioners because these various adaptations to stress can identify who is has innate resilience, who has the capacity for PTG and under what circumstances, and what vulnerabilities exist in children and adolescents when confronted by traumatic events.

The PTG Inventory (PTGI) (Tedeschi & Calhoun, 1996) is one instrument that can help to identify PTG. It uses five PTG domains: relating to others, seeing new possibilities, appreciation for life, personal strength, and spiritual change. Positive changes are noted in each of these domains when PTG exists. In a more recent and shorter version (PTG-SF), there are two items included in each of the five original domains (Cann, Calhoun, Tedeschi et al., 2010). Two examples include, "I changed my priorities of what is important in my life" and "I learned a great deal about how wonderful people are" (p. 130).

Overall, references to PTG are still limited and most PTG experiences have related it with exposure to singular incidents such as terrorist attacks, hurricanes, fires, and terminal illness. There is very little understanding of PTG in terms of chronic, cumulative, or developmental trauma and post-traumatic stress reactions within these categories. As previously mentioned, forms of resilience may exist with children and adolescents who have experienced even lifelong abuse, domestic violence, or war. However, the existing research does indicate that the highest level of PTG is generally achieved by those experiencing average, mild, or moderate levels of PTSD (Levine, Laufer et al., 2008; Solomon & Dekel, 2007).

Kilmer and Gil-Rivas (2010) note that there are probably certain children who are more likely than others to achieve PTG after a disaster or tragedy because they may be able to understand that there are both positive and negative feelings about a distressful event. The authors note that children as young as 7 years may develop this capacity, but that PTG may take a number of years to manifest, with no average time period yet identified. Like resilience, hope, and an optimistic outlook are also important factors.

The development of PTG with survivors of chronic trauma is much less clear and improvements that include PTG are not well understood. Trauma-informed practice emphasizes safety and self-regulation, relationships, and positive environments in response to chronic and developmental trauma; because these types of traumas are cumulative and severe, it is believed that PTG may not be possible. In contrast, other studies indicate that critical situations trigger strong survival instincts and that many individuals actually do bounce back and see growth in various areas in their lives (Bonanno, Wortman et al., 2002; Bonanno, Wortman, & Nesse, 2004).

There are many unanswered questions and even controversies about PTG, particularly in children and adolescents. For example, the relationship between PTG and overall well-being is not understood, evidence is mixed (Tedeschi & Calhoun, 2004), and may even be illusionary; others have observed that there is no connection between PTG and positive emotional outcomes (Hobfoll et al., 2006). It may be that growth, post-trauma, is more complex and may include other factors such as temperament and culture beliefs. Others note that people who report positive change may have actually manufactured a more optimistic response in order to cope with trauma and reduce helplessness and psychological distress similar to the adaptive coping skills found in survivors of chronic trauma. Timing is also a consideration; for example, a longer time period posttrauma may be needed for the development of PTG (Helgeson et al., 2006) and therefore, it may go unnoticed or unrecorded. Finally, unlike resilience, PTG may be more of a process than a stable outcome with several phases of coping.

PTG Intervention

Despite a lack of consistent information and research on PTG and controversies, the principles of posttrauma growth are still worth consideration within the context of trauma-informed practice. Overall, the focus of initial intervention should be on amelioration of existing trauma reactions, while supporting the characteristics of PTG that Tedeschi and Calhoun (1996) included in five domains of their PTG Inventory. Interventions directed at PTG can easily be integrated with concurrent interventions addressing trauma reactions and PTSD.

Some studies and clinical observations support that short-term intervention of 8 to 10 weeks can result in significant PTSD symptom reduction and improvement in the five domains measured by the PTGI, even in cases involving multiple exposures (Raider, 2010; Steele, Kuban, & Raider, 2009). However, in these cases, children will definitely benefit from additional intervention that focuses on social skills, conflict resolution, problem solving, how to learn, language skills, and other impaired functions that assessment reveals need attending. For those experiencing the more severe symptoms of cumulative trauma, remedial interventions are needed because of developmental delays caused by trauma (such as in Michael's case presented in Chapter 2). In general, most chronic trauma survivors do need support to experience PTG, while resilient individuals may already have developed effective ways to overcome challenges and sustain that resilience to stress over time.

PTG also appears to demand a much more structured, long-term form of trauma-specific assistance that involves a narrative process (Neimeyer, 2005).

This process is best suited to adolescents who have the cognitive capacity to engage in it. It provides the opportunity for self-expression and helps individuals reframe experiences in positive terms. Unlike the creation of trauma narratives in addressing PTSD, the PTG narrative process does not focus on the details of trauma, but instead on the meaning resulting from those experiences. Here are several views for adolescents to consider and reframe within a PTG context:

- How I see myself now, and what I think of myself now as a result of these experiences (PTG view supporting growth—If you survived this, you will survive other tragedies).
- How I see others now, and what I think of others now (PTG view—It was wonderful that my teacher was so nice when this happened; I know when similar things happen to others I will be really helpful in some way because I know what it was like for me).
- How I now see myself in the future, and what I think about life, about my future (PTG view—Having gone through this, I am not so worried about my future; I know I can do good things in my life).

Helping professionals can assist adolescents in reframing their thoughts to match the PTG characteristics cited earlier in this section. A narrative approach can be used with most adolescents, although some simply will not want to talk, have limited abilities to abstract, or have difficulty finding words to adequately express their thoughts. Narratives can, in these cases, be in the form of journaling, creating music or lyrics, or making a CD cover that lists a set of songs that reflects how they have grown because of "what happened."

While there are a number of creative interventions to enhance PTG (Malchiodi, Steele, & Kuban, 2008), bibliotherapy and therapeutic storytelling are particularly helpful to promote resilience-related learning in children and adolescents. The healing power of stories is often effective with trauma and loss issues because the inherent metaphors in a well-chosen story can communicate how others have met challenges and overcome them in various ways. Bibliotherapy has a long history of application as a resilience-enhancing intervention because it is widely accepted as a way to communicate how problems have affected others and alternate solutions to problems. Stories can also support the development of empathy through understanding the experiences of others and encourage a deeper understanding of the struggles faced by others.

BIBLIOTHERAPY AND POSTTRAUMATIC GROWTH

Deanne Ginns-Gruenberg

In the days following September 11, 2001, trauma specialists scrambled to find resources to help young clients. There were numerous requests for resources to manage nightmares, decrease stress levels, locate ideas for altruistic activities, and address bigotry and hatred. The need to reach out to others and bring people together to share common concerns was also expressed.

Sailing Through the Storm by Edie Julik (1996) is a story that is helpful in developing a sense of empowerment after a disaster or episode of violence. In this story, a sailboat on the water of life is happily sailing along in calm, blue water until suddenly there is a big boom. At that point everything changes because of a bad and hurtful event. The message of the story is that once trauma happens, nothing is the same but that things do eventually get better. The overall narrative moves from one of tragedy to eventual empowerment and hopefulness. *Sailing Through the Storm* is a good book to use as a springboard for creative activities and affirms that within each of us lies the power to make a difference and sail toward an ocean of peace.

A second book worth using in work with resilience and posttraumatic growth is *Brave Bart: A Story for Traumatized and Grieving Children* by Caroline Sheppard (1998), published by the National Institute for Trauma and Loss in Children. The story's main character is a small cat, Bart, who teaches readers that with the assistance of Helping Hannah, his trauma specialist, children can overcome traumatic events and feel better. Even more importantly, children identify with the animal characters in this story and are encouraged to believe that they too can confront challenges with success and hopefulness.

Benchmarks for Resilience and PTG

Table 7.1, PTG and Resilience, provides a summary of thoughts and behaviors of the survivors and thrivers encountered by the National Institute for Trauma and Loss in Children over the past 20 years. Although not formally validated from a research perspective, it presents clinical observations of the most common responses of those who have identified themselves as

Table 7.1 Resilience and Posttraumatic Growth (PTG)

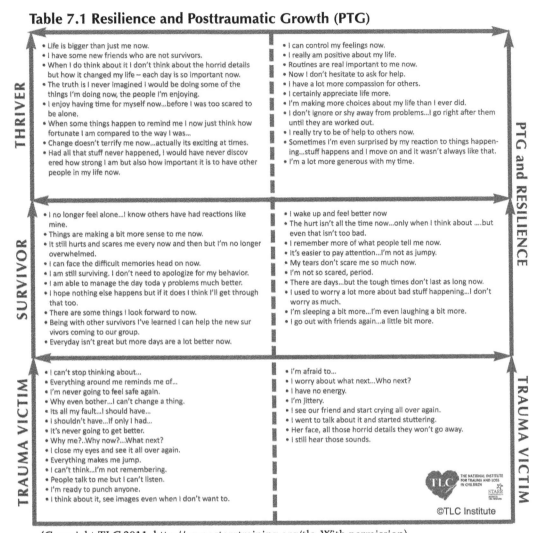

THRIVER

- Life is bigger than just me now.
- I have some new friends who are not survivors.
- When I do think about it I don't think about the horrid details but how it changed my life – each day is so important now.
- The truth is I never imagined I would be doing some of the things I'm doing now, the people I'm enjoying.
- I enjoy having time for myself now...before I was too scared to be alone.
- When some things happen to remind me I now just think how fortunate I am compared to the way I was...
- Change doesn't terrify me now...actually its exciting at times.
- Had all that stuff never happened, I would have never discovered how strong I am but also how important it is to have other people in my life now.

- I can control my feelings now.
- I really am positive about my life.
- Routines are real important to me now.
- Now I don't hesitate to ask for help.
- I have a lot more compassion for others.
- I certainly appreciate life more.
- I'm making more choices about my life than I ever did.
- I don't ignore or shy away from problems...I go right after them until they are worked out.
- I really try to be of help to others now.
- Sometimes I'm even surprised by my reaction to things happening...stuff happens and I move on and it wasn't always like that.
- I'm a lot more generous with my time.

SURVIVOR

- i no longer feel alone...I know others have had reactions like mine.
- Things are making a bit more sense to me now.
- It still hurts and scares me every now and then but I'm no longer overwhelmed.
- I can face the difficult memories head on now.
- I am still surviving. I don't need to apologize for my behavior.
- I am able to manage the day toda y problems much better.
- I hope nothing else happens but if it does I think I'll get through that too.
- There are some things I look forward to now.
- Being with other survivors I've learned I can help the new survivors coming to our group.
- Everyday isn't great but more days are a lot better now.

- I wake up and feel better now
- The hurt isn't all the time now...only when I think about ....but even that isn't too bad.
- I remember more of what people tell me now.
- It's easier to pay attention...I'm not as jumpy.
- My tears don't scare me so much now.
- I'm not so scared, period.
- There are days...but the tough times don't last as long now.
- I used to worry a lot more about bad stuff happening...I don't worry as much.
- I'm sleeping a bit more...I'm even laughing a bit more.
- I go out with friends again...a little bit more.

TRAUMA VICTIM

- I can't stop thinking about...
- Everything around me reminds me of...
- I'm never going to feel safe again.
- Why even bother...I can't change a thing.
- Its all my fault...I should have...
- I shouldn't have...If only I had...
- It's never going to get better.
- Why me?..Why now?...What next?
- I close my eyes and see it all over again.
- Everything makes me jump.
- I can't think...I'm not remembering.
- People talk to me but I can't listen.
- I'm ready to punch anyone.
- I think about it, see images even when I don't want to.

- I'm afraid to...
- I worry about what next...Who next?
- I have no energy.
- I'm jittery.
- I see our friend and start crying all over again.
- I went to talk about it and started stuttering.
- Her face, all those horrid details they won't go away.
- I still hear those sounds.

PTG and RESILIENCE

TRAUMA VICTIM

TLC THE NATIONAL INSTITUTE FOR TRAUMA AND LOSS IN CHILDREN
STARR
©TLC Institute

survivors and thrivers. In this context, survivors refer to individuals who have bounced back and who are functioning, but whose identity is still partially that of a victim and with a focus on the past. On the other hand, thrivers have a more positive outlook with a focus more on the present and future than on the past. In all cases, personal accounts of individuals who have experienced trauma help define the distinctions between these categories and the worldviews, statements, and behaviors that indicate that growth and change have taken place.

Cultural Aspects of Resilience and PTG

While everyone has the potential for resilience and growth, posttrauma, trauma-informed practice includes sensitivity to the cultural meanings and preferences for these experiences. Research on resilience and PTG comes mostly from a Western perspective and these concepts may not hold the same meaning for all cultural groups, including children, adolescents, and families. For example, while resilience is related to self-efficacy, some individuals may not value or prefer to achieve self-efficacy because of their community's values and beliefs.

One of resilience's core factors—optimism—is an experience that holds multi-meaning for different cultural groups. In some, being optimistic or happy is a low priority while Western cultures usually see the pursuit of happiness as a central motivation for all actions (Snyder, Lopez et al., 2010). Additionally, behaviors like self-criticism that might be defined as a threat to resilience are actually believed by many cultures to strengthen personal character and show respect for the greater community's expectations. It is also widely accepted that emotions and values do not have the same meaning across cultures and that there are very specific differences due to ethnicity, social environment, life experiences, and religion or other beliefs (Kubokawa & Ottaway, 2009).

What does this mean to trauma-informed practice with children and adolescents when promoting resilience and PTG? Similar to previous discussions of cultural sensitivity, it means that practitioners should attempt to fully understand their young clients' cultural backgrounds and worldviews in applying interventions. If possible, this should include talking with parents and caregivers to understand their values and beliefs about resilience and how they define its meaning. Finally, it is always wise to discuss with all individuals their cultural preferences for the terms *victim* and *survivor*. Because these words are ubiquitous in mental health and healthcare, helping professionals often forget that calling someone a "survivor" may have multiple meanings that are not necessarily acceptable or positive for some. For example, for some individuals this term may be associated with shame because it implies that others may not have survived a similar incident or experience. In brief, any resilience-enhancement or PTG intervention undertaken will be more successful if practitioners get a clear understanding of what these concepts mean to their young clients and their families.

Developing and Sustaining Resilience and PTG

As previously described, trauma-informed environments that enhance resilience include many factors. They promote core values of respect, generosity, and cooperation among members and interactions and make emotional and physical safety paramount. They provide opportunities to learn, pursue interests, and experience success without fear of failure. They honor individual beliefs and values and encourage individuals to embrace personal beliefs and values that help them to find self-worth, confidence, and stability.

Trauma-informed environments can produce remarkable changes in children and adolescents, particularly in the area of resilience enhancement and support of PTG. How resilience and PTG are sustained over time is less well understood. Recovery from trauma does not imply that changes are permanent or long term. Being resilient one month following a traumatic exposure only addresses the immediate response and not the responses to the challenges and changes in the months that follow. Sustainability speaks to the ongoing ability to consistently adapt positively and over time. Research has yet to capture longitudinal data that would correlate the current practices supporting resilience and PTG with long-term outcomes. Common sense says that the longer we cope effectively either following past traumatic experience or in the face of ongoing trauma, the greater our resilience and PTG gains will be in increasing quality of life and satisfaction. The old saying "it takes time to heal" is filled with the wisdom of those who discovered that healing and learning from tragic and terrifying experiences is an ongoing journey. Until more is known about the coping skills involved in resilience and PTG, all practitioners who work with traumatized individuals can apply the current knowledge of these concepts to trauma-informed care.

Conclusion

Ongoing adaptation to extreme stress necessitates a balanced integration of the varied components of trauma-informed care—safety, self-regulation, ongoing trauma-informed relationships, and environments that provide supportive resources during times of greatest stress. Recovery is an integrative process itself. We can recover from an illness, but if the cause is not treated, the illness returns. We can survive a traumatic experience, but if we have not become stronger in some way as a result, then we become less resilient in the face of future trauma. All trauma-informed practitioners want children and adolescents to recover from their traumas, but even more so, they want them to integrate all that they have learned in ways that sustain their ability to consistently adapt in positive ways over time. The final chapter discusses what constitutes trauma integration and the importance of adaptation and sustainability in resilience to future trauma.

Chapter 8

Trauma Integration

The ultimate goal in all trauma-informed work is to help children and adolescents master the impact of traumatic events and become what we call *thrivers*. Individuals who can move from surviving to thriving have developed a sense of wholeness, balance, and satisfaction and respond to others and the environment in a more productive way. Because of their experiences and trauma-informed intervention, they are able to meet new challenges with resilience and new skills in dealing with any future distressful experiences. However, these changes are not a result of merely moving beyond traumatic events or replacing what has happened with new experiences; they are signs of trauma integration.

Determining if trauma-informed interventions are working is the most important objective for helping professionals and the young clients they see. Recognizing the signs of trauma integration is central to that determination. This chapter addresses the concept of trauma integration in children and adolescents with reference to the major concepts of trauma-informed practice presented throughout this book. Throughout this text we have presented various practices and core elements of what constitutes trauma-informed practice, supplemented by expert commentary and guidance by noted trauma experts. The subsequent sections provide a summary of aspects of trauma integration including biopsychosocial signs of trauma integration and concepts of balance, adaptability, and sustainability, concluding with a discussion of the future of trauma-informed care.

Biopsychosocial Signs of Trauma Integration

While adults may be able to answer the question, "is this intervention working," children and adolescents may show practitioners that treatment is effective in different ways. Jose, 9 years old, is a good example of trauma integration. Jose entered residential treatment at age 6 years after three months of foster care for recurrent child abuse by his father and grandfather. Like many abused children, Jose had trouble sleeping due to hyperarousal and recurrent memories; his prominent trauma reactions included sleeping in a closet or contained space when fearful and fighting when feeling threatened in any way by others. When in foster care, he assaulted his caregivers and their children regularly; they simply could not continue taking care of Jose. Additionally, he responded like a much younger child, his language and communication skills were poor; due to his lifelong experiences of abuse, he understandably did not initially bond well with staff and helping professionals.

After 2½ years of consistent trauma-informed care, Jose is now quite a different individual. On occasion he still finds himself acting aggressively toward other children and staff, but now he shows concern and makes an "I'm sorry" card, showing an emerging capacity for empathy. He has learned a variety of ways to express his feelings more clearly, is able to communicate with adults at close to his age level, and has more secure attachments with his counselors and childcare workers. In particular, he is able to respond appropriately to men who initially frightened him and triggered recurrent memories of physical punishment. Once in a while, Jose will become upset and rip up paper or throw toys around the playroom, but he realizes more about why he does this and is able to take his own time out to practice relaxation skills.

Jose also now sleeps deeply, has nontraumatic dreams, and enjoys a good bedtime story before sleep. He takes pride in his appearance and likes to wear his favorite team shirts. He shows good manners during meals and recreational activities and tries new things; when he first became a resident at the facility, Jose could not tolerate sitting at the same table with other children. His physical skills have improved as well, including coordination, attention span, and ability to collaborate with other children. Most of all, Jose is confident when he encounters new challenges and learning experiences and is proud of who he is. Overall, he has achieved improvement in how his body (biological) responds to perceived threats, in his cognitive and emotional functioning (psychological), and in his relationships with both peers and adults (social).

CHILDREN DRAW AND TELL US ABOUT
TRAUMA INTEGRATION

Cathy Malchiodi

While a standardized trauma-informed assessment is essential to evaluating progress in children like Jose, trauma-informed practice also includes empowerment of the individual to advise helping professionals about their progress, too. Just as nonverbal sensory-based interventions work to help children and adolescents address trauma reactions, similar activities can be used to help practitioners understand changes that happen as a result of intervention over time. These activities are really clinical interviews, but they can provide valuable information not found through standard measures. Most importantly, children and adolescents generally enjoy these approaches because they often seem more like *fun* than *work*.

Show Me Your Worry is one simple technique used within the National Institute for Trauma and Loss in Children protocol for trauma-informed intervention (Steele, 2003). I use this technique regularly with children and adolescents because it really gives me an immediate understanding of what worries individuals are struggling with and postintervention, if those worries have been addressed. There are a number of ways to approach it, but I like to use a worksheet that has a series of different size boxes on it and ask the following questions:

■ What is your biggest worry right now?
■ How big is your worry on a scale of 1 to 5, with 5 being the biggest worry?

I encourage the individual to then choose the box that is closest to the size of the worry and use felt markers, crayons, or colored pencils to show me what the worry looks like with colors, lines, and/or shapes. Some children may select more than one box; it's OK to have more than one worry, and of course many children do have several worries that are troubling them. Some additional questions to ask the individual include

■ What is happening to you when you worry about this (the event or situation) the most?
■ What makes the worry go away, even for a little while?

■ Have you told anyone else about your worry?

This activity can be adapted to other feeling states too, including fear (what is your biggest fear right now?), anger, or sadness. It also is adaptable to a number of trauma-informed settings including medical environments where, for example, a child might be able to show a counselor or therapist what a particular symptom (pain, body temperature, headache) looks like. The nice thing about this activity is that it can be repeated over the course of intervention and used an informal measure of how the child or adolescent perceived progress. In brief, it helps me understand if the worry has gotten larger and more disruptive, has been reduced, has turned into other worries, or is no longer a problem. Because it is a hands-on, simple activity, it meets the trauma-informed goal of empowering the individual to be active in intervention and gives young clients a developmentally appropriate means to do so.

Trauma integration will probably be a lifelong journey for Jose as it is for many children. When he becomes a teenager, he will likely face new situations that may once again create trauma reactions or other emotional responses. Jose's trauma-informed care spans more than three years and is still in progress. Some children may respond more quickly, depending on the circumstances, exposure to multiple events, and age of initial intervention; in all cases, successful trauma-informed care is adapted to the needs and pace of the child.

Looking back to the initial chapters of this book, trauma in children and adolescents can be defined as simply feeling afraid, unprotected, unsafe, helpless, and in danger because of one or multiple events including abuse, neglect, witness to violence, medical illness, abandonment/separation, homelessness, or disaster, among other circumstances. When trauma reactions are present, they manifest themselves through the body's response to these feelings and to the belief that the next bad, sad, or frightening thing is about to happen again. In brief, feeling terrified, unprotected, and helpless hurts individuals' health and development in numerous ways. Children and adolescents are at greater risks for depression, self-harm, overeating, addictions, inappropriate sexual behavior and teenage pregnancy, anxiety disorders, dissociative disorder, crime and truancy, and of course, posttraumatic stress disorder. They may lack empathy for others, may become suspicious of kindness and affection, and develop unproductive and even dangerous behaviors that distress everyone around them, but serve a purpose for the traumatized child or adolescent. Overall, the goal of trauma-informed practice is to transform the body's learned reactions to traumatic experiences to responses that include resilience and posttraumatic growth.

In brief, signs of recovery and trauma integration in traumatized children include

1. Development of a sense of self and the ability to appropriately express oneself
2. Ability to show appropriate reactions, problem solve, and make good choices
3. Ability to make appropriate relationships with adults and peers
4. Ability to take responsibility appropriate to developmental level
5. No longer physically or emotionally hurting self or others
6. Development of insight and conscience
7. Development of cause-and-effect thinking
8. Improvement in motor skills and cognition appropriate to developmental level
9. Development of appropriate sleeping patterns, personal hygiene, and eating behavior
10. Ability to make positive contributions

These signs may show themselves in a number of ways—behavior, cognitive improvements, speech and language, gross and fine motor skills, interpersonal skills, and developmental gains. Most importantly, what the body remembers about trauma through nonproductive adaptive coping skills has changed and hyperarousal, avoidance behaviors, and disturbing memories are measurably reduced (including through evaluation as described in Chapters 2 and 3). Rothschild (2011) summarizes this by stating, "It is clear that traumatic events exact a toll on the body as well as the mind. The DSM-IV includes several somatic symptoms alongside the psychological symptoms in its definition of PTSD. However, the body is often missed in trauma treatment. On the other hand, some body-approaches neglect the importance of psychological integration. Neither aspect can be neglected. Trauma treatment must regard the whole person and integrate trauma's impact on both body and mind" (Rothschild, n.d.). Rothschild and others concur that one major factor in trauma integration is the reduction of trauma-related symptoms expressed by the body as hyperarousal, avoidance, and intrusive memories.

FIVE PRINCIPLES TO GUIDE CHILDREN'S PLAY TOWARD RESOLUTION

Peter Levine and Maggie Kline

The following analysis of Sammy's experience (Chapter 4) will help clarify and apply the following principles for using therapeutic play:

Let the Child Control the Pace of the Game

Healing takes place in a moment-by-moment slowing down of time. In order to help the child you are working with feel safe, follow her pace and rhythm. If you put yourself in the child's shoes (through careful observation of her behavior), you will learn quickly how to resonate with her. Let's return to the story to see exactly how we did that with Sammy:

By running out of the room when Pooh Bear fell off the chair, Sammy indicated loud and clear that he was not ready to engage in this new activating game. Sammy had to be rescued by his parents, comforted, and brought back to the scene before continuing. In order to make him feel safe, we all assured him that we would be there to protect Pooh Bear. By offering this support and reassurance, we helped Sammy move closer to playing the game—*in his own time at his own pace.*

After this reassurance, Sammy ran into the bedroom instead of out the door. This was a clear signal that he felt less threatened and more confident of our support. Children may not state verbally whether they want to continue, so take cues from their behavior and responses. Respect their wishes in whatever way they choose to communicate them. Children should never be rushed to move through an episode too fast or forced to do more than they are willing and able to do. Just like with Sammy, it is important to slow down the process if you notice signs of fear, constricted breathing, stiffening, or a dazed (dissociated) demeanor. These reactions will dissipate if you simply wait, quietly and patiently, while reassuring the child that you are still by his side and on his side. Usually, the youngster's eyes and breathing pattern will indicate when it's time to continue.

Distinguish Between Fear, Terror, and Excitement

Experiencing fear or terror for more than a brief moment during traumatic play will not help the child move through the trauma. Most children will take action to avoid it. Let them! At the same time, try and discern whether it is avoidance or escape. The following is a clear-cut example to help in developing the skill of "reading" when a break is needed and when it's time to guide the momentum forward.

When Sammy ran down to the creek, he was demonstrating avoidance behavior. In order to resolve his traumatic reaction, Sammy had to feel that he was in control of his actions rather than driven to act by his emotions. Avoidance behavior occurs when fear and terror threaten to overwhelm the child. This behavior is typically accompanied by some sign of emotional distress (crying, frightened eyes, screaming). Active escape, on the other hand, is exhilarating. Children become excited by their small triumphs and often show pleasure by glowing with smiles, clapping their hands, or laughing heartily. Overall, the response is much different from avoidance behavior. Excitement is evidence of the child's successful discharge of emotions that accompanied the original experience. This is positive, desirable, and necessary.

Trauma is transformed by changing intolerable feelings and sensations into pleasurable ones. This can only happen at a level of activation that is similar to the activation that led to the traumatic reaction in the first place. If the child appears excited, it is OK to offer encouragement and continue as we did when we clapped and danced with Sammy. However, if the child appears frightened or cowed, give reassurance, but don't encourage any further movement. Instead, be present with your full attention and support, waiting patiently until a substantial amount of the fear subsides. If the child shows signs of fatigue, take a rest break.

Take One Small Step at a Time

You can never move too slowly in renegotiating a traumatic event whatever the age, but this is especially true with a young child. Traumatic play is repetitious almost by definition. Make use of this cyclical characteristic. The key difference between *renegotiation* and traumatic play (reenactment) is that in renegotiation there are incremental differences in the child's responses and behaviors in moving toward mastery and resolution. The following illustrates how I noticed these small changes with Sammy.

When Sammy ran into the bedroom instead of out the door, he was responding with a different behavior, indicative that progress had been made. No matter how many repetitions it takes, if the child you are helping is responding differently—such as with a slight increase in excitement, with more speech, or with more spontaneous movements—he is moving through the trauma. If the child's responses appear to be moving in the direction of constriction or compulsive repetition instead of expansion and variety, you may be attempting to renegotiate the event with scenarios that involve too much arousal for the child to make progress. If you notice that your attempts at playful renegotiation are backfiring, ground yourself and pay attention to your sensations until your breathing brings a sense of calm, confidence, and spontaneity. Then, slow down the rate of change by breaking the play into smaller increments. This may seem contradictory to what was stated earlier about following the child's pace. However, attuning to children's needs sometimes means setting limits to prevent them from getting wound up, overwhelmed, and collapsing. If the child appears tense or frightened, it's OK to invite some healing steps. For example, when renegotiating a medical trauma, you might say, "Let's see, I wonder what we can do so that Pooh Bear (Dolly, GI Joe, etc.) doesn't get so scared before you (the pretend doctor/nurse) give him the shot?" Often children will come up with creative solutions showing you exactly what they *needed—the missing ingredient* that would have helped them settle more during their experience.

Don't be concerned about how many times you have to go through what seems to be the "same old thing." (We engaged Sammy in playing the game with Pooh Bear at least 10 times.) Sammy was able to renegotiate his traumatic responses fairly quickly. Another child in your care might require more time. You don't need to do it all in one day! Resting and time are needed to help internally reorganize the child's experience at subtle levels. Be assured that if the resolution is not complete, the child will return to a similar phase when given the opportunity to play during the next session.

Become a Safe Container

Remember that biology and instinct are on your side. Perhaps the most difficult and important aspect of renegotiating a traumatic event with a child is maintaining your own belief that things will turn out OK. This feeling comes from inside you and is projected out to the child. It becomes a container that surrounds the child with a feeling of confidence. This may be particularly difficult if the child resists your attempts to renegotiate the trauma.

If the child resists, be patient and reassuring. The instinctive part of your child wants to rework this experience. All you have to do is wait for that part to feel confident and safe enough to assert itself. If you are excessively worried about whether the child's traumatic reaction can be transformed, you may inadvertently send a conflicting message. Adults with their own unresolved childhood trauma may be particularly susceptible to falling into this trap.

Stop If You Feel That the Child Is Genuinely Not Benefiting From the Play

The reworking or *renegotiation* of a traumatic experience, as we saw with Sammy, represents a process that is fundamentally different from traumatic play or reenactment. Left to their own devices, most children will attempt to avoid the traumatic feelings that their play evokes. With guidance, Sammy was able to "live his feelings through" by gradually and sequentially mastering his fear. Using this stepwise renegotiation of the traumatic event and Pooh Bear's support, Sammy was able to emerge as the victor and hero. A sense of triumph and heroism almost always signals the successful conclusion of a renegotiated traumatic event. By following Sammy's lead after setting up a potentially activating scenario, joining in his play, and making the game up as we went along, Sammy got to let go of his fear.

TRAUMA INTEGRATION AND MICHELLE
Caelan Kuban

Michelle is a 16 year old with a history of abuse, neglect, sexual assault, and rape. Her case helps illustrate the importance of structured sensory trauma interventions that provide adolescents with opportunities to make connections, have fun, and master something they enjoy doing.

One of the trauma-specific questions that helped to encourage Michelle to tell her story and focus on specific details was, "Of all that has happened that brought you here today, what was the worst part for you?" Upon asking this question the clinician anticipated what the "worst part" must have been for Michelle. What we as observers often consider as the worst part is not necessarily experienced by the victim. Only by giving the victim the opportunity to make us a witness can we truly know the experience as he or she knows it. The use of trauma-specific questions helps provide this opportunity. When asked about the worst thing that had happened to her, Michelle clearly stated, "The rape but not the rape itself. I am an outgoing, strong girl. I was the only girl on our school football team my sophomore year—I am tough! Every day I look back and just hate myself for letting the rape happen." By asking this one trauma-specific question, the specialist was able to help this teen work through the cognitive distortion she experienced; a focus that likely would have otherwise been missed. The guilt and shame of this experience weighed heavily on Michelle. Depression, substance abuse, difficulty paying attention in school, and verbal and physical aggression toward others were her presenting problems. Michelle's current view of herself was certainly obvious—this was all her fault.

Providing Michelle with an opportunity to tell her story, while encouraging her to provide a visual representation of her experience by drawing, was a turning point. Even after months of talking through her rape experience with a very caring aunt and good friends, it was only when Michelle started to draw images to help detail her experience along with answering trauma-specific questions that she had a shift in her view of self. Michelle looked up from her paper after drawing and said, "I *did* do everything I could to try to stop the rape from happening. It *wasn't* my fault." The drawing provided Michelle with a visual representation that allowed her to now see that she did everything she could do to escape that situation. Others had told her this but she did not believe them.

Talking did not provide Michelle with the relief from the guilt and shame she had been experiencing for months; it was the ability to "see" her experience from a different perspective, provided by drawing, which shifted her distorted perception of her experience to a more realistic realization of what happened. She now wasn't only hearing from others that the rape was not her fault, she actually believed herself that she indeed was not at fault but rather did do everything she could do in her power to escape the awful experience.

Over the months that followed the trauma intervention, Michelle joined the school choir and really found her voice. She knew she enjoyed singing but as she indicated, "I didn't know that I was actually good at it!" Michelle's participation in the choir provided her with a sense of belonging. She was part of a peer group with similar interests, many of whom she connected with immediately. After a few weeks, Michelle was practicing to sing a solo for a board member retreat. Michelle recalls the day of her performance vividly. She described in detail, "It was scary but I just knew I could do it. As soon as I started caring about and believing in myself I noticed that other people do too—even adults care about me! All the things I did in the past, all the bad things, well, I am bigger than that now, there is more to me than that." Singing with the choir provided Michelle with an opportunity to master one of her interests in the company of like-minded peers. Michelle is now not only in the school choir but also a travel choir that participates in events across the country. When Michelle was asked to provide one or two words to describe herself before she started her treatment, she indicated, "Sad and ignorant." When asked to use one or two words to describe herself now she exclaimed, "Pretty amazing!"

When asked what made the most impact on the change of Michelle's view of herself and the world around her, she credited two things: first was the opportunity to tell her story, which helped her realize that her experience was only an experience and not her fault, and second, being in the choir. Telling her story only took an hour, but it was life changing. Singing is something Michelle "has to do every day" and she asserts, "Singing makes me feel good about myself and it makes other people feel good too, what is better than that?"

Positive Developmental Outcomes

Another way to think about trauma integration involves positive developmental gains as a result of trauma-informed intervention. Perry (2002) proposes six developmental outcomes that also serve as a guideline for informally evaluating psychosocial growth:

1. **Attachment**—the capacity to form healthy relationships with others
2. **Self-regulation**—the ability to notice and regulate physical responses (eating patterns and sleep) and trauma reactions (anger, fear, and anxiety)
3. **Affiliation**—the capacity to join with others and contribute to a group
4. **Attunement**—the recognition of needs, strengths, preferences, interests, and values of others
5. **Tolerance**—the capacity to understand and accept how others are different than you
6. **Respect**—the appreciation of one's worth and the worth of others

Residential staff and counselors observed that Jose demonstrated positive changes in all these outcomes. For example, Jose began to enjoy making friends with peers and established appropriate attachment to helping professionals, including male counselors who he previously feared. He gradually was able to control behavioral responses and when he found it impossible, he was able to use self-regulating methods to calm him and reduce his frustration and anger. Jose learned to enjoy and look forward to group activities and tolerated (as much as the average nine-year-old can) the behaviors, personalities, and values of others. As a result of intervention during his time at residential care he also has discovered some of his own self-worth and has started to show respect for the strengths, interests, and needs of others.

The Ecology of Trauma Integration

In previous chapters, the importance of five areas of trauma-informed practice were described: (1) understanding of the individual through comprehensive assessment; (2) enhancing safety and introducing self-regulation skills; (3) establishing secure, consistent, and meaningful relationships with adults and peers; (4) creating environments that not only emphasize safety, self-regulation, and relationships, but also values and beliefs; and (5) promoting and enhancing resilience and posttraumatic growth. These five areas form a *trauma-informed ecology* whose end result leads to trauma integration, the sense of balance, wholeness, and satisfaction that increase the chances that individuals will have more productive lives and be free of distressing symptoms over time.

In addition, this trauma-informed ecology reflects many of the principles of positive psychology that includes not only traditional amelioration of emotional distress, but also emphasizes interventions that help individuals discover what makes life most worth living in the process. Like positive psychology, trauma-informed approaches focus on strengths as well as weaknesses and on creating good things in life while repairing the worst (Peterson, 2006; Seligman, 1994). For children and adolescents, this means helping to not only integrate the mastery of trauma responses, but additionally helping to enhance qualities of human goodness and excellence.

As a result of the positive psychology movement (Aspinwall & Strudinger, 2003; Keyes & Haidt, 2003), the support for a more consilient (holistic and inclusive) approach to trauma intervention has emerged. In many ways, the terms *consilience* and *integration* are synonymous and represent outcomes that are based upon the blending of multiple sources to lead to a more adaptable and sustainable approach to stressful, terrifying situations. In trauma-informed practice, balance, adaptability, and sustainability are key aspects of working toward integration. These elements form an *ecology* of approaches and objectives that work together to enhance recovery and reparation. In contrast, attempting to manage difficult challenges through only one approach simply creates a rigid, very vulnerable, tenuous, and frequently unsuccessful resolution of challenges. For example, much emphasis is placed on the sole use of evidence-based practices. This is a nonintegrative view that excludes *evidence-supported* practices (including many discussed in this book) because they are categorized as less valuable. There are many excellent evidence-based practices available today, but also many excellent evidence-supported practices that have emerged from body–mind, biology, anthropology, social sciences, and even humanities. Trauma-informed practices in trauma integration recognize and apply multiple resources to help children and adolescents utilize their unique strengths and abilities to thrive instead of merely survive.

Balance

In brief, trauma-informed care seeks to help individuals find an equilibrium in their lives that enhances the ability to self-regulate body and mind and enhance developmental and personal strengths while resolving challenges; above all, the preferences, values, beliefs, pace, and style of trauma-informed intervention are respected. As demonstrated throughout this book, this is achieved through attention to four major areas—comprehensive assessment; self-regulation skills; relationships that promote attachment, attunement, respect and affiliation; and exposure to positive environments.

The case example of Michelle (see the "Trauma Integration and Michelle" text box) underscores how traditional outpatient efforts that did not include these principles were used with little success. Initially, Michelle was unable to regulate her body and resorted to drug abuse to self-regulate. She was unable to establish relationships except those that were controlling and manipulative. Her life was void of opportunities to discover strengths and potentials; she viewed others as barriers or only as a means to get what she needed or wanted. In helping Michelle to find balance in multiple areas of functioning, intervention included developing opportunities for her to experience what it was like to belong to a set of peers and to interact within a community that valued respect, generosity, and cooperation. Additionally, she needed experiences to assist her in discovering the value of helping herself and others versus hurting herself and others. She also required opportunities to discover what she was good at doing to increase her self-worth. Finally, Michelle needed professional guidance to help her understand the impact that traumatic experiences had on thinking and behavior and to practice new ways to manage (regulate) her fear reactions. In contrast, previous outpatient treatment focused only on her deficits and attempted to control her behavior, a treatment plan that was not balanced and ultimately failed to produce change.

TRAUMA INTEGRATION—HAVE PATIENCE

P. Gussie Klorer

Children with histories of maltreatment protect themselves by not attaching. They have learned that relationships are painful and do not last, and therefore it is far better to stay superficial and aloof. The relationship with the therapist is no exception. It is vitally important that the therapist stay with the child's level of comfort in the relationship, and not push. This means being immensely patient. I'll never forget Joseph, a 9-year-old boy referred because his foster home placement was failing due to his inability to integrate himself into a family. He had no desire to be adopted with his siblings and was doing everything he could to sabotage this plan.

In our first session, it was clear that Joseph had no interest in my art supplies, games, puzzles, books, sand tray, or anything else in my highly stimulating office, because he had no interest in me. Joseph came into the office, sat down at the art table, closed his eyes, and did not move for 45 minutes. No talking and no seeing for this young man. It was clear he was not going to engage after my initial attempts at conversation, so I quickly abandoned the talking plan. I decided to just share the space with him. I sat too, said nothing, and tried to stay attentive to him. I felt it was very important that I not do paper work or be distracted by things in the office that I could have attended to, but rather, just stay with him and focus my thinking on what it must be like to be him.

After 45 minutes, I told him we had five minutes left and I would like to bring in his foster father so we could make another appointment. He opened his eyes and I brought in his foster father, a grandfatherly man who was quite aware that Joseph did not want to come to the session. He asked how Joseph did. I told him that Joseph was pretty quiet, but he did fine. Only then did Joseph briefly look at me, perhaps confused or surprised at my answer. The next week, Joseph announced boldly that he wasn't talking, and I couldn't make him. To me, this was progress: he talked! I said that was fine. This time he opened his eyes and looked around the office while he did not talk. In the ensuing weeks, he argued about how stupid this was, and what a waste of time it was. Now we were getting somewhere; we were having real conversations.

I ended up working with Joseph for six years, through his transition from foster care into residential treatment. At first his resistance was our way of interacting, providing a safe way for him to enter the relationship. Over six years, he eventually made a few art projects, but most of them were stereotypic doodles that he threw away.

He did make one important piece of art when he was 14. It was a box to contain his feelings about his father, an abusive man who elicited fear and intense anxiety in his three children. Joseph wanted the box to appear painful when you looked at it, and it was never to be opened. He nailed, taped, and glued it shut using three different kinds of glue, then wrapped it in sandpaper, then put nails all around the outside of the box. Needless to say, he never talked about this box, and never told me what the piece of paper inside of it said.

After we terminated therapy, Joseph moved into an independent living program. That might have been the end of our relationship, but once a year, always near his birthday, Joseph emails me and his former residential therapist and reminds us that his birthday is coming up. We continue an old tradition of taking him out for ice cream for his birthday. Joseph just turned 24, and he likes chocolate chip. Patience.

Adaptability and Sustainability

Adaptability and sustainability are long-term goals of trauma integration with children and adolescents. *Adaptability* refers to the ability to apply learning to other experiences; it also is part of enhancement of resilience and encouragement of posttraumatic growth. The ultimate goal of all trauma-informed care is to see children and adolescents flourish, to realize an array of strengths, and to be able to use these strengths to maintain a balance intrapersonally (self-worth and self-efficacy) as well as interpersonally (interaction with others) throughout their lives.

Michelle's story reflects adaptation. For example, she has developed some mastery through singing and delighting others with her skill. By joining the choir, she developed a sense of belonging and learned the value of working together as well as being connected in a positive way to others. By volunteering for service groups like helping seniors, she discovered the value of generosity. Life was not just about her anymore, but also about her community; her aggressive and challenging behavior went from hurting others to helping others. Intervention in Michelle's case not only revisited her trauma experiences, but also focused on development of strengths and connection with others through placement in a residential program.

When Michelle graduates from the residential community, she will return to an environment that is not as protected, and it will not have the same level of social support. However, she has learned skills in adaptation because of experiences with meaningful attachments, emphasis on personal achievements, being altruistic, and autonomous through learning to take care of herself. She discovered that as she began taking responsibility for herself and how she looked and acted, others began to care about her, too. This balanced adaptation will provide her with valuable resources when faced with any new stress in her life.

Sustainability refers to how well and how long someone can maintain adaptations over time. Once Michelle leaves her residential community, will she be able to sustain her gains, and if so, for how long? The only way to answer these questions is through additional periodic evaluation. Unfortunately, such evaluations are rarely funded more than three to six months after treatment ends. Only a few studies have captured data over longer time periods and have increased understanding of the presence of significant adults and repressive coping that seems to protect some individuals. Currently, there is a need for more longitudinal research that helps to identify trauma survivors who become thrivers and go on to lead successful lives and those who continue to struggle with developmental gains.

The collective wisdom of long-term survivors and thrivers can provide reliable information that could be used in continuing efforts to help individuals like Michelle. Recalling T's story (Chapter 4), T turned his life around after very traumatic early years of childhood. All trauma specialists should be curious as to what helped him emotionally survive his experiences and what allowed him to adapt when he returned to his community. This is the kind of information that would help validate and define trauma-informed care as well as what specifically allows a survivor to sustain gains across developmental life stages.

The Future of Trauma-Informed Practice

The Western view of treatment and what constitutes healing is quite narrow and far from integrative. For example, the practice of mindfulness has been supported in Eastern cultures for years and is only now gaining some recognition for its value in self-regulation practices. In recent years, prescriptive responses like debriefing have been recommended for everyone exposed to a traumatic incident, ignoring the fact that many people are innately resilient and do well without intrusive insistence that such an intervention is necessary for reparation. Many centers have invested thousands of dollars on training staff in the use of one strategy, like cognitive-behavioral therapy (CBT), only to find that CBT alone is not beneficial for every client. This is not meant to suggest that evidence-based programs are of little value because many do target specific areas affected by trauma with positive outcomes and evidence of efficacy. However, when used as a single or predominant approach to trauma, they often fall short in addressing children and adolescents in their ecologies. No one medicine heals everyone with the same ailment. Similarly, there is no one intervention that addresses the complexities of every traumatized individual.

Some propose that the only good intervention is an evidence-based intervention, disregarding that even though "research may show statistical significance, the amount of change may be insignificant" (Brendtro & Mitchell, 2010, p. 2). Additionally, outcomes are often only measured at the end of the intervention and not 3, 6, or 12 months later; this fails to address sustainability of gains, thereby skewing the real value of initial outcomes. From this perspective, a practice that is said to be evidence based today may be very narrow in its application when addressing the complexities of trauma and meeting the practical needs and challenges of traumatized children and adolescents. There are many aspects to trauma integration that cannot be addressed by one program or even measured by evidence-based formats.

Despite these challenges, fortunately trauma-informed practice, including evidence-based and emerging interventions, is more widely recognized and implemented in mental health, medical, community, residential, and educational settings than even a few years ago. While funding and system-wide change are always a challenge, there is a growing acceptance and knowledge of neuroscience and sensory-based approaches in work with traumatized individuals of all ages. As practitioners continue to work with and adapt these approaches, it is certain that more data will be generated that will enhance the understanding of how children and adolescents can benefit from trauma-informed practice and provide all helping professionals with more effective ways to assist all traumatized individuals with integration and recovery.

SOME FINAL THOUGHTS ON TRAUMA INTEGRATION

William Steele

In 1976 while involved in my own treatment, I was fortunate to meet Alexander Lowen, founder of Bioenergetics. He evaluated (scanned) my body structure for indicators of emotional blocking and provided my psychotherapist with several body activities to help discharge what talk alone could never accomplish. My therapist was amazing, given her appreciation that there were many ways to heal other than talk, and she integrated bodywork ("resourcing") into my treatment. This was by no means conventional wisdom or well-accepted treatment at the time. But talk simply was unable to provide me with a way to express my own trauma. The personal growth and resilience that followed was amazing.

In the early 21st century, technology has now clearly documented the importance of using the body as a resource in healing from trauma. The works of van der Kolk; Levine and Kline; Ogden; Perry; Rothschild, and so many others cited in this text have led to the development of excellent methods for integrating the use of the body in treating trauma. We have science to thank for what is now accepted as essential treatment within the context of trauma-informed care.

In 1990, I was introduced to Cathy Malchiodi and the power of art in facilitating the healing process through her book *Breaking the Silence* (Malchiodi, 1990). If you were to look at my copy of her work, you would find highlighted content on every page. So fascinated and impressed with the work she was doing with children from violent homes, I invited her to present to the professionals participating in training at the National Institute for Trauma and Loss in Children (TLC). That was in 1994. Similar to bodywork, art therapy at the time was seen as a questionable treatment by traditional disciplines. However once again, thanks to neuroscience, and the realization that many traumatized children are navigating their world in the lower, midbrain regions where reason and logic do not exist, art therapy, drawing, play, sand tray, and other sensory modalities are now being integrated into trauma treatment within the context of trauma-informed care. Her recent work, *Creative Interventions With Traumatized Children* (Malchiodi, 2008), reflects today's neurological affirmation that this approach is essential to significantly influence and modify the impact of trauma on key neural systems and traumatized children's responses to the stressful and threatening situations they face in today's world.

Having lived for six years in a residential setting, from 1968 through 1973, I know all too well the powerful influence the environment has on our behavior, our attitudes, our private logic, relationships, performance, view of self, others, and life. The importance of environment on development began to gain formal support in the early 1980s when micro and macro systems were introduced into graduate school curriculums, but really did not attract a great deal of attention until Bronfenbrenner's work on ecology was published in 2005. However, once again science, and recently the study of epigenetics, has documented the importance of integrating into trauma treatment, environmental strategies within a trauma-informed context. This is now taking place in clinics, schools, childcare agencies, community programs, statewide systems of child care like juvenile justice, and protective services systems. Tremendous advances have been made in the ways services are now being delivered to traumatized children.

Now that the principles of trauma-informed care are being widely accepted, there is more that needs to be done to help organizations, systems programs, communities, and practitioners become proficient at trauma-informed practices. We hope the information in this book supports the ongoing integration of trauma-informed care and practices wherever children are being served. What is most exciting is that the greatest benefit of this major shift in treatment is the array of brain-based practices we now have available to integrate into our efforts to help traumatized children. Sammy, T, Michelle, and so many others are examples of what can happen with a trauma-informed, integrated approach to care.

References

Achenbach, T. M., & Rescorla, L. A. (2001). *Manual for the ASEBA school-age: Forms & profiles*. Burlington, VT: University of Vermont, Research Center for Children, Youth, & Families.

Adler, A. (1930). *The problem child*. New York: P. G. Putnam's Sons.

Ainsworth, M. D. S. (1967). *Infancy in Uganda: Infant care and the growth of attachment*. Baltimore, MD: Johns Hopkins University Press.

Allen, J., & Klein, R. (1997). *Ready, set, relax: A research-based program of relaxation, learning and self-esteem for children*. Watertown, WI: Inner Coaching.

American Psychiatric Association (APA). (1994). *Diagnostic and statistical manual of mental disorders (DSM-IV)* (4th ed.). Washington, DC: Author.

American Psychiatric Association. (APA) (2000). *Diagnostic and statistical manual of mental disorders (DSM-IVTR)* (5th ed.). Washington, DC: Author.

Aspinwall, L. G., & Staudinger, U. M. (2003). *A psychology of human strengths: Fundamental questions and future directions for a positive psychology*. Washington, DC: American Psychological Association.

Bath, H. (2008). The three pillars of trauma-informed care. *Reclaiming Children and Youth, 17*(3), 5.

Berg, I. K. (1994). *Family-based services: A solution-focused approach*. Scranton, PA: W. W. Norton.

Berkman, L. F., & Glass, T. A. (2000). Social integration, social networks, social support, and health. In L. F. Berkman & I. Kawachi (Eds.), *Social epidemiology* (pp. 137–173). New York: Oxford University Press.

Betancourt, T. S., & Khan, K. T. (2008). The mental health of children affected by armed conflict: Protective processes and pathways to resilience. *International Review of Psychiatry, 20*(3), 317–328.

Bisson, J., Jenkins., P. L., Alexander, J., & Bannister, C. (1997). Randomised controlled trial of psychological debriefing for victims of burn trauma. *British Journal of Psychiatry, 171*, 78–81.

Bloom, S. (1997). *Creating sanctuary: Toward the evolution of sane societies*. New York: Routledge.

Bloom, S. (2000). The sanctuary model. *Therapeutic Communities, 21*(2), 67–91.

Bloom, S. L., & Farragher, B. (2010). *Destroying sanctuary: The crisis in human service delivery systems*. New York: Oxford University Press.

Bloom, S. L., & Farragher, B. (in press). *Restoring sanctuary*. New York: Oxford University Press.

Boden, J. M., Horwood, L. J., & Ferguesson, D. M. (2007). Exposure to childhood sexual and physical abuse and subsequent educational achievement outcomes. *Child Abuse & Neglect, 31*(10), 1101–1114.

Bonanno, G. A., & Field, N. P. (2001). Examining the delayed grief hypothesis across five years of bereavement. *American Behavioral Scientist, 44,* 798–806.

Bonanno, G. A., Papa, A., & O'Neill, K. (2001). Loss and human resilience. *Applied and Preventive Psychology, 10,* 193–206.

Bonanno, G. A., Wortman, C. B., Lehman, D. R., Tweed, R. G., Haring, M., Sonnega, J., et al. (2002). Resilience to loss and chronic grief: A prospective study from pre-loss to 18-months post-loss. *Journal of Personality and Social Psychology, 83,* 1150–1164.

Bonanno, G. A., Wortman, C. B., & Nesse, R. M. (2004). Prospective patterns of resilience and maladjustment during widowhood. *Psychology and Aging, 19,* 260–271.

Booth, P. B., & Jernberg, A. M. (2009). *Theraplay: Helping parents and children build better relationships through attachment-based play*. San Francisco: Jossey-Bass.

Bowen, M. (1990). *Research at the Georgetown Family Center*. Retrieved December 27, 2010 from http://www.thebowmencenter.org/page/research.

Bowlby, J., & Winton, J. (1998). *Attachment and loss: Separation, anger and anxiety*. New York: Basic Books.

Brendtro, L., Brokenleg, M., & Van Bockern, S. (2002). *Reclaiming youth at risk: Our hope for the future*. Indianapolis, IN: Solution Tree.

Brendtro, L., & Du Toit, L. (2005). *Response ability pathways: Restoring bonds of respect*. Cape Town: Pretext.

Brendtro, L., & Long, N. J. (2002). Controls from within: The enduring challenge. *Reclaiming Children and Youth, 11*(1), 5–9.

Brendtro, L., & Longhurst, J. (2005). The resilient brain. *Reclaiming Children and Youth, 14*(1), 52–60.

Brendtro, L., & Mitchell, M. (2010). Weighing the evidence: From chaos to consilience. *Reclaiming Children and Youth, 19*(2), 3–9.

Brendtro, L., Mitchell, M., & McCall, H. (2009). *Deep brain learning: Pathways to potential with challenging youth*. Albion, MI: Starr Commonwealth.

Brendtro, L., Ness, A., & Mitchell, M. (2001). *No disposable kids*. Longmont, CO: Sopris West.

Brendtro, L. K., & Shahbazian, M. (2004). *Troubled children and youth: Turning problems into opportunities*. Champaign, IL: Research Press Publishing.

Briere, J. (1996). *Trauma symptom checklist for children*. Odessa, FL: Psychological Assessment Resources.

Briere, J., & Scott, J. G. (2006). *Principles of trauma therapy: A guide to symptoms, evaluation, and treatment*. Thousand Oaks, CA: Sage.

Bronfenbrenner, U. (Ed.). (2005). *Making human beings human: Bioecological perspectives on human development*. Thousand Oaks, CA: Sage.

Burnham, J. J. (2009). Contemporary fears of children and adolescents: Coping and resiliency in the 21st century. *Journal of Counseling & Development, 87*(1), 28–35.

Cahn, B. R., & Polich, J. (2006). Meditation states and traits: EEG, ERP, and neuro-imaging studies. *Psychological Bulletin, 132*(2), 180.

Calhoun, L. G., & Tedeschi, R. G. (2006). *The assessment of posttraumatic growth in different cultural contexts.* Symposium presented at the annual meeting of the International Society for Traumatic Stress Studies, Hollywood, California.

Cann, A., Calhoun, L. G., et al. (2010). Posttraumatic growth and depreciation as independent experiences and predictors of well-being. *Journal of Loss and Trauma, 15*(3), 16.

Carter, C. S. (2007). Neuropeptides and the protective effects of social bonds. In E. Harmon-Jones & P. Winkielman (Eds.), *Social neuroscience: Integrating biological and psychological explanations of social behavior* (pp. 425–437). New York: Guilford Press.

Centers for Disease Control and Prevention. (2011). Adverse child experiences (ACE) study. Retrieved March 30, 2011, from http://www.cdc.gov/ace/index.htm.

Chapman, D. P., Dube, S. R., et al. (2007). Adverse childhood events as risk factors for negative mental health outcomes. *Psychiatric Annals, 37*(5), 359.

Chapman, L. M., Morabito, D., et al. (2001). The effectiveness of art therapy interventions in reducing post traumatic stress disorder (PTSD) symptoms in pediatric trauma patients. *Art Therapy: Journal of the American Art Therapy Association, 18*(2), 100–104.

Charney, D. S. (2004). Psychobiological mechanisms of resilience and vulnerability: Implications for successful adaptation to extreme stress. *American Journal of Psychiatry, 161*(2), 195–216.

Cheever, K. H., & Hardin, S. B. (1999). Effects of traumatic events, social support, and self-efficacy on adolescents' self-health assessments. *Western Journal of Nursing Research, 21*(5), 673.

Cicchetti, D., Rogosch, F. A., & Toth, S. L. (2006). Fostering secure attachments in infants in maltreating families through preventive interventions. *Development and Psychopathology, 18*(3), 623–649.

Cloitre, M., Morin, N., et al. (2004). *Children's resilience in the face of trauma.* New York: New York University Child Study Center.

Cloud, J. (January, 2010). *Why your DNA isn't your destiny.* Retrieved from http://www.time.com/time/health/articles/0,8599,1951968,00.html.

Cohen, J. A., Mannarino, A. P., Deblinger, E. (2006). *Treating trauma and traumatic grief in children and adolescents.* New York: Guilford Press.

Cohen, J. A., Mannarino, A. P., Greenberg, T., Padlo, S., & Shipley, C. (2002). Childhood traumatic grief: Concepts and controversies. *Trauma, Violence and Abuse, 3*(4), 307–327.

Coifman, K. G., Bonnano, G. A., Ray, R. D., & Gross, J. J. (2007). Does repressive coping promote resilience? Affective-autonomic response discrepancy during bereavement. *Journal of Personality and Social Psychology, 92*(4), 745–758.

Collins, D. (2009). *Essentials of business ethics: Creating an organization of high integrity and superior performance*. New York: John Wiley & Sons.

Conley, D. (2011). Wired for distraction? *Time*, February 21, 55–56.

Connors, R., & Smith, T. (2009). *How did that happen? Holding people accountable for results the positive principled way*. New York: PenguinGroup.

Conradi, L., Kletzka, N. T., & Oliver, T. (2010). A case study using the Trauma Assessment Pathway (TAP) model. *Journal of Child and Adolescent Trauma, 3*, 1–18.

Cook, A., Blaustein, M., et al. (2003). *Complex trauma in children and adolescents*. White paper from the National Child Traumatic Stress Network, Complex Trauma Task Force. Retrieved April 29, 2011, from http://www.nctsnet.org/nctsn_assets/pdfs/edu_materials/ComplexTrauma_All.pdf.

Cook, A., Spinazzola, J., Ford, J., Lanktree, C., Blaustein, M., Cloitre, M., et al. (2005). Complex trauma in children and adolescents. *Psychiatric Annals, 35*(5), 390–398.

Corso, P. S., Edwards, V. J., et al. (2008). Health-related quality of life among adults who experienced maltreatment during childhood. *American Journal of Public Health, 98*(6), 1094.

Coulter, S. J. (2000). Effect of song writing versus recreational music on posttraumatic stress disorder (PTSD) symptoms and abuse attribution in abused children. *Journal of Poetry Therapy, 13*(4), 189–208.

Cox, M., & Catte, M. (2000). Severely disturbed children's human figure drawings: Are they unusual or just poor drawings? *European Child & Adolescent Psychiatry, 9*(4), 301–306.

Csikszentmihalyi, M. (1996). *Flow: The psychology of optimal experience*. New York: HarperCollins.

Damasio, A. R. (1999). *The feeling of what happens: Body and emotion in the making on consciousness*. New York: Harcourt Brace.

Damasio, A. R., Grabowski, T. J., Bechara, A., et al. (2000). Subcortical and cortical brain activity during the feeling of self-generated emotions. *National Neuroscience, 3*, 1049–1056.

Davis, K. M. (2010). Music and expressive arts with children experiencing trauma. *Journal of Creativity in Mental Health, 5*(2), 125–133.

Deblinger, E., Lippman, J., & Steer, R. (1996). Sexually abused children suffering posttraumatic stress symptoms: Initial treatment outcomes findings. *Child Maltreatment, 1*, 310–321.

Deblinger, E., Stauffer, L. B., et al. (2001). Comparative efficacies of supportive and cognitive behavioral group therapies for young children who have been sexually abused and their non-offending mothers. *Child Maltreatment, 6*(4): 332–343.

De Boer, C., & Coady, N. (2007). Good helping relationships in child welfare: Learning from stories of success. *Child & Family Social Work, 12*(1), 32–42.

DeWaal, F. (2009). Bodies in sync. *Natural History, 118*(7), 20–25.

Donovan, D. M., & McIntyre, D. (1990). *Healing the hurt child: A developmental contextual approach*. New York: W. W. Norton.

Drewes, A. (2001). The possibilities and challenges in using play therapy in schools. In A. A. Drewes, L. J. Carey, & C. E. Schaefer (Eds.), *School-based play therapy* (pp. 41–51). New York: John Wiley & Sons.

Duggal, H. S., Berezkin, G., et al. (2002). PTSD and TV viewing of World Trade Center. *Journal of the American Academy of Child & Adolescent Psychiatry, 41*(5), 494–495.

Echterling, L. G., Presbury, J. H., et al. (2005). *Crisis intervention: Promoting resilience and resolution in troubled times.* Upper Saddle River, NJ: Prentice Hall.

Edgar, A., & Sedgwick, P. R. (1999). *Key concepts in cultural theory.* New York: Routledge.

Else, B. A. (2009) Disaster events and young children. *Early Childhood Newsletter, 15,* 17–18.

Epstein, M. H., Mooney, P., et al. (2004). Validity and reliability of the behavioral and emotional rating scale: Youth rating scale. *Research on Social Work Practice, 14*(5), 358.

Eth, S., & Pynoos, R. (Eds). (1986). *Post-traumatic stress disorder in children.* Washington, DC: American Psychiatric Press.

Eyberg, S. M. (1988). Parent-child interaction therapy: Integration of traditional and behavioral concerns. *Child and Family Behavior Therapy, 10,* 33–46.

Fallot, R. D., & Harris, M. (2006). *Trauma-informed services: A self-assessment and planning protocol, version 1.4.* Washington, DC: Community Connections.

Famularo, R., Kinscherff, R., & Fenton, T. (1992). Psychiatric diagnosis of maltreated children: Preliminary findings. *Journal of American Academy of Child and Adolescent Psychiatry, 31,* 863–867.

Figley, C. (1995). Compassion fatigue as secondary traumatic stress disorder: An overview. In C. Figley (Ed.), *Compassion fatigue: Coping with secondary traumatic stress disorder in those who treat the traumatized* (pp. 1–20). Philadelphia: Brunner/Mazel.

Foa, E. B., Keane, T., & Friedman, M. (2000). *Effective treatment for PTSD: Practice guidelines from the International Society for Traumatic Stress Studies.* New York: Guilford Press.

Foa, E. B., Keane, T. M., et al. (2008). *Effective treatments for PTSD: Practice guidelines from the International Society for Traumatic Stress Studies.* New York: Guilford Press.

Foa, E. B., & Kozak, M. (1986a). Emotional processing of fear: Exposure to corrective information. *Psychological Bulletin, 99,* 20–35.

Foa, E. B., & Kozak, M. (1986b). Treatment of anxiety disorders: Implications for psychopathology. In A. Hussein & J. D. Maser (Eds.), *Anxiety and the anxiety disorders.* Hillsdale, NJ: Erlbaum.

Foa, E. B., Rothbaum, B.O., Riggs, D. S., & Murdock, T. (1991). Treatment of post-traumatic stress disorder in rape victims: A comparison between cognitive-behavioral procedures and counseling. *Journal of Consulting and Clinical Psychology, 59,* 715–723.

Frazier, P. A., & Kaler, M. E. (2006). Assessing the validity of self-reported stress-related growth. *Journal of Consulting and Clinical Psychology, 74,* 859–869.

Frederick, C. J., Pynoos, R., & Nader, K. (1992). Child post-traumatic stress reaction index. In S. Eth & R. Pynoos (Eds.) *Posttraumatic stress disorder in children* (pp. 171–183). Washington, DC: American Psychiatric Press.

Freier, N., & Kahn, P. (2009). The fast-paced change of children's technological environments. *Children, Youth and Environments, 19*(1): 1–11.

Freudenberger, H. J. (1974). Staff burn-out. *Journal of Social Issues, 30*(1), 159–165.

Funderburk, B. W., Eyberg, S. M., et al. (1998). Parent-child interaction therapy with behavior problem children: Maintenance of treatment effects in the school setting. *Child & Family Behavior Therapy 20*(2), 17–38.

Gao, T. (2008). *Music therapy and crisis intervention with survivors of the China earthquake of May 12, 2008*. Retrieved February 15, 2011 from http://www. chinamusictherapy.org/html/data/en/a38.html.

Garbarino, J. (1992). *Children in danger: Coping with the consequences of community violence*. San Francisco: Jossey-Bass.

Garmezy, N. (1991). Resiliency and vulnerability to adverse developmental outcomes associated with poverty. *American Behavioral Scientist, 34*, 416–430.

Gharabaghi, K. (2008). Reclaiming our "toughest" youth. *Reclaiming Children and Youth, 17*(3), 30–32.

Gil, E. (1991). *The healing power of play: Working with abused children*. New York: Guilford Press.

Gil, E. (2000). *Family play therapy: Rational and techniques*. Fairfax, VA: Starbright Training Institute for Family and Child Play Therapy.

Gil, E. (2003a). Art and play therapy with sexually abused children. In C. Malchiodi (Ed.) *Handbook of art therapy* (pp. 152–166). New York: Guilford Press.

Gil, E. (2003b). Play genograms. In C. F. Sori, L. L. Hecker & Associates (Eds.), *The therapist's notebook for children and adolescents: Homework, handouts, and activities for use in psychotherapy* (pp. 49–56). New York: The Haworth Clinical Practice Press.

Gil, E. (2006). *Helping abused and traumatized children: Integrating directive and nondirective approaches*. New York: Guilford Press.

Gil, E. (Ed.) (2010). *Working with children to heal interpersonal trauma: The power of play*. New York: Guilford Press.

Gil, E., & Drewes, A. A. (2006). *Cultural issues in play therapy*. New York: Guilford Press.

Gil, E., & Green, N. (n.d.) *Extended play-based developmental assessments: Clinicians guide*. Springfield, VA: Multicultural Clinical Center.

Ginsburg, K. R., & Jablow, M. M. (2006). *A parent's guide to building resilience in children and teens: Giving your child roots and wings*. Elk Grove Village, IL: American Academy of Pediatrics.

Gluckman, P., & Haonson, M. (2006). *Mismatch: Why our world no longer fits our bodies*. Oxford, UK: Oxford University Press.

Golumb, C. (1990). *The child's creation of a pictorial world*. Berkeley: University of California Press.

Grafton, S. T. (2007). Evidence for a distributed hierarchy of action representation in the brain. *Human Movement Science, 26*(4), 590–616.

Greenspan, S. I., & Lewis, N. B. (2000). *Building healthy minds: The six experiences that create intelligence and emotional growth in babies and young children.* Cambridge, MA: Perseus.

Greenwald, R. (2005). *Child trauma handbook: A guide for helping trauma-exposed children and adolescents.* New York: The Haworth Maltreatment and Trauma Press.

Griffith, J., & Powers, R. L. (1984). *An Adlerian lexicon: Fifty-nine terms associated with the individual psychology of Alfred Adler.* Chicago: Americas Institute of Adlerian Studies.

Gross, J., & Haynes, H. (1998). Drawing facilitates children's verbal reports of emotionally laden events. *Journal of Experimental Psychology, 4,* 163–179.

Harris, M. E., & Fallot, R. D., (2001). *Using trauma theory to design service systems.* San Francisco: Jossey-Bass.

Harvey, M. (2007). Towards an ecological understanding of resilience in trauma survivors: Implications for theory, research and practice. *Journal of Aggression, Maltreatment and Trauma, 14*(1), 9–32.

Hass-Cohen, N., & Carr, R. (2008). *Art therapy and clinical neuroscience.* London: Jessica Kingsley.

Helgeson, V. S., Reynolds, K. A., & Tomich, P. L. (2006). A meta-analytic review of benefit finding and growth. *Journal of Consulting and Clinical Psychology, 74,* 797–816.

Henry, J., Sloane, M., et al. (2007). Neurobiology and neurodevelopmental impact of childhood traumatic stress and prenatal alcohol exposure. *Language, Speech, and Hearing Services in Schools, 38*(2), 99.

Herman, J. (1992). *Trauma and recovery.* New York: Basic Books.

Hobfoll, S. E., Tracy, M., et al. (2006). The impact of resource loss and traumatic growth on probable PTSD and depression following terrorist attacks. *Journal of Traumatic Stress, 19*(6), 867–878.

Howard, G. S. (1991). Culture tales: A narrative approach to thinking, cross-cultural psychology, and psychotherapy. *American Psychologist, 46,* 187–197.

Hummer, V., & Dollard, N. (2010). *Creating trauma-informed care environments: An organizational self-assessment.* Tampa, FL: University of South Florida.

Hyman, I. A., & Snook, P. A. (1999). *Dangerous schools: What we can do about the physical and emotional abuse of our children.* San Francisco: Jossey-Bass.

Hyter, Y., Atchison, B., Henry, J., Sloane, M., & Black-Pond, C. (2001). A response to traumatized children: Developing a best practices model. *Occupational Therapy in Health Care, 15,* 113–140.

Imber-Black, E., & Roberts, J. (1992). *Rituals for our times: Celebrating, healing, and changing our lives and our relationships.* New York: Harper Perennial.

James, B. (1989). *Treating traumatized children: New insights and creative interventions.* New York: Free Press.

Janoff-Bulman, R., & Berg, M. (1998). Disillusionment and the creation of values. In J. H. Harvey (Ed.), *Perspectives on loss* (pp. 35–47). Philadelphia: Brunner/Mazel.

Julik, E. (1996). *Sailing through the storm to the ocean of peace.* Lakeville, MN: Galde Press.

Kabat-Zinn, J. (1994). *Wherever you go, there you are.* New York: Hyperion.

Kantor, D., & Neal, J. H. (1985). Integrative shifts for the theory and practice of family systems therapy. *Family Process, 24*(1), 13–30.

Kato, P. M., & Mann, T. (1999). A synthesis of psychological interventions for the bereaved. *Clinical Psychology Review, 19,* 275–296.

Keyes, C. L. M., & Haidt, J. E. (2003). *Flourishing: Positive psychology and the life well-lived,* Washington, DC: American Psychological Association.

Kilmer, R. P., & Gill-Rivas, V. (2010). Building safe, humane, and responsive communities for children and families. *American Journal of Orthopsychiatry, 80*(1), 135–142.

Klein, R., & Klein, N. (2011). *Relaxation and success imagery* (CD). www.inner-coaching.com.

Klorer, P. G. (2000). *Expressive therapy with troubled children.* Northvale, NJ: Jason Aronson Inc.

Klorer, P. G. (2008). Expressive therapy for severe maltreatment and attachment disorders. In C. Malchiodi (Ed.), *Creative interventions with traumatized children* (p. 43). New York: Guilford Press.

Klorer, P., & Malchiodi, C. (2003). Acute incident vs. long-term trauma: Therapeutic interventions. In *Proceedings of the 34th Annual Conference of the American Art Therapy Association,* Mundelein, IL: AATA Inc.

Koppitz, E. (1968). *Psychological evaluation of children's human figure drawings.* New York: Grune & Stratton.

Kramer, E. (1998). *Childhood and art therapy.* Chicago: Magnolia Street.

Kruger, D. (2002). *Integrating body self and psychological self.* New York: Brunner-Routledge.

Kuban, C., & Steele, W. (2009). *A time for resilience—Raising resilient children in a traumatic world: A guide for professionals.* Clinton Township, MI: TLC—The National Institute for Trauma and Loss in Children.

Kubokawa, A., & Ottaway, A. (2009). Positive psychology and cultural sensitivity: A review of the literature. *Graduate Journal of Counseling Psychology, 1*(2), 2–6.

Lakes, K. D., & Hoyt, W. T. (2004). Promoting self-regulation through school-based martial arts training. *Applied Developmental Psychology, 25,* 283–302.

Landreth, G. (2002). *Play therapy: The art of the relationship* (2nd ed.). New York: Brunner-Routledge.

Larson, S. (2008). The relationship trauma crisis. *Reclaiming Children and Youth, 17*(3), 4.

Latham, V., Dollard, N., et al. (2010). Innovations in implementation of trauma-informed care practices in youth residential treatment: A curriculum for organizational change. *Child Welfare, 89*(2), 79–95.

Laughlin, P., Hatch, E., Silver, J., & Both, L. (2006). Groups perform better than the best individuals on letters-to-numbers problems: Effects of group size. *Journal of Personality and Social Psychology, 90*(4), 644–651.

Lazar, S. W., Kerr, C. E., et al. (2005). Meditation experience is associated with increased cortical thickness. *Neuroreport, 16*(17), 1893.

Levin, D. (2008). Building peaceable classroom communities: Counteracting the impact of violence on young children. *Exchange.* Retrieved from http://child careexchange.com.

Levine, P. A., & Frederick, A. (1997). *Waking the tiger.* Berkeley, CA: North Atlantic Books.

Levine, P. & Kline, M. (2008). *Trauma proofing your kids.* Berkeley, CA: North Atlantic Books.

Levine, S. Z., Laufer, A., et al. (2008). Posttraumatic growth in adolescence: Examining its components and relationship with PTSD. *Journal of Traumatic Stress, 21*(5), 492–496.

Lev-Wcisel, R. (2007). Intergenerational transmission of trauma across three generations: A preliminary study. *Qualitative Social Work, 61,* 75–94.

Lieberman, A., Van Horn, P., et al. (2005). The impact of domestic violence on preschoolers: Predictive and mediating factors. *Developmental Psychopathology, 17*(2), 385–396.

Long, N., Wood, M., & Fecser, F. (2001). *Life space crisis intervention.* Austin, TX: Pro-ED Publishers.

Lonigan, C., Shannon, M., Finch, A., Daugherty, T., & Taylor, C. (1991). Children's reactions to a natural disaster: Symptom severity and degree of exposure. *Advances in Behavior Research and Therapy, 13,* 135–154.

Lowenfeld, V., & Brittain, W. (1987). *Creative and mental growth* (7th ed.). New York: MacMillan.

Lowen, A. (1967). *Betrayal of the body.* Alachua, FL: Bioenergetics Press.

Malchiodi, C. (1990). *Breaking the silence.* New York: Brunner/Mazel.

Malchiodi, C. A. (1997). *Breaking the silence: Art therapy with children from violent homes,* (2nd ed.). New York: Routledge.

Malchiodi, C. A. (1998). *Understanding children's drawings.* New York: Guilford Press.

Malchiodi, C. A. (2001). Using drawing as intervention with traumatized children. *Trauma and Loss: Research and Interventions, 1*(1), 21–28.

Malchiodi, C. A. (2005). The impact of culture on art therapy with children. In E. Gil & A. Drews (Eds.), *Cultural issues in play therapy* (pp. 96–111). New York: Guilford Press.

Malchiodi, C. A. (2008). Creative interventions and childhood trauma. In C. Malchiodi (Ed.), *Creative interventions with traumatized children* (pp. 3–21). New York: Guilford Press.

Malchiodi, C. A. (2009). *The effects of posttraumatic stress disorder on children's human figure drawings.* Dissertation Abstracts, #AAT 3368184.

Malchiodi, C. A. (2010). *Cool art therapy intervention #1: The art therapist's third hand.* Retrieved March 17, 2011 from http://www.psychologytoday.com/blog/the-healing-arts/201010/cool-art-therapy-intervention-1-the-art-therapist-s-third-hand

Malchiodi, C. A. (2011a). Art therapy and the brain. In C. Malchiodi (Ed.), *Handbook of art therapy.* New York: Guilford Press.

Malchiodi, C. A. (2011b). Trauma-informed art therapy with children who have been sexually abused. In P. Goodyear-Brown (Ed.), *Handbook of sexual abuse treatment*. New York: Wiley.

Malchiodi, C. A., & Steele, W. (2008). Resilience and posttraumatic growth in traumatized children. In C. Malchiodi (Ed.), *Creative interventions with traumatized children* (pp. 285–301). New York: Guilford Press.

Malinowski, B. (1960). *A scientific theory of culture and other essays*. New York: Oxford University Press. (Original work published 1944.)

March, J., Amaya-Jackson, L., Costanzo, P., Terry, R., & The Hamlet Fire Consortium. (1993). Posttraumatic stress in children and adolescents after an industrial fire. *Selected Abstracts PTSD Research Quarterly* (January). Paper presented at the Lake George Conference on PTSD.

Mayou, R. A., Ehlers, A., & Hobbs, M. (2000). Psychological debriefing for road traffic accident victims. *British Journal of Psychiatry, 176,* 589–593.

McCann, I. L., & Pearlman, L. A. (1990). Vicarious traumatization: A framework for understanding the psychological effects of working with victims. *Journal of Traumatic Stress, 3*(1), 131–149.

McCormick, L., & Schiefelbusch, R. (1990). *Early language intervention: An introduction* (2nd ed.). Columbus, OH: Merrill.

McFarlane, A., Policansky, S., & Irwin, C. (1987). A longitudinal study of the psychological morbidity in children due to a natural disaster. *Psychological Medicine, 17,* 727–738.

McGoldrick, M., Gerson, R., & Petry, N. (2008). *Genograms: Assessment and intervention*. New York: Norton.

McGowan, P. O., Sasaki, A., D'Alesso, A. C., Dymov, S., et al. (2009). Epigenetic regulation of the glucorticoid receptor in human brain associates with child abuse. *Nature Neuroscience, 12,* 342–348.

McMahon, R. (2009). Anthropological race psychology 1820–1945: A common European system of ethnic identity narratives. *Nations and Nationalism, 15*(4): 575–596.

Melillo, R. (2009). *Disconnected kids: The groundbreaking brain balance program for children with autism, ADHD, dyslexia, and other neurological disorders*. New York: Perigee.

Menninger, K. (1963). *The vital balance: The life process in mental health & illness*. New York: Viking Press.

Mihaescu, G., & Baettig, D, (1996). An integrated model of post-traumatic stress disorder. *The European Journal of Psychiatry, 10*(4), 233–242.

Miller Kunaneck, H., Henry, D. A., & Glennon, T. J. (2007). *Sensory processing measure*. Los Angeles: Western Psychological Services.

Monahon, C. (1997). *Children and trauma: A guide for parents and professionals*. San Francisco: Jossey Bass.

Morris, B. A., Shakespeare-Finch, J., et al. (2007). Coping processes and dimensions of posttraumatic growth. *The Australasian Journal of Disaster and Trauma Studies 2007-1,* 1–12.

Morse, W. C. (2008). *Connecting to kids in conflict: A life space legacy.* Albion, MI: Starr Commonwealth.

Nader, K., Pynoos, R. S., Fairbans, L., & Frederick, C. (1990). Children's PTSD reactions one year after a sniper attack at their school. *American Journal of Psychiatry, 147,* 1526–1530.

National Child Traumatic Stress Network (NCTSN). (2005). *Mental health interventions for refugee children in resettlement.* (White Paper II) Los Angeles, CA: National Child Traumatic Stress Network.

National Center for Trauma Informed Care. (2011). *What's trauma-informed care?* Retrieved June 30, 2011 from http://www.samhsa.gov/nctic/trauma.asp.

Neimeyer, R. A. (2002). Meaning reconstruction theory. In N. Thompson (Ed.), *Loss and grief: A guide for human service practitioners* (pp. 45–64). New York: Palgrave.

Neimeyer, R. A. (2005). Widowhood, grief and quest for meaning: A narrative perspective on resilience. In D. Carr, R. M. Nesse, & C. B. Wortman (Eds.), *Late life widowhood in the United States.* New York: Springer.

Nelson, E. E., & Panksepp, J. (1998). Brain substrates of infant-mother attachment: Contributions of opioids, oxytocin, and norepinephrine. *Neuroscience & Biobehavioral Reviews, 22*(3), 437–452.

OACAS (Ontario Association of Children's Aid Societies). (2006). *Youth leaving care: An OACAS survey of youth and CAS staff.* Toronto, Ontario, Canada: OACAS. Retrieved April, 17, 2008 from http://www.oacas.org/about/programs/youthcan/07conference/youthleavingcare07oct25.pdf.

Ogden, P., Minton, K., et al. (2006). *Trauma and the body: A sensorimotor approach to psychotherapy.* New York: W. W. Norton.

Olafson, E., & Kenniston, J. (2008). Obtaining information from children in the justice system. *Juvenile and Family Court Journal, 59*(4), 71–89.

Osofsky, J. (Ed.) (2004). *Young children and trauma.* New York: Guilford Press.

Piaget, J., & Inhelder, B. (1969). *The psychology of the child.* New York: Basic Books.

Perry, B. (2009). Examining child maltreatment through a neurodevelopmental lens: Clinical applications of the neurosequential model of therapeutics. *Journal of Loss and Trauma, 14*(4), 16.

Perry, B., & Szalavitz, M. (2006). *The boy who was raised as a dog and other stories from a child psychiatrist's notebook.* New York: Basic Books.

Perry, B. D. (2002). Childhood experience and the expression of genetic potential: What childhood neglect tells us about nature and nurture. *Brain and Mind, 3*(1), 79–100.

Perry, B. D. (2006). Applying principles of neurodevelopment to clinical work with maltreated and traumatized children. In N. B. Webb (Ed.), *Working with traumatized youth in child welfare* (pp. 27–52). New York: Guilford Press.

Perry, B. D., & Hambrick, E. P. (2008). The neurosequential model of therapeutics. *Reclaiming Children and Youth, 17*(3): 38–43.

Peterson, C. (2006). *Primer in positive psychology.* New York: Oxford University Press.

Pfefferbaum, B., Nixon, S. J., et al. (1999). Posttraumatic stress responses in bereaved children after the Oklahoma City bombing. *Journal of the American Academy of Child & Adolescent Psychiatry, 38*(11), 1372–1379.

Pifalo, T. (2002). Pulling out the thorns: Art therapy with sexually abused children and adolescents. *Art Therapy: Journal of the American Art Therapy Association, 19*(1), 12–22.

Pynoos, R., Nader, K., Arroyo, E., Steinberg, A., Eth, S., Nunez, F., et al. (1987). Life threat and posttraumatic stress in school age children. *Archives General Psychiatry, 44*, 1057–1063.

Raider, M., Steele, W., & Santiago, A. (1999). *Trauma response kit: Short-term trauma intervention model evaluation.* Detroit, MI: Wayne State University School of Social Work.

Raider, M. C. (2010). Structured sensory trauma intervention program for elementary school children. *National Social Science Journal, 34*(2), 167–185.

Ramachandran, V. (2011). *The tell-tale brain: A neuroscientist's quest for what makes us human.* New York: W. W. Norton.

Ratey, J. J. (2002). *A user's guide to the brain: Perception, attention, and the four theatres of the brain.* New York: Vintage Books.

Reich, W. (1972). *Character analysis.* New York: Farrar, Straus, & Giroux. (Original work published 1945.)

Riley, S. (1997). Children's art and narratives: An opportunity to enhance therapy and a supervisory challenge. *The Supervision Bulletin, 9,* 2–3.

Riley, S. (2001). *Group process made visible: Group art therapy.* New York: Routledge.

Rothschild, B. (2000). *The body remembers: The psychophysiology of trauma and trauma treatment.* New York: W. W. Norton.

Rothschild, B. (2004). *The body remembers casebook.* New York: W. W. Norton.

Rothschild, B. (2009). *8 keys to safe trauma recovery: Take-charge strategies to empower your healing.* New York: W. W. Norton.

Rothschild, B. (2011). *An open letter to visitors of Babette's website.* Retrieved March 20, 2011 from http://home.webuniverse.net/babette/.

Rubin, D. C., & Greenberg, D. L. (2003). The role of narrative in recollection: A view from cognitive psychology and neuropsychology. In G. D. Fireman, T. E. McVay, & O. J. Flanagan (Eds.), *Narrative and consciousness* (pp. 53–85). New York: Oxford University Press.

Saigh, P., & Bremner, J. (1999). *Posttraumatic stress disorder.* Boston: Allyn and Bacon.

Schrierer, H., Ladakakos, C., Morabito, D., Chapman, L., & Knudson, M. (2005). Posttraumatic stress symptoms in children after mild to moderate pediatric trauma: A longitudinal examination of symptom prevalence. *Journal of Trauma, 58*(2), 353–363.

Seligman, M. E. P. (1994). *What you can change and what you can't.* New York: Knopf.

Shapiro, F. (2001). *Eye movement desensitization and reprocessing: Basic principles, protocols, and procedures.* New York: Guilford Press.

Shelden, D., Angell, M., Stoner, J., & Roseland, B. (2010). School principal's influence on trust: Perspectives of mothers of children with disabilities. *The Journal of Educational Research, 103*(3), 159–170.

Sheppard, C. (1998). *Brave Bart: A story for traumatized and grieving children*. Clinton Township, MI: National Institute for Trauma and Loss in Children (TLC).

Siegel, D. (1999). *The developing mind*. New York: Guilford Press.

Siegel, D. (2003). An interpersonal neurobiology of psychotherapy: The developing mind and the resolution of trauma. In M. Solomon & D. Siegel (Eds.), *Healing trauma: Attachment, mind, body, and brain* (pp. 1–5). New York: Norton.

Siegel, D., & Hartzell, M. (2003). *Parenting from the inside out*. New York: Jeremy P. Tarcher/Penguin.

Sieta, J. R., & Brendtro, L. (2005). *Kids who outwit adults*. Bloomington, IN: National Education Services.

Silver, R. A. (2007). *The Silver drawing test and draw a story: Assessing depression, aggression, and cognitive skills*. Boca Raton, FL: CRC Press.

Snowden, L. R., Hu, T., & Jerrell, M. (1995). Emergency care avoidance: Ethnic matching and participation in minority-serving program. *Community Mental Health Journal, 31*(5), 463–473.

Snyder, C. R., Lopez, S. J., et al. (2010). *Positive psychology: The scientific and practical explorations of human strengths*. Thousand Oaks, CA: Sage.

Solomon, Z., Berger, R., et al. (2007). Resilience of Israeli body handlers: Implications of repressive coping style. *Traumatology, 13*(4), 64.

Solomon, Z., & Dekel, R. (2007). Posttraumatic stress disorder and posttraumatic growth among Israeli ex-POWS. *Journal of Traumatic Stress, 20*(3), 303–312.

Steele, W. (2003). Helping traumatized children. In S. L. A. Strausner & N. K. Philips (Eds.), *Understanding mass violence: A social work perspective* (pp. 41–56). New York: Allyn and Bacon.

Steele, W. (2003). Using drawing in short-term trauma resolution. In C. Malchiodi (Ed.), *Handbook of art therapy*, (pp. 139–151). New York: Guilford Press.

Steele, W. (2009). Trauma-informed care: A history of helping, a history of excellence. Retrieved April 29, 2011 from http://www.tlcinst.org/pdfs/TICare5.28.09.pdf.

Steele, W., Kuban, C., & Raider, L. M. (2009). Connections, continuity, dignity, opportunities model: Follow-up of children who completed the I Feel Better Now! Trauma Intervention Program. *School Social Work Journal, 33*(2), 98–111.

Steele, W., & Malchiodi, C. (2008). Interventions for parents of traumatized children. In C. Malchiodi (Ed.), *Creative interventions with traumatized children* (pp. 264–281). New York: Guilford Press.

Steele, W., & Raider, M. (1991). *Working with families in crisis: School-based intervention*. New York: Guilford Press.

Steele, W., & Raider, M. (2001). *Structured sensory interventions for children, adolescents and parents* (SITCAP™). New York: Edwin Mellen Press.

Steele, W., & Raider, M. (2003). Drawing as intervention with child witnesses to violence research study. *Journal of Social Sciences, 1*(2), 127–140.

Steele, W., Raider, M., Delillo-Storey, M., Jacobs, J., & Kuban, C. (2008). Structured sensory therapy (SITCAP-ART) for traumatized adjudicated adolescents in residential treatment. *Residential Treatment for Children and Youth, 25*(2), 167–185.

Steinberg, A. M., Brymer, M. J., et al. (2004). The University of California at Los Angeles post-traumatic stress disorder reaction index. *Current Psychiatry Reports, 6*(2), 96–100.

Stien, P. T., & Kendall, J. C. (2004). *Psychological trauma and the developing brain: Neurologically based interventions for troubled children.* New York: Routledge.

Stubner, M., Nader, K., Yasuda, P., Pynoos, R., & Cohen, S. (1991). Stress responses after pediatric bone-marrow transplantation: Preliminary results of a prospective longitudinal study. *Journal of the American Academy of Child and Adolescent Psychiatry, 30,* 952–957.

Sweatt, J. D. (2009). *Mechanisms of memory.* Waltham, MA: Academic Press.

Szalavitz, M., & Perry, B. (2010). *Born for love.* New York: Harper Collins.

Tancredi, L. R. (2005). *Hardwired behavior: What neuroscience reveals about morality.* Cambridge: Cambridge University Press.

Taylor, N., Gilbert, A., Mann, G., & Ryan, B. E. (2005). *Assessment-based treatment for traumatized children: A trauma assessment pathway.* Unpublished Manuscript, Chadwick Center for Children & Families, Rady Children's Hospital, San Diego, CA.

Tedeschi, R., & Calhoun, L. (1995). *Trauma and transformation.* Thousand Oaks, CA: Sage.

Tedeschi, R. G., & Calhoun, L. G. (1996). The posttraumatic growth inventory: Measuring the positive legacy of trauma. *Journal of Traumatic Stress, 9,* 455–471.

Tedeschi, R. G., & Calhoun, L. (2004). Posttraumatic growth: Conceptual foundations and empirical evidence. *Psychological Inquiry, 15*(1), 1–18.

Tedeschi, R. G., Park, C. L., et al. (1998). Posttraumatic growth: Conceptual issues. In R. G. Tedeschi, C. L. Park, & L. G. Calhoun (Eds.) *Posttraumatic growth: Positive changes in the aftermath of crisis* (pp. 1–22). Mahwah, NJ: Erlbaum.

Terr, L. (1990). *Too scared to cry.* New York: Harper & Row.

Terr, L. (1994). *Unchained memories.* New York: Basic Books.

Terr, L. C. (1979). Children of Chowchilla study of psychic trauma. *Psychoanalytic Study of the Child, 34,* 547–623.

Thames, B. J. (2008). *Building family strengths: Values.* Retrieved from http://www.education.com/partner/articles/clemson.

Traumatic Stress Institute of Klingberg Family Centers (2008). *Trauma-informed care in youth serving settings: Organizational self assessment.* New Britain, CT: Author.

Trickett, P., & Putnam, F. (1993). Impact of sexual abuse in females: Toward a developmental psychobiological integration. *Psychological Science, 4,* 81–87.

Turner, D., & Cox, H. (2004). Facilitating posttraumatic growth. *Health and Quality of Life Outcome, 2,* 43.

Tweddle, A. (2007). Youth leaving care: How do they fare? *New Directions for Youth Development* (113), 15–31.

Ungerleider, S. (2003). Posttraumatic growth: Understanding a new field of research: An interview with Dr. Mark Chesler. *The Prevention Researcher, 10*, 10–12.

van der Kolk, B. (2006). Clinical implications of neuroscience research in PTSD. *Annals: New York Academy of Sciences, 1*, 1–17.

van der Kolk, B. A. (1994). The body keeps the score: Memory and the evolving psychobiology of posttraumatic stress. *Harvard Review of Psychiatry, 1*(5), 253–265.

van der Kolk, B. A. (2005). Developmental trauma. *Psychiatric Annals, 35*, 401.

van der Kolk, B. A., McFarlane, A. C., & Weisaeth, L. (Eds.) (1996). *Traumatic stress: The effects of overwhelming experience on mind, body, and society.* New York: Guilford Press.

van der Kolk, B. A., Pynoos, R. S., et al. (2009). Proposal to include a developmental trauma disorder diagnosis for children and adolescents in *DSM-V.* Official submission from the National Child Traumatic Stress Network Developmental Trauma Disorder Taskforce to the American Psychiatric Association.

van der Kolk, B., Roth, S., Pelcovitz, D., & Mandel, F. (1993). Complex post traumatic stress disorder: Results from the *DSM-IV* field trial of PTSD. In D. Meichenbaum (Ed.), *A clinical handbook/practical therapist manual: For assessing and treating adults with post-traumatic stress disorder (PTSD)*, Waterloo, Ontario, Canada: Institute Press.

Van Dyk, A., & Wiedis, D. (2001). Sandplay and assessment techniques with preschool-age children. In G. L. Landreth (Ed.), *Innovations in play therapy: Issues, process, and special populations* (pp. 16–37). Philadelphia: Brunner- Routledge.

Vernberg, E., LaGreca, A., Silverman, W., & Prinstein, M. (1996). Prediction of posttraumatic stress symptoms in children after hurricane Andrew. *Journal of Abnormal Psychology, 105*, 237–248.

Wallen, J. (1993). Protecting the mental health of children in dangerous neighborhoods. *Children Today, 22*, 24–27.

Webb, N. B. (2007). *Play therapy with children in crisis: Individual, group, and family treatment.* (3rd ed.) New York: Guilford Press.

Webb, N. B. (2010). *Helping bereaved children: A handbook for practitioners.* (3rd ed.) New York: Guilford Press.

Weinberger, D. A. (1990). The construct validity of the repressive coping style. In J. L. Singer (Ed.), *Repression and dissociation: Implications for personality theory, psychopathology, and health* (pp. 337–386). Chicago: University of Chicago Press.

Weinberger, D. A., Schwartz, G. E., et al. (1979). Low-anxious, high-anxious, and repressive coping styles: Psychometric patterns and behavioral and physiological responses to stress. *Journal of Abnormal Psychology, 88*, 369–380.

Weine, S., Danieli, Y., et al. (2002). Guidelines for international training in mental health and psychosocial interventions for trauma exposed populations in clinical and community settings. *Psychiatry-New York, 65*(2), 156–164.

Werner, E. E., & Smith, R. S. (1992). *Overcoming the odds: High-risk children from birth to adulthood*. Ithaca, NY: Cornell University Press.

Werner, S. R. S. (1989). *Vulnerable but invincible: A longitudinal study of resilient children and youth*. New York: Adams, Banister, Cox. (Original work published 1982.)

Wilkinson, M. (2003). Undoing trauma: Contemporary neuroscience. *Journal of Analytical Psychology, 48*(2): 235–253.

Willard, C. (2010). *Child's mind: Mindfulness practices to help our children be more focused, calm, and relaxed*. Berkeley, CA: Parallax Press.

Witness Justice. (2010). *Trauma is the common denominator: New discoveries in the science of traumatic behavior*. Retrieved from http://www.witnessjustice. org/resources/trauma.cfm.

Wolin, S. (2004). *Presenting a resilience paradigm for teachers: Educational resiliency: Student, teacher, and school perspectives*. Washington, DC: Project Resilience.

Wolin, S., & Wolin, S. J. (2000). Shifting paradigms: Easier said than done. *Strength Based Services Intervention Newsletter*, 1–4.

Yehuda, R. (2002). Post-traumatic stress disorder. *New England Journal of Medicine, 346*(2), 108–114.

Yule, W. (1992). Post-traumatic stress disorder in child survivors of shipping disasters: The sinking of the *Jupiter. Psychotherapy and Psychosomatics, 57*(4), 200–205.

Zak, P. J., Stanton, A. A., & Ahmadi, S. (2007). *Oxytocin increases generosity in humans*. Retrieved from http://www.PLoS ONE 2(11):e 1128.doi:10. 1371/journal. Pone.ooo1128.

Zautra, A., Hall, J.S., & Murray, K. (2010). Resilience: A new definition of health for people and communities. In Reich, J., Zautra, A., & Hall, J.S. (Eds.) *Handbook of adult resilience*, pp. 3–29. New York: Guilford Press.

Ziegler, D. (2002). *Traumatic experience and the brain: A handbook for understanding and treating those traumatized as children*. Phoenix, AZ: Acacia Publishing.

Organizational Resources

Chadwick Center for Children and Families, Rady Children's Hospital, San Diego, CA. 3020 Children's Way, MC 5131, San Diego, CA 92123. Tel: 858-576-1700 ext. 6008, Fax: 858-966-7524.

Children's Trauma Assessment Center, Western Michigan University. http://www. wmich.edu/hhs/unifiedclinics/ctac/

Circle of Courage. http://www.circleofouragenz.org

Substance Abuse and Mental Health Services Administration, National Center for Trauma-Informed Care; http://samhsa.gov/nctic

The National Institute for Trauma and Loss in Children; http://www.starrtraining. org/tlc.

Traumatic Stress Institute of Klingberg Family Centers. 370 Linwood Ave., New Britain, CT, 06052, 860-832-5507.

WISQARS™ (Web-based Injury Statistics Query and Reporting System). (2010). Centers for Disease Control and Prevention, Atlanta, GA. http://cdc.gov/injury/ wisqars/index.html

Index